A DICTIONARY OF
CLICHÉS

A DICTIONARY OF CLICHÉS

WITH AN INTRODUCTORY ESSAY

By
ERIC PARTRIDGE

Occidit miseros crambe repetita scriptores
Juvenal emendatus.

ROUTLEDGE & KEGAN PAUL

London and New York

First published in Great Britain September 1940
2nd Edition January 1941
3rd Edition (Revised) January 1947
4th Edition January 1950
Reprinted (with some additions) November 1962
Reprinted (with some additions) June 1966
5th Edition and first published
as a paperback in 1978
Reprinted in 1979, 1980, 1981, 1985 and 1987
by Routledge & Kegan Paul Ltd
11 New Fetter Lane, London EC4P 4EE

Published in the USA by
Routledge & Kegan Paul Inc.
in association with Methuen Inc.
29 West 35th Street, New York NY 10001

Printed in Great Britain by
Redwood Burn Ltd
Trowbridge, Wiltshire

British Library Cataloguing in Publication Data
Partridge, Eric
A dictionary of clichés.—5th ed.
1. English Language – Terms and phrases
I. Title
423'.1   PE1689   78–40557

ISBN 0 7100 0088 X

ISBN 0 7100 0049 9 Pbk.

TO THE MEMORY OF
THE LATE
A. W. STEWART
PROFESSOR OF CHEMISTRY
WRITER OF THRILLERS
LOVER OF GOOD ENGLISH

GRATEFULLY FROM THE AUTHOR
WHOM HE CONSIDERABLY HELPED
IN THAT EXCELLENT BLOOD SPORT: CLICHÉ-HUNTING

CONTENTS

PREFACE TO THE 5TH EDITION

SINCE the latest edition of this book appeared a few years ago, the situation seems to have become worse. As we advance scientifically and technologically, and as standards of living improve, we tend to become lazier and slacker in our attitude towards speech and writing: instead of being more alert and adventurous, we resort more and more to 'the good old cliché'.

Not only in the Press, radio, TV, but also—and not only as a result of their insidious influence—in everyday life, we remain faithful to all the old clichés and adopt the new, foisted on us by politicians and publicists. Only those of us who are concerned to keep the language fresh and vigorous regard, with dismay, the persistence of these well-worn substitutes for thinking and the mindless adoption of new ones.

The danger is seen at its clearest when we listen to public figures of undoubted ability and read the works of well-known writers of every sort—and suddenly we realize how often they bore us by employing a cliché when they could so easily have delighted us with something vivid or, at the least, precise.

Among the newer clichés, two stand out from among the 'things better left unsaid': *in this day and age*, which, originally possessing sonority and dignity, now implies mental decrepitude and marks a man for the rest of his life; and its mentally retarded offspring, *at this point in time*: 'at present', or 'nowadays' or, usually, the simple 'now' would suffice.

Notably, the new edition is available as a paperback. And so, besides the general intelligent public, teachers and, our torch-bearers, students will find it much more accessible. ˙

PREFACE

THAT some such book as this is needed has been indicated, shown, proved to me in several ways and on many occasions: the most important occasion could not be made public without a gross breach of good faith and a sad lack of tact. (A pity; for it was so startling as to be almost indecently convincing.) Having formerly been a graceless sinner in this matter of clichés, I know how useful a dictionary of clichés *could* be to others.

To the clichés I have subjoined a synonym or an explanation only where necessary; but I have in many instances established the etymological or semantic origin, determined the status, and named the author (or work) in whom (or which) the phrase first occurred; to quotation-clichés I have added the context and, sometimes, amplified the quotation. By the extremely border-line cases, I have done my best.

A note of authentic (and authenticated) omissions will be gratefully received; to collect clichés is not an easy job—after the first three or four hundred. I gladly thank Professor A. W. Stewart, Mr Wilson Benington, and Mr Allen Walker Read (American clichés) for their assistance in accumulating clichés, but they are not to be held responsible for anything, either in the Introduction or in the Dictionary itself.

London.   February 28, 1940.

INTRODUCTION

CLICHÉS*

IN an address delivered in December 1938 to the Institute of Journalists, Mr Frank Whitaker remarked, 'As to clichés, I daresay we are all in agreement'. But are we? If you ask the averagely well educated person, 'What is a cliché?', he will look at you in pity and say 'Oh, well! *you* know what a cliché is', and hesitate, and stumble, and become incoherent. In November 1939, there met in conference a body of learned and able men: someone brought up the subject of clichés: everyone's opinion was different: what one included, another excluded; what one excluded, another included. In short, *it is a vexed question* (cliché).

In 1902, Edmund Gosse scathingly said that 'All but the most obvious motives tend to express themselves no longer as thoughts but as clichés'; in 1910, O. Henry in *Whirligigs* invented a story based on the widespread use of clichés, and in it he wrote, 'It was wonderful . . . And most wonderful of all are words, and how they make friends one with another, being oft associated, until not even obituary notices do them part' ('until death do them part': cliché); and in 1932, that acute dialectician and admirable prose-writer, Mr Frank Binder, *went so far as to say* (cliché) that 'There is no bigger peril either to thinking or to education than the popular phrase', in which he included both catch-phrase and cliché.

What, therefore, is a cliché? Perhaps intellectual and intelligent opinion has not yet been so far crystallized as to justify a definition. *The Oxford English Dictionary* says that it is 'a stereotyped expression, a commonplace phrase'. I

*An abridged version (seven-thirteenths the length of this) appeared in *John o' London's Weekly* in March, 1940.

I

should (*ex cathedra ignorantiæ*, as Mr Humbert Wolfe once said wittily of someone else) like to enlarge on that definition and render it more practical, more comprehensive. The origin of the term may help, for, as Littré shows, *cliché* is the substantivized participle of *clicher*, a variant of *cliquer*, 'to click'; *clicher* is a die-sinkers' term for 'to strike melted lead in order to obtain a cast'; hence, a cliché is a stereotyped expression—a phrase 'on tap' as it were—and this derivative sense, which has been current in France since the early 'eighties, came to England ca. 1890. *Revenons à nos moutons* (cliché). A cliché is an outworn commonplace; a phrase, or short sentence, that has become so hackneyed that careful speakers and scrupulous writers shrink from it because they feel that its use is an insult to the intelligence of their audience or public: 'a coin so battered by use as to be defaced' (George Baker). Clichés range from fly-blown phrases ('much of a muchness'; 'to all intents and purposes'), metaphors that are now pointless ('lock, stock and barrel'), formulas that have become mere counters ('far be it from me to . . .')—through sobriquets that have lost all their freshness and most of their significance ('the Iron Duke')—to quotations that are nauseating ('cups that cheer but not inebriate'), and foreign phrases that are tags ('longo intervallo', 'bête noire').

Why are clichés so extensively used? Their ubiquity is remarkable and rather frightening. 'Haste encourages them, but more often they spring from mental laziness' (Frank Whitaker); then, too, they are a convenience, *of which more anon* (cliché). A half-education—that snare of the half-baked and the ready-made—accounts for many: an uncultured, little-reading person sees a stock phrase and thinks it apt and smart; he forgets that its aptness should put him on guard. The love of display often manifests itself in the adoption of foreign phrases (especially French) and Classical tags (Latin, not Greek). The use of clichés approximates to the use of proverbs, and certain proverbial phrases lie on the Tom Tiddler's Ground or No Man's Land between the forces of Style and Conscience entrenched on the one side and those of Lack of

Style and Consciencelessness on the other: but proverbs are instances of racial wisdom, whereas clichés are instances of racial inanition. It is perhaps not irrelevant to note that with the rapidly decreasing popularity of proverbs among the middle and upper classes, clichés are, there, becoming increasingly popular.

But are not clichés sometimes justifiable? To say 'Never' would be going too far. In the address from which I have already quoted twice, an address reprinted in *The Journal of the Institute of Journalists*, January 1939, Mr Whitaker says that he has 'heard their use in [Association] football reports defended on the ground that the public expects them and would feel lost without them. I may be wrong,' he adds, 'but I don't believe it. Can anything be said in favour of this specimen ... :—"Stung by this reverse, the speedy left-winger propelled the sphere straight into the home custodian's hands. He found it a rare handful and was glad to let go".' Politicians look on the cliché as *a friend in need*: the late Mr Ramsay MacDonald, the Rt. Hon. David Lloyd George, and the late Rt. Hon. Neville Chamberlain are *passed masters at the art*, though they are much less conscious artists than the Rt. Hon. Winston Churchill and the Rt. Hon. Anthony Eden. Politicians address great audiences; on the majority of whose individual members subtlety and style would be wasted. Royalty, too, in its speeches to the British Empire, *has constant recourse to* clichés; in a speech delivered on July 8, 1939, occurred this typical passage:—'I hope that *this historic occasion* will be *the beginning of a new era*, when agriculture *will come into her own*.' Poets have found the literate, the cultured cliché (*rosy-fingered dawn*) invaluable for the eking-out of the metric and the conquest of the evasive rhyme; a convenient *faute de mieux*.

Let us, however, *get down to brass tacks*. I classify clichés—very roughly and (I fear) unsatisfactorily, yet in the hope of clarifying a penumbral subject—into four groups, of which the second often overlaps the first, and the fourth occasionally overlaps the third:

1. Idioms that have become clichés.
2. Other hackneyed phrases.
    Groups (1) and (2) form at least four-fifths of the aggregate.
3. Stock phrases and familiar quotations from foreign languages.
4. Quotations from English literature.

Idiom-clichés are those idioms which have been so indiscriminately used that the original point has been blunted or even removed entirely. That most idioms are metaphors is irrelevant; that some non-idiomatic clichés are metaphors is equally irrelevant. (Is not every transferred sense—originally at least—a metaphor?) Idiom-clichés are the most catholic of all clichés: they constitute the common stock, known to *the man in the street*, the journalist, the scholar. A cursory reading of Dr Logan Pearsall Smith's wholly admirable essay, 'English Idioms' (a recast of an S.P.E. tract published in 1922) in *Words and Idioms*, will show that many indubitable idioms have indubitably become clichés. I stress this point, for certain writers and certain scholars would like to confine clichés to the non-idiomatic hackneyed phrases that constitute my second group. Doublets afford easy examples: 'dust and ashes'—'enough and to spare'—'far and wide'—'for good and all'—'heart and soul'—'by leaps and bounds'—'a man and a brother'—'null and void'—'to pick and choose'—'sackcloth and ashes'—'six of one and half a dozen of another'—'tooth and nail'—'ways and means'. So do such repetitions of the same word as: 'again and again'—'to share and share about'—'through and through'. Alliteration accounts for: 'bag and baggage'—'to chop and change'—'with (all one's) might and main'—'rack and ruin'—'safe and sound'—'slow and (or, but) sure'. So rhyme: 'fair and square'—'high and dry'—'wear and tear'. Alternatives supply: 'ever and anon'—'fast and loose'—'kill or cure'—'the long and the short of it'—'for love or money'—'neither here nor there'—'one and all'. Battered similes: 'as cool as a cucumber'—'as fit as a fiddle'—'as large as life' (elaborated by a wit to '. . . and twice as natural')—'as old as

4

the hills'—'as steady as a rock'—'as thick as thieves'. And there are many clichés from among the idioms based on occupations, trades and professions, sports and games, the weather, domestic life and national polity. To mention but a few: 'to leave the sinking ship'—'to know the ropes'—'to stick to one's guns'—'at daggers drawn'—'to lead a dog's life'—'a bolt from the blue'—'to darken the door of'—'to take pot-luck'—'to stick to one's last'—'behind the scenes'—'to set one's hand to the plough'.

Group II consists of non-idiomatic clichés: phrases so hackneyed as to be knock-kneed and spavined. These may be roughly divided into General; Sociological, Economic, Political; Journalistic (often overlapping the preceding division); Literary. To the first of these sub-divisions belong such clichés as 'add insult to injury'—'alive and kicking' (from Billingsgate?)—'(something does someone) all the good in the world' —'all the world and his wife'—'all to the good'—'and (or, with) something to spare'—'any port in a storm'—'armed to the teeth'—'as a matter of fact'—'at one's last gasp'—'an awkward predicament'—'baptism of fire'—'one's better half' —'blank amazement'—'blissful ignorance'—'the brave and the fair'—'(it is) by no means certain'—'the call of the wild'— 'castles in Spain'—'cheer to the echo'—'circumstances over which one has no control'—'the coast is clear'—'(it is my) considered opinion that'—'dead and gone'—'in deadly earnest'— '(in the) dim and distant past'—'down to the last detail'—'at the eleventh hour'—'an errand of mercy'—'to fall on deaf ears' —'(to suffer) a fate worse than death'—'the finishing touch'— 'the friend of man' (the dog)—'from the bottom of one's heart'—'generous to a fault'—'a glorious victory'—'the golden mean'—'good Queen Bess'—'a grievous error'—'to grow no younger'—'halcyon days'—'a hearty British cheer'—'here to-day and gone to-morrow'—'highly improbable'—'Hobson's choice'—'imagination runs riot'—'a kindred spirit'—'to know for a fact'—'last but not least'—'mine host'—'a miraculous escape'—'a moot point'—'to nip in the bud'—'of a certain age' —'the open road'—'the picture of health'—'(at) the psycho-

logical moment'—'quite the opposite'—'it runs in the blood'
—'the salt of the earth'—'scantily clad'—'second to none'—
'sick at heart'—'the soul of honour'—'the staff of life'—'a
superhuman effort'—'to take it as read'—'(some affair) terminated fatally'—'twelve good men and true'—'to venture an
opinion'—'to welcome with open arms'—'the why and the
wherefore'—'you could have knocked me down with a
feather'.

A few of those clichés were originally either journalistic or
political. In the political and sociological sub-division we find
such tattered phrases as 'ancestral acres'—'beyond the pale'—
'blue blood'—'bloated plutocrat'—'the economic factor'—'to
explore every avenue'—'a far-reaching policy'—'to leave a
door open'. Journalistic are, or were originally: 'a Barmecide
feast' (obsolescent)—'captains of industry' and 'the life-blood
of industry'—'the Dark Continent' (obsolescent)—'(to flout
or transgress) every canon of international law' (also political)
—'every principle of decency and humanity'—'a gay Lothario'
—'the Fourth Estate' and 'the power of the Press'—'the Grand
Old Man'—'the incident passed without further comment'—
'John Bull'—'Jupiter Pluvius' and 'the clerk of the weather'—
'laying heretical hands on our imperishable constitution'
(American journalists' and politicians')—'to maintain the
status quo'—'the march of time'—'a modern classic'—'of that
ilk' (but only as incorrectly used: it generally *is* misused)—'the
police have the matter well in hand'—'(we learn from) a reliable source of information'—'Scylla and Charybdis' (obsolescent)—'a social butterfly'—but let us in kindness give no
more examples. Rather literary than journalistic are the fol-
lowing formulas: 'all things considered'—'be that as it may'—
'curious to relate'—'I may mention in this connexion'; and
such phrases as 'an apostle of culture'—'Attic salt'—'Earth, the
Great Mother' (obsolescent)—'the eternal verities'—'the
golden age' (especially if written with capitals)—'Pandora's
box'—'Rabelaisian humour'—'a sop to Cerberus'. There are,
obviously, other sub-divisions. Among legal clichés, for
instance, are: 'it appears to be without foundation'—'we must

assume as proved' and 'the burden of proof'. Sporting clichés include 'Eclipse first and the rest nowhere' and 'neck and neck'.

Group III: Phrases and quotations from dead and foreign languages. These are of two kinds: phrases apprehended without reference to an author, phrases adopted bodily and unreflectingly; and quotations proper, i.e. quotations apprehended as such and not as tags. Among the outworn phrases taken from Latin are these: 'aqua pura' (as though it signified merely 'water')—'ceteris paribus'—'cui bono?'—'de mortuis' (with a pregnant pause)—'Deo volente'—'deus ex machina' (originally theatrical)—'in flagrante delicto'—'laudator temporis acti'—'longo intervallo' (Virgil's 'longo intervallo insequi' is not even a quotation-proper cliché)—'meum et tuum'—'mutatis mutandis'—'persona grata'—'pro bono publico'—'saeva indignatio'—'terra firma'. French has given us 'à l'outrance'—'bête noire'—'carte blanche'—'cherchez la femme'—'coup de grâce'—'fait accompli'—'fin de siècle'—'je ne sais quoi'—'sans cérémonie'—'toujours la politesse'. From Italian come 'al fresco'—'con amore'—'sotto voce'.

The foreign quotations, properly so termed, are numerous. Many (perhaps most) scholars would reject such quotations as are self-contained sentences, complete with a principal verb. But is not the primary criterion of a cliché its commonplaceness, its too frequent employment, rather than its phrasenature? In short, the excessive use, not the phrasal quality, determines the cliché. Moreover, the cliché is often uneconomical and nearly always unnecessary. *I do not wish to labour the point:* but is not 'to all intents and purposes' inferior to 'virtually', 'bête noire' to 'bugbear', 'to have neither chick nor child' to 'to be childless'? That test is as valid for conscious quotations as for unconscious phrases. Here are several full-blooded quotations that, to me, are clichés; to be full-blooded, however, they may, in essence, be phrases. 'Arcades ambo' and 'et in Arcadia ego vixi'—'facilis descensus Averni' (the preferable 'f.d. Averno' is not a cliché)—'pulvis et umbra'—'quis custodiet ipsos custodes?'—'sic transit gloria mundi'—

'timeo Danaos et dona ferentes'; the French 'nous avons changé tout cela' and 'plus ça change, plus ça reste la même chose': two from at least a dozen. 'All hope abandon ye who enter here' is Italian—in Cary's translation.

The English quotation-clichés are numerous. Many from the Bible have become so encrusted in the language that we remember that they are Biblical only because of the archaic phraseology; 'balm in Gilead'—'gall and wormwood'—'a howling wilderness'—'the flesh-pots of Egypt'—'the law of the Medes and Persians'—'the Mammon of unrighteousness'—'their name is Legion' (generally misapprehended)—'to spoil the Egyptians'. Shakespeare quotation-clichés abound: 'to be or not to be, that is the question'—to 'minister to a mind diseased'—'there are more things in heaven and earth . . .': are among the best known. Milton's 'a dim religious light', Keats's 'A thing of beauty is a joy for ever', and Dickens's 'Barkis is willin' ' are hardly less popular. But some English quotations are clichés only when they are misquoted: 'cribbed, cabined and confined' (on Shakespeare); 'fresh fields and pastures new' (on Milton); 'when Greek meets Greek' (on Nathaniel Lee); 'A little knowledge is a dangerous thing' (on Pope); 'Water, water everywhere, and not a drop to drink' (on Coleridge). Even 'of the making of books there is no end' is a misquotation: the Bible has 'of making many books there is no end'.

But of the recording of clichés there must be an end here.

A DICTIONARY OF CLICHÉS

The dates indicate, approximately, the period during which the phrases have been clichés.

A query (?) indicates a border-line case or an incipient cliché.

A ★ before a cliché indicates that it is a particularly hackneyed or objectionable one.

A

à l'outrance (?). Incorrect for the French *à outrance* or *à toute outrance*, 'to excess', (of a fight) 'to the end, to extremity': mid C. 19–20.

A1 at Lloyd's. A cliché (from ca. 1870) only as applied to persons or to things other than—the correct usage—ships. Often shortened to *A1*.

à propos des bottes. An introductory formula: 'With regard to nothing in particular': C. 19–20. Literally, 'on the subject of boots', it was used by Regnard in late C. 17. (Benham.)

abject apology, an. A too low-spirited, hence a despicable, apology: late C. 19–20.—Cf. the next.

abject terror. Panic: C. 20. The original sense of *abject* (C. 15–17) is 'cast out; rejected' (L. *abjicere*, 'to cast off or away').

able to make head or tail of, not (or **unable**). To understand nothing of: C. 19–20. Fielding, 1729 (O.E.D.). A thing that has neither head nor tail is difficult to determine or classify.

'abomination of desolation, the.' Abominable desolation; a desolate and abominable thing: C. 19–20. *Matthew*, xxiv. 15, 'When therefore ye shall see the abomination of desolation, spoken of by Daniel the prophet, stand in the market place,' where it means 'a cause of pollution; an idol'.

absit omen! 'Absent be the omen!' is a too literal rendering of the Latin; 'let that be no omen!' is nearer the mark, but 'I hope that *that* won't happen' goes closer still, as in 'If he dies soon (*absit omen!*), his nephews will rejoice'. C. 19–20.

accidents will (or do) happen. These mishaps will occur no matter how careful one may be: late C. 19–20.

*according to Cocker. According to the acknowledged authority; hence, correct or regular: C. 18–20. Edward Cocker's *Arithmetic*, 1664, went into more than a hundred editions. Variants that have not become clichés are *according to Gunter* (of 'Gunter's Law'), an Americanism, and *according to Hoyle* (the authority on card-games).

ace up one's sleeve, an; esp., **have an ...** To have something effective in reserve: a C. 20 colloquial variant of *to have something up one's sleeve*, itself a cliché of late C. 19–20.

Achilles' heel, the; the heel of Achilles. The (or one's) weak spot. '*His* Achilles' heel was his pride.' C. 18–20; literary; since ca. 1920, obsolescent. Achilles had one vulnerable spot—his heel.

aching void, an. With reference to peaceful hours, Cowper, in *Olney Hymns*, 1779, wrote, 'But they have left an aching void, | The world can never fill' (Benham): C. 19–20. A sense of loss and emptiness.

acid test, the. A severe test: from ca. 1915. Woodrow Wilson, at the beginning of 1918, 'The acid test of their good will' (O.E.D.). Technically and originally it means 'testing, with aquafortis, for gold'.

act in cold blood, to. To do, coolly, something that looks like a cruel deed of passion: from ca. 1880. *Murdered in cold blood* is an incipient cliché. *In cold blood* is a full cliché, dating from ca. 1870: with cool deliberateness

acute agony and **acute shock;** esp. *to suffer* the former, *to be suffering from* the latter: respectively late C. 19–20 and C. 20. *Acute pleasure*, 'intense or poignant pleasure', is a border-line case, for it has been very general since ca. 1860.

ad infinitum; ad libitum; ad nauseam. These Latin phrases may be rendered 'infinitely, never-endingly'—'at choice' (as much as one desires)—'sickeningly' (to an extent that nauseates one): respectively mid C. 17–20, C. 19–20, C. 18–20.

*add insult to injury, to; esp., **adding ...** (whether participial or substantival). To harm or hurt a person and then insult him: C. 20. Perhaps originally an etymologist's pun: *injury* (cf. Fr. *injure* and L. *injuria*), in C. 16–18, meant both 'harm, wrong' and 'insult'.

admirable Crichton, an. A particularly fine all-rounder; one who is extremely good at many things (physical and/or intellectual): C. 20. James Crichton of Clunie (1560–?85) was a prodigy of knightly and intellectual accomplishments (O.E.D.). 'Julius Cæsar, Michelangelo, and Napoleon are the admirable Crichtons, *par excellence*, of history.'

admit ... See **soft impeachment.**

affront to national honour, an. A journalistic and political cliché of the 20th century—the century of nationalistic insults.

after one's own heart; e.g. 'That's a man after my own heart', either one that I admire or one much like myself: from ca. 1880. Here, *after = after the nature of*, 'like; according to'.

again and again. Frequently; repetitiously: C. 18–20. Shakespeare, 'I have told thee often, and I re-tell thee again and again' (*Othello*, I, iii, 372: O.E.D.).

airy nothings; esp., **to whisper airy nothings.** Trivial or superficial remarks, empty compliments: from ca. 1870.— Cf. Byron's 'To his gay nothings, nothing was replied' (*Don Juan*, XV: 1824) and Shakespeare's 'Trifles, light as air' (*Othello*, III, iii).

al fresco. This Italian phrase, literally 'in the fresh', i.e. 'in the open air', is a cliché only when adverbial, as in 'We dined al fresco'; very common ca. 1880–1910, but now regarded as an affectation.

'alarums and excursions.' A C. 20 literary cliché or vague meaning (something like 'alarms and sorties'), in reminiscence of a frequent stage-direction of Elizabethan and Jacobean dramatists.

*'alas, poor Yorick!' Poor fellow, he's dead now!: C. 19–20. In allusion to the Shakespeare passage (*Hamlet*, V, i), 'Alas, poor Yorick! I knew him, Horatio: a fellow of infinite jest, of most excellent fancy.'

alive and kicking; all alive. Alert and active: mid C. 19–20; the latter, obsolescent; both, colloquial. From fish-vending.

all and sundry. All, both collectively and individually: from ca. 1830. Scott uses it in *Old Mortality*, 1816.—Cf. **one and all.**

'all hope abandon ye who enter here.' From ca. 1820. A translation of Dante's *lasciate ogni speranza, voi ch'entrate* (verse 9, Canto III, of the *Inferno*).

all in a lifetime; esp. **it's all . . .,** one must expect these things; it happens to all of us: late C. 19–20.

all in the day's work, it (etc.) **is** (or **was**). Such a mishap, such hard work, is in the natural course of a day's labour: C. 20.—Cf. the preceding.

all sorts and conditions of men. Men (and women) of all the different kinds of character and social condition: C. 19–20. From *The Book of Common Prayer*.

all that in him lay (or **lies**), **he** (etc.) **did** (or **does**); **so far as in one lies** (or **lay**). He did all he could; so far as one can: respectively mid C. 19–20 and mid C. 18–20. The latter is the original (mid C. 16). In C. 14, *lie in one's might*; in C. 15–20, *lie in one's power*.

all the good in the world; esp. **something does someone all . . .** It is extremely beneficial to him: C. 20. I.e. all possible good.

all the relevant considerations (?). Every pertinent aspect of a case: from ca. 1910.—Cf. **all things considered**.

all the world and his wife. Everybody from a mentioned village, town, city, district: recorded in 1832: a cliché since ca. 1860.—Cf. the synonymous Northants *all the world and little Billing*.

all things considered. Everything being taken into account: a cautious or precautionary formula, either at the beginning or at the end of a judicious statement: late C. 19–20. It is the title of one of G. K. Chesterton's volumes of essays.—Cf. the absolute *considered* that became obsolete ca. 1800 (see O.E.D., *consider*, last paragraph).

all things to all men, to be. To make onself indispensable to everyone: C. 19–20. 'I am made'—R.V., 'become'—'all things to all men' (1 *Corinthians*, ix. 22): τοῖς πᾶσι γέγονα πάντα: Vulgate, *omnibus omnia factus sum* ('je me suis fait tout à tous', Verdunoy's *Bible Latine-Française*).

all through the ages. Since man's recorded history began: from ca. 1880.—Cf. Tennyson's 'Yet I doubt not thro' the ages one increasing purpose runs' (*Locksley Hall*, 1860).

all to the good, it (or **that**) **is** (or **was** or **will be**). It is, etc., ultimately an advantage: late C. 19–20. Originally commercial: net profit.

all (one's) **worldly goods.** Late C. 19–20, as in 'He lost all his worldly goods'. From the marriage service ('With all my worldly goods I thee endow'), *The Book of Common Prayer*.

almighty dollar, the. The power of wealth: from ca. 1840; originally American. Used by Washington Irving, *The Creole Village*, 1836.—Cf. Ben Jonson's 'almighty gold' (Benham).

almost incredible (?). Hardly credible: late C. 19–20. 'Why! it's almost incredible that *he* should have committed murder.'

alpha and omega; the . . . of. The beginning and the end: learned and literary: C. 19–20. Herschel, 1830, 'The alpha and omega of science' (O.E.D.); 'In Physics, this principle is alpha and omega'. From the Biblical *alpha and omega*, applied (with capital letters) to the Deity: see, e.g., *Revelation*, i. 8, 'I am Alpha and Omega, the beginning and the ending, saith the Lord, which is, and was, and is to come, the Almighty' and, in verse 11, 'I am Alpha and Omega, the first and the last': 'Ἐγώ εἰμι τὸ A καὶ τὸ Ω, ὁ πρῶτος καὶ ὁ ἔσχατος. Alpha is the first, omega the last letter of the Greek alphabet.

'am I my brother's keeper?' See **I am not . . .**

ambulance responds (usually **responded**), **the.** American newspaper reporters: C. 20. (Frank Sullivan.)

amende honorable. A public apology (and, if necessary, material reparation) made to re-establish the offended or injured honour of a person wronged: from ca. 1860. Literally, the French phrase = 'honourable compensation'.

amiable qualities (?). Lovable qualities: mid C. 19–20. 'For all his faults, he has many amiable qualities.'

ample opportunity. Unrestricted opportunity; numerous opportunities: late C. 19–20.

*ample sufficiency, an. A liberal sufficiency; an unstinted supply: from ca. 1880.

ancestral acres. Land inherited from ancestors: C. 20. O'Connor, *Beaconsfield*, 1879, 'The extent of their ancestral acres and the splendour of their ancestral halls' (O.E.D.); now often jocular (e.g. in Denis Mackail's novels).—Cf. **stately homes,** q.v.

and how! (Not in dialogue, where it is a catch-phrase; but in narrative.) 'He was a wise guy—and how': to a notable extent. American: C. 20. From Italian *e come !*

and I don't mean maybe! I say it emphatically—without reservation. 'He fell for that dame, and I don't mean maybe!' This Americanism began as a catch-phrase; since ca. 1936, however, it has been a cliché.

'and so to bed!' C. 20: with the connotation of a jocular 'so that's that' or of satisfaction with a pleasant evening or a well-filled day. Pepy's *Diary*, e.g. on July 22, 1660.

. . . and something to spare. And something left over: late C. 19–20. 'There was enough, and something to spare.'

(and) that's flat! And I mean it!; that's frank!: mid C. 19–20.

angry passions. Angry feelings; anger: mid C. 19–20; obsolescent. Not tautological, for *passion* = 'feeling'.

animated scene, an (or **the, this, that**); e.g. 'The circus presented an animated scene'; mid C. 19–20. Reeve, *Brittany*,

1859, 'The scene was one of the most animated we had met with' (O.E.D.).

another Richmond in the field. Someone else engaged in the same work or in a similar enterprise: C. 19–20. Originally in allusion to Shakespeare's 'I think there be six Richmonds in the field' (*King Richard III*, v, iv).

answer . . . See **in the affirmative.**

answer a fool according to his folly, to. C. 19–20. *Proverbs*, xxvi. 5, 'Answer a fool according to his folly, lest he be wise in his own conceit'—in proportion to his folly, lest he be wise in his own opinion.

any port in a storm (?). Perhaps rather a proverbial saying than a (C. 19–20) cliché. Recorded ca. 1780 in Apperson.

apostle of culture, an. One who, missionary-like, does much—and does it very ably—to spread culture: from ca. 1870. There was originally an allusion to Matthew Arnold, whose *Culture and Anarchy* appeared in 1859.

appeal from Philip drunk to Philip sober, to. To appeal to a person 'in his right mind': literary: C. 19–20. From *provocarem ad Philippum, sed sobrium* ('I would appeal to Philip, but when he is sober', Benham): Valerius Maximus, fl. A.D. 14.

*appear on the scene, to. To appear; to arrive: mid C. 19–20. From an actor's appearing on the stage, esp. for the first time in the performance of a play.

appears to be without foundation, it. Applied to a theory, rumour, statement, complaint: late C. 19–20. Verbose for 'it is apparently baseless'.

apple of discord, the. A source of contention: C. 18–20. From that apple which was given by Paris to the most beautiful of the three Graces; around this apple there has grown a corpus of imagery and symbolism.

16

*apple of one's eye, to be the. (Of a person—or a pet animal) to be precious to a person: C. 18–20. From 'Keep me as the apple of the eye', *Psalms*, xvii. 8.

approximately correct. Sufficiently correct for practical purposes; correct in essentials: C. 20.

après moi le déluge; après nous . . . Literally 'after me (or, us) the deluge', it means 'I (or we) don't care: the trouble will come after we die': C. 19–20. The former is a proverbial form, recorded in a French dictionary of proverbs in 1758, one year after Madame de Pompadour uttered the latter to Louis XV. Benham remarks that the prototype is the Greek saying, ἐμοῦ θανόντος (I being dead), denounced by Cicero as inhuman and disgraceful.—Cf. 'a sailor's farewell'.

apron-strings, as in **tied to someone's . . .,** wholly under a person's influence: mid C. 19–20.

*aqua pura is a cliché when used as equivalent to water (as a beverage): mid C. 19–20; slightly obsolescent. Properly this Latin phrase = 'pure water'.

arbiter elegantiarum. An acknowledged authority on—properly, judge of—matters of taste: C. 18–20. An adaptation of Tacitus's *elegantiæ arbiter*. (Benham.)

'Arcades ambo.' Arcadians both: C. 18–20. Virgil, 'Arcades ambo, | Et cantare pares, et respondere parati' (*Eclogues*, vii, 4).—Cf. **et in Arcadia ego vixi.**

Argus-eyed. Sharp-sighted and extremely watchful: mid C. 19–20; slightly obsolescent. Argus: a mythological person with a hundred eyes.

*armed to the teeth. Fully armed; fully equipped for war or for a particular battle: from ca. 1840. Cobden, 1849 (in a speech), 'Is there any reason why we should be armed to the teeth?' (O.E.D.)

arrangements (esp. **suitable arrangements**) **have been made.** There have been preparations; it is prepared: late C. 19–20.

artful deceiver, an. A cunning wheedler (or attractive swindler); often jocular: mid C. 19–20. Applied only to men.

as a matter of fact. In point of fact: C. 19–20. Usually the prelude to a lie—or, at best, an evasion.

as a matter of form. As a piece of routine; merely routine: C. 20. 'Yes, you must sign it; just as a matter of form, you know.' *A matter of form*, 'a mere formality', is likewise a cliché.

as ... as makes no matter. See **as makes no matter.**

(as) 'every schoolboy knows.' As a cliché, since ca. 1850. 'The frequency of Macaulay's reference to somewhat abstruse matters as subjects which any public schoolboy would know, has led to his being credited with the phrase. It is to be found, however, in many earlier authors', e.g. R. Burton, 1621, and Swift. (Benham.)

as (or **so**) **far as in me lies.** See **all that in him lay.**

as far as that goes ... See **so far as that goes.**

as good luck would have it, something happened—existed—prevailed: late C. 19–20.

as makes no matter, in, e.g., 'It is correct—as near as makes no matter', as makes no difference; i.e. virtually correct: late C. 19–20.

(as) man to man. Frankly; with frank friendliness (as befits one man speaking to another): late C. 19–20.

as one man (?). Unanimously: C. 19–20. 'The vast crowd applauded as one man.' Cf. *Judges*, xx. 8 and other passages in the Bible, although there the sense is rather 'altogether' than 'unanimously'.

*as the crow flies. Direct; in a straight line, i.e. without allowing for topographical obstacles: from ca. 1840.

as well as can (or **could**) **be expected,** as in 'She's doing as well as can be expected' (almost obligatory on husbands speaking of wives within a week of parturition): late C. 19–20.

as ye sow, so shall ye reap. An adaptation of *as you sow, so will you reap*, a proverb dating from C. 18 and occurring in various forms (see Apperson). There seem to be allusions to Cicero's *ut sementem feceris ita metes* ('as you do your sowing, so shall you reap', Benham) and 'By their fruits ye shall know them', *Matthew*, vii. 16 (R.V.).

ask for bread and receive a stone, to. To receive very much less than one asks for; to seek compassion and find hard-heartedness: mid C. 18–20. Perhaps from an epigram by the Rev. Samuel Wesley († 1739); cf. *Matthew*, viii. 9.

assume as proved, we must. A legal cliché of C. 19–20.

assume heavy responsibilities, to. See **heavy responsibilities.**

at a loose end; e.g. 'I was at a loose end', without anything particular (or planned) to do: colloquial: late C. 19–20. From a horse whose tether has broken or slipped.

*at (a person's) **beck and call, to be.** Obliged or willing to attend to somebody's every order, to satisfy his every whim: from ca. 1880. Here, *beck* is a nod indicative of command.

at daggers drawn. Hostile to each other; at the point—actual or potential—of quarrelling; mid C. 19–20. Originally, *at daggers' drawing*, characteristic of an age when quarrels were settled by a fight with daggers.

at death's door, to be or **lie; to bring to death's door.** To be, to bring, to the point of death; to be extremely ill: mid C. 19–20. Current in C 16 (and after).

---

at long last. Ultimately; at last: C. 20, though Carlyle used it in 1864 and *at the long last* was current in C. 16–17.

*at one fell swoop. At one blow: C. 19–20. 'What, all my pretty chickens and their dam, | At one fell swoop', Shakspeare, *Macbeth*, IV, iii.

at one's earliest convenience is a cliché only in the form *at your . . .* , q.v. at **your . . .**

at one's last gasp, to be. To be at the point of death; or loosely, to be utterly exhausted: C. 20. I.e. at one's last (gasping) breath.

at one's wit's (or **wits'**) **end, to be.** To be utterly perplexed; at a complete loss what to do: C. 18–20, though common even in C. 16–17. *Wit* = 'mental capacity'.

at (a person's) **own sweet will.** As and when one pleases; as it suits one: mid C. 19–20. Fathered by Wordsworth, 1802, in a sonnet. In 1902, H. Littledale, in the Preface to Dyce's glossary of Shakespeare, writes, 'Now that each edition of **Shak**espeare seems to number the lines of prose and verse at its own sweet will, a chaos of line-numberings will be upon us unless some agreement is arrived at before long'.

at sixes and sevens, to be. To be in a state of confusion, disorder, or neglect: late C. 18–20. From dicing.

at the cross-roads. At a critical point in one's career or spiritual life: from ca. 1890. Not knowing one's way, one comes to a cross-roads: which road is one to take?—Cf. Meredith's *Diana of the Crossways*, 1883.

*at the end of one's tether, to be. To be unable, physically, financially, or mentally, to do anything more to relieve the situation: C. 19–20. (A tethered animal.)

at the first blush. At the first glance; at first sight (but not on detailed examination): C. 19–20, though fairly common in

C. 16–17. *Blush* is in its otherwise obsolete sense, 'a glance, a look'.

*at the psychological moment. In the nick of time; at the critical moment; incorrect uses and senses, which constitute the cliché: from ca. 1895. 'The Prince . . . always . . . turns up at the psychological moment—to use a very hard-worked and sometimes misused phrase', *The Westminster Gazette*, October 30, 1897. For the correct use, see the O.E.D.

at this juncture. At this (critical) point; at this conjuncture of affairs: journalistic: C. 20.

atmosphere of doubt, an. A general feeling of doubt; a pervasive feeling of doubt: C. 20.

Attic salt. Refined yet trenchant wit; subtle, delicate wit: late C. 18–20; slightly obsolescent. A translation of *sal Atticum.*

au courant, as in 'She likes to be au courant with'—acquainted with—'the latest gossip': from ca. 1860. (Many French phrases became popular in England ca. 1850–1900.)

auspicious occasion; esp. **on this . . .** At this happy time; on this important social occasion: public speakers': late C. 19–20.

average ability (?). Ability of the prevalent standard: C. 20. 'All I want is a man of average ability and more than average honesty.'

avoid . . . See **plague.**

awkward alternative, an. An embarrassing alternative: late C. 19–20.—Cf. the next.

awkward fix, an (colloquial); **an awkward predicament.** An embarrassing, unpleasant, or even dangerous predicament: C. 20.

*axe to grind, an; esp. **to have no . . . ,** to be disinterested. Recorded in 1811, it became a cliché in mid C. 19.

B

back the wrong horse, to (colloquial). To support the wrong cause, uphold the wrong man: from ca. 1860.

back to the wall; esp. **to have one's back to the wall** or **stand with one's . . .** C. 19–20, but especially since Haig's famous *backs to the wall* order of 1918.

*bag and baggage. With all one's impedimenta: 1552, Huloet; it became a stock phrase in C. 18. Like so many 'reduplications', it was generated, in part at least, by a desire to alliterate.

baker's dozen, a. Thirteen: C. 19–20; slightly obsolescent.

balm in Gilead; esp. as a quotation, **'is there no balm in Gilead?'**—of which the completion is, 'is there no physician there' (*Jeremiah*, viii. 22): a comfort, a soothing agency: C. 18–20.

balmy breezes; balmy weather. Very mild, pleasant breezes or weather: late C. 19–20; the latter is only a borderline case.

baptism of fire; esp. **to receive one's baptism of fire,** to be exposed, for the first time, to rifle and/or gun fire: late C. 19–20. Perhaps originally with allusion to the *baptism of blood* (violent death) of unbaptized martyrs.

'Barkis is willin'.' A phrase that indicates one's willingness and readiness: mid C. 19–20. Dickens, *David Copperfield*, ch. v (published in 1849): Barkis's quietly persistent courtship of Peggotty.

Barmecide feast, a. An imaginary sumptuous feast; great illusory benefits: mid C. 19–20; obsolescent. The Barmecides, a princely family of Bagdad, once put before a beggar a succession of magnificent dishes—all empty.

*battle royal, a. A general engagement, a free-for-all fight, a general squabble: C. 19–20. From cock-fighting: a battle royal was one in which more than two birds were engaged.

be-all and (the) end-all, the. The thing that matters far more than anything else: an aim or purpose to which all else is subordinate: C. 19–20. Very few apprehend it as coming, in the longer form, from Shakespeare's *Macbeth* (I, vii).

be in good hands, to. To be well cared for, trustworthily guarded or treated: from ca. 1870.

*be in the same boat with, to. To be in the same position, enterprise, circumstances: mid C. 19–20.

be of good cheer! See **good cheer . . .**

*be that as it may is an introductory formula, meaning 'nevertheless': from ca. 1880. ' "Be that as it may," said the Duke, unconsciously supporting himself on what had been the pivotal phrase of his celebrated speech in the House of Lords in 1908 . . .', Michael Innes, *Hamlet, Revenge!*, 1937.

bear the brunt (of the battle), to. The chief stress, most violent part, of the battle, hence metaphorically of any struggle, hardship, misfortune: mid C. 19–20. *Brunt* = 'violence; shock'.

beard the lion in his den, to; hence, **to beard a person in his den.** Respectively mid C. 19–20 and late C. 19–20. Scott, in *Marmion*, 1808, has 'And darest thou then to beard the lion in his den, | The Douglas in his hall?' (adduced by Benham). With an allusion to Daniel in the den of lions.

'bears his blushing honours . . .' See **blushing honours.**

beat a retreat, to, is a cliché only in its figurative sense, which is simply 'to retreat': from ca. 1860. From sounding retreat on the drum.

*beat about the bush, to. To hum and haw before saying (or doing) that which one wishes to say (or do); to approach a matter over-cautiously or circuitously: late C. 18–20. From hunting.

beat swords into ploughshares, to. To turn the armaments of war into the implements of peace; to become pacific: mid C. 19–20. 'They shall beat their swords into ploughshares, and their spears into pruning hooks', *Isaiah*, ii. 4 (cf. *Micah*, iv. 3), or, as the Vulgate has it, 'Conflabunt [they will forge] gladios suos in vomeres, et lanceas suas in falces'.

beaten at the post (colloquial). Defeated when success is almost within one's grasp: from ca. 1870. From horse-racing.

beaten track, the. The well-trod way: a cliché only when employed figuratively: from ca. 1870; apparently American originally, Emerson having used it in 1855.

bed and board; esp. **at bed and board,** in bed and at table; i.e. lodging and food: C. 15–20, but a cliché only in C. 19–20.

bed of roses, a; usually, **no bed of roses,** a far from comfortable resting-place or position, a most unpleasant employment: mid C. 19–20.—Cf. the obsolete *bed of down*.

*bee in one's bonnet, a; esp. **to have a . . .** To be a crank about something: C. 18–20. Semi-proverbial. A bee so placed, excites and flusters the person.

beer and skittles; esp. ***not all beer and skittles.** Self-indulgence and amusement: mid C. 19–20. In the positive, it occurs in C. S. Calverley's *Fly Leaves*, 1872.

before we—more frequently, **you—know where you are,** something will have happened. 'Christmas will be here before you know where you are.' A colloquial cliché dating from ca. 1860.

before you are many years (occasionally, **months) older; before you are much older.** Before long; soon:

from ca. 1870. ' "There's some that gossip. . . . You'll find that, Dr Law, before you are many months older" ', J. Storer Clouston, *Scotland Expects*, 1936.

before you were born . . . See **born** . . .

beg and petition, to. To ask (a person) earnestly: C. 19–20; obsolescent. Alexander Bain notes it in his *Rhetoric.*

beggars (or **beggared**) **description, it;** esp. **. . . all description,** it is (or was) utterly beyond the powers of description to picture; it was indescribable: late C. 18–20. 'For her own person | It beggared all description', Shakespeare, concerning Cleopatra.

beginning of a new era, the; often, **it marks the . . .,** it is epoch-making, a mountain-divide in historical geography: from ca. 1880.

*beginning of the end, the. The initial phase of decay, degeneration, ruin, death; an unmistakable adumbration of disaster or finality or cessation: mid C. 19–20. A rendering of *le commencement de la fin,* Talleyrand's attributed epigram made in respect—and during the course—of the Hundred Days (Benham).

behind the scenes. In private; behind what the public sees, esp. in relation to important events: mid C. 19–20. The origin appears in: 'Murders and executions are always transacted behind the scenes in the French theatre': 1711, Addison, *The Spectator*, No. 44.

believe it or not, . . . ; you may (etc.) **not believe it, but** (e.g., **it's true**). Introductory formulas: late C. 19–20. In late 1939–40, there was running in London a theatrical entertainment entitled *Believe It or Not.*

believe one's (own) eyes, to; esp. **cannot believe . . .,** not to trust one's sight: from ca. 1870. 'I could not believe my eyes: there was the shy Lancelot with a girl on each arm.' (If seeing's believing, then much *believing* is mere folly.)

belong to—to live in—a world apart, to. To belong to a (much) higher social class or to have a much more comfortable home; to be otherworldly: respectively C. 20 and late C. 19–20.

belted earl, a. An earl; an aristocrat: mid C. 19–20; in C. 20, often jocular. *Belted* refers to that cincture which distinguishes an earl.

beneath contempt. Utterly contemptible: from ca. 1870.

benefit of the doubt, the; esp. **to give someone the benefit . . .,** to treat him as innocent because, though there is doubt, he has not been proved guilty: from ca. 1890. From the law-courts.

'best is yet to be, the.' Late C. 19–20. Browning, *Rabbi Ben-Ezra*, 'The best is yet to be, | Grow old along with me!'

'best-laid schemes o' mice an' men | Gang aft a-gly, the.' Our plans often miscarry: late C. 18–20. Robert Burns, *To a Mouse*, 1785; the quotation is concluded thus, 'And lea'e us nought but grief and pain | For promised joy'.

'best of all possible worlds, in the' and **'all's for the best in the . . .'** The latter is a C. 20 elaboration of the C. 19–20 cliché—the former. 'Dans le meilleur des mondes possibles', Voltaire, *Candide*, ch. vi.—Cf. Chaucer's 'I woot wel clerkes wol seyn, as hem leste | By arguments, that all is for the best' ('The Franklin's Tale', 158–9).

*bête noire. A bugbear: mid C. 19–20. This Gallicism means 'black beast' and is frequently misspelt *bête noir*. Equally a cliché is **pet aversion** (late C. 19–20), *aversion* being 'an object of aversion'.

better and better. Increasingly good: C. 19–20. It found its culmination in 'Émile Coué's formula of "Auto-Suggestion", as propounded in London, June, 1922' (Benham): *Every day and in every way, I am getting better and better.*

---

*better half, one's; esp. **my better half:** my wife: mid C. 19–20, though used as early as 1580 (by Sidney in *Arcadia*). In C. 17–18, also of husband. Originally a Latinism: see the O.E.D. at *better*, adj., 3c.

better left unsaid. (It is) better unsaid: late C. 19–20.

better or ... See **for better ...**

better than a play, it is (or **was**). It is (or was) most entertaining: mid C. 19. There is an adumbration in the Latin of Aretino († 1557): see Benham.

between Scylla ... See **Scylla ...**

between the cup and the lip. Between plan and realization, expectation and fulfilment, with the connotation of prevention at the last moment: C. 19–20, though used as early as C. 16.

between the devil and the deep sea. Between two dangers; faced with two considerable difficulties: mid C. 18–20. In C. 20, often ... *deep blue sea.*

between two fires. Exposed to an assault or a danger (literal or figurative) on both sides or from front and rear: from ca. 1880. I.e. gun-fire.

between you and me and the bed-post (or **gate-post**). In confidence: colloquial: late C. 19–20. An elaboration of *between you and me* or *between ourselves.*

beyond a (or **any possible**) **shadow of doubt.** Indubitable, certain: late C. 19–20. The *possible* form is a Gilbertian allusion.

beyond belief (?). Incredible: mid C. 19–20. 'It is beyond belief that he should have failed to see it.'

beyond the ken of mortal man. Beyond the vision (hence, knowledge) of man: mid C. 19–20.

*beyond the pale. Beyond the bounds of decency (moral or social); no longer acceptable to Society or respectable people: late C. 19–20; since ca. 1920, often ironic of ostracism. *Pale* is 'a district or country subject to a certain jurisdiction'.

'big fleas have little fleas . . .', where the dots represent a dying fall or a significant pause. In full, 'Great fleas have little fleas upon their backs to bite 'em, | And little fleas have lesser fleas, and so *ad infinitum*', adumbrated in Swift's poem, *Poetry, a Rhapsody* (Benham): mid C. 19–20; in C. 20, generally misquoted as *big fleas* . . .

bird has or **had flown.** The sought person has (had) decamped: mid C. 19–20.

bird of ill omen, a. A person that augurs ill, a 'Jonah': C. 19–20. From Roman augury by birds: *bonis avibus*; *malis avibus*, 'with happy omens; with bad omens' (literally, 'birds'). (Benham.)

bird of passage, a. A person always on the move from one place (or country) to another: mid C. 19–20. From migrant birds.

*birds of a feather is the cliché-shortening (C. 19–20) of the proverb, 'birds of a feather flock together' (C. 17–20; in C. 16, '. . . fly . . .'; 'the Greeks had a word for it', and so had the Romans of Cicero's day).

bite off more than one can chew, to. To undertake more than one can deal with or perform: late C. 19–20.

bitter complaint, a; bitter complaints. A harsh or trenchant or sharply reproachful complaint or complaints: C. 19–20.

bitter irony. Trenchant or virulent irony: mid C. 19–20.— Cf. **scathing sarcasm.**

blank amazement. Utter or unrelieved amazement; utterly prostrating amazement: from ca. 1870. Esp. *a look of blank amazement.*—Cf. the next.

blank despair. Helpless or nonplussed or prostrating despair: from ca. 1880.

blaze a (or **the**) **trail, to.** To show the way, to be a pioneer: American from ca. 1890; English from ca. 1905. From blazing (marking) trees to determine a path.

blazing inferno, a. See **inferno.**

bless one's lucky star (or **one's stars**), **to.** To be grateful for one's good luck: respectively late C. 19–20 and late C. 18–20. From astrology.

blessed word 'Mesopotamia', the. A magic word: from ca. 1870. (See esp. Benham.) It owes much of its charm and potency to its sonority.

*****blessing in disguise, a.** Good issuing from evil, good fortune (etc.) from misfortune: from ca. 1890.

*****blind leading the blind, the.** A cliché formed from the proverb, 'when the blind leads the blind, both fall into the ditch', dating from C. 16 and adumbrated in *Luke*, vi. 39, as a parable (Apperson, *English Proverbs*).

blissful ignorance was generated by 'Where ignorance is bliss, 'tis folly to be wise' (Gray's *Ode on Eton College*, 1747): mid C. 18–20.

bloated armaments (?). Swollen or over-large armaments: journalistic: from ca. 1880. Disraeli, 1862, 'Those bloated armaments which naturally involve states in financial embarrassments' (O.E.D.).

bloated plutocrat, a. A rich man: Socialistic: C. 20; since ca. 1925, generally jocular. Literally, a plutocrat too proud or excessively pampered.

blood and iron. This phrase (*Blut und Eisen*), 'military force as opposed to diplomacy', used by Bismarck in a speech delivered to the Diet in 1862, was taken up by Tennyson in his poem, *A Word for the Country*, thus: 'Not with dreams, but with blood and with iron, shall a nation be moulded at last'; a cliché since ca. 1880. (Benham.)

blood and treasure. See **expense of . . .**

blood-curdling yell, a. A horrible and/or eery yell: late C. 19–20. A requisite in shockers and melodramas.

'bloody but unbowed.' Since ca. 1890. From 'Under the bludgeonings of fate | My head is bloody, but unbowed' (W. E. Henley, *Invictus*).

bloody Mary. Mary, Queen of England: a Protestant cliché: C. 19–20. Thomas Hood the Elder, (of coins) 'Now stamped with the image of good Queen Bess, | And now of a Bloody Mary'. From her stake-burnings of protestant Protestants.

blot on the landscape, a. Something that spoils the scenery, disfigures the landscape: late C. 19–20; now often jocularly applied to a person.

blow hot and cold, to. To be enthusiastic and then, very soon, apathetic: semi-proverbial: C. 18–20. Recorded in C. 16. Apperson compares a passage in Plautus. See also *soon hot, soon cold*, in Benham (1936 edition, p. 884a).

blow off steam, to To rid oneself of one's indignation or superfluous energy: colloquial: from ca. 1860. From an engine's blowing off excess steam.

blow one's own trumpet, to. To brag; to advertise oneself: mid C. 19–20.

blown to smithereens (colloquial). Blown to pieces: utterly shattered and destroyed by an explosion: late C. 19–20.

*blue blood. Aristocratic blood; hence, aristocratic rank or condition: from ca. 1870. A translation of the Spanish *sangre azul* (Castilian families uncontaminated by admixture of Jewish or Moorish): veins show in the fair much more than in the dark. (O.E.D.)

*blue Mediterranean, the. The Mediterranean, which usually isn't: from ca. 1910.

blunt instrument, a. A detective-story writers' cliché, dating from ca. 1920. A very vague phrase, covering anything from a club to a spanner.

'blushing honours thick upon him'; usually, **he bears his . . . ;** occasionally, **with his . . .** A cliché of C. 19–20. From Shakespeare, *King Henry VIII*, III, ii.

bolt from the blue, a. A figurative thunderbolt from a blue sky; a blow, a misfortune that is unexpected, unannounced: mid C. 19–20.

bonds. See **holy matrimony.**

bone of contention, a. A cause of discord, a subject that leads to dissension or bitter argument: C. 19–20. A marrowy or juicy bone may cause strife between dogs.

*boon companion, a. Properly, a companion in drinking; loosely, a pleasant, merry companion at any time: C. 19–20. Benham cites *nulli te facias nimis sodalem*, 'make yourself too much a companion to no one'.

boot is on the other leg, the. The case is altered; the responsibility is the other party's: C. 19–20.

booted and spurred. Prepared; ready for something: mid C. 19–20; in C. 20, often jocular. Macaulay, *History of England*, attributes it to Richard Rumbold, 1685. (Benham.)

bored to death (or **tears**). Extremely bored: late C. 19–20. In 1782, Fanny Burney, in *Cecilia*, wrote, 'He really bores me to a degree' (*ibid.*)

*born and bred; esp. **he was a . . . born and bred** or **born and bred in** (some place). 'He was a Lancashire man born and bred', a native of Lancashire and reared there. From ca. 1870.

31

born in the purple. See **purple . . .**

born or thought of, before you were. Before your parents became sexually intimate: late C. 19–20.

born under a lucky star. Born lucky: C. 19–20. The planet presiding at one's birth being a favourable one: astrology.

*born with a silver spoon in one's mouth. Born in prosperous circumstances: C. 18–20. Semi-proverbial.—Cf. **cradled . . .**

borrowed plumes. With fine but borrowed clothes; metaphorically, bright with a lustre shed by another: C. 19–20.—Cf. Horace's *furtivis nudata coloribus*, 'stripped of its stolen colours' (Benham).

bottom of the deep blue sea, the; esp. at the . . ., on the sea-bed; drowned: late C. 19–20.

bottomless pit, the. Hell: late C. 18–20. The phrase occurs seven times in *Revelation*, e.g. 'To him was given the key of the bottomless pit': ἐδόθη αὐτῷ ἡ κλεὶς τοῦ φρέατος τῆς ἀβύσσον, literally 'there was given to him the key of the well of the abyss'.

bounden duty, one's. One's clear duty, indubitable obligation: C. 18–20, though common enough in C. 16–17. The duty by which one is bound.

bow and scrape, to. See **bowing and scraping.**

bowels of the earth, the; esp. in the, deep in the earth, in a mine: C. 19–20. Recorded for ca. 1593 (O.E.D.).

bowing and scraping, n.; to bow and scrape, to be too ceremoniously polite; to be obsequiously polite or reverent: mid C. 19–20. To bow the head and scrape the ground in drawing back one foot.

Box and Cox. Applied (a cliché since the 1880's) to 'an arrangement in which two persons take turns in sustaining a part, occupying a position, or the like' (O.E.D.). From J. H. Morton's farce, *Box and Cox*, 1847.

brand of Cain, the. The stigma (*signum*) of murder, esp. of a brother: mid C. 19–20. Cain was the first fratricide, indeed the first murderer, to be mentioned in the Bible (*Genesis*, iv. 15, 'Posuitque Dominus Cain signum').

brave and the fair, the. Heroes (actual or potential) and lovely women: late C. 19–20.—Cf. the next.

*brave men and fair women. A transposition of the quotation-cliché, **'fair women and brave men'**, q.v.: mid C. 1920.

break the ice, to (figurative). To make a beginning, pre-pare the way: mid C. 18–20, though Cotgrave (at *acheminer*) shows that it was an accepted phrase as early as 1611. In mid C. 19–20, generally applied to overcoming coldness or stiffness between strangers. (O.E.D.)

breath of heaven (or **Spring**), **a;** generally as a simile, **like a . . .,** applied to something that is as pure and beneficent as an emanation from heaven or as refreshing (and well-omened) as an exhalation of Spring: mid C. 19–20. Byron has the former.

breath of one's (or **the**) **nostrils, the.** Breathing, as tantamount to life; life as indicated or constituted by the act of breathing; 'the breath of life': literary: C. 19–20; obsolescent. Perhaps originally in allusion to *Genesis*, vii. 22, 'All in whose nostrils was the breath of life'.

breathe freely, to (figurative). To be at ease, esp. after risk or danger or excitement: mid C. 19–20.

breathe one's last, to. To die: C. 19–20. Shakespeare, in 3 *Henry VI*, v, ii, 40, 'Montague hath breath'd his last'.

bred in the bone. From the proverb, 'what is bred in the bone will not out of the flesh' (C. 15 onwards; recorded in C. 13 in a Latin form, *teste* Apperson).

bribery and corruption. Bribery, esp. political or legal: mid C. 19–20.

bright and early (colloquial), 'early in the morning', applied to rising from bed or to matutinal arrival: C. 20.

bright orb of day, the. The sun: C. 19–20; in C. 19, thought to be poetical; in C. 20, slightly ludicrous; except as an elegancy, it is now somewhat archaic.

*bring grist to one's (or the) mill, to; it is all grist to one's (or the) mill. To obtain work that brings in money; it all helps financially: C. 19–20. From a semi-proverbial saying recorded in C. 17.

bring home to, to (?). To make a person fully realize something: from ca. 1880. 'His mother's death brought home to him how much he had loved her.'

bring (someone) **to his knees, to.** To humble or abase him: C. 19–20.

British Lion, the. The British nation: mid C. 19–20. (Dryden, 1687; Burke, 1796.) From the lion as the national emblem of Great Britain. (O.E.D.)

British phlegm. Calm and stolidity: late C. 19–20. 'L'Anglais avec son sangfroid perpétuel.'

British raj, the. British rule (in India): pukka sahibs': from ca. 1880. Hindi *raj*, 'rule; sovereignty': cf. *raja*(*h*), 'a prince'.

broke to the wide, wide world (colloquial); **broke to the wide** (slangy). Penniless; ruined, bankrupt: late C. 19–20; from ca. 1910.

broken reed, a. An undependable person (or thing): C. 19–20. Young, *Night Thoughts*, 1742, 'Lean not on Earth . . . A broken reed at best' (Benham).

34

Brother Jonathan and **Uncle Sam.** A typical American, and the United States of America personified: C. 19–20; mid C. 19–20. *Brother Jonathan*: from a remark frequently made by George Washington. (Benham.)

*brown study, a; esp., in a . . . Absorbed in (melancholy) thought, serious thought: mid C. 18–20. Brown is a sober colour.

bruit about (or abroad), to (?). To report widely, to rumour in many quarters: mid C. 19–20. *Bruit abroad* has much the longer history and is rather the commoner: it would, therefore, be more precise to classify *bruit about* as a potential, *bruit abroad* as an actual, cliché.

brutal atrocity, a. A brutally cruel and heinous act: C. 20: originally and, in the main, still journalistic (hence also political).

brute force. Force and violence employed without intelligence; senseless force; sheer or mere force: mid C. 19–20. Recorded in 1736 (O.E.D.): cf. *brute matter*, insentient matter.

buffeted by fate; the buffeting (or buffets) of fate. Battered—the batterings of—misfortune: late C. 19–20.—Cf. Shakespeare's 'Whom the vile blows and buffets of the world | Hath so incens'd, that . . .' (*Macbeth*, III, i, 109–10).

build castles in the air, to. See **castle in Spain.**

build upon sand, to. To build insecurely; to do something with inadequate preparations or on an insecure basis: C. 19–20. *Matthew*, vii. 26, 'A foolish man, which built his house upon the sand'.

bulwark of the State, a. A person that is a powerful safeguard of the State's prosperity and/or liberty: mid C. 19–20. —Cf. **pillar of the Church.**

bundle of nerves, to be a. To be in an extremely nervous condition; to start at every noise, show irritation at every mishap or hindrance and fear at every alarm: from ca. 1910.

burden and heat of the day, bear the. To do all the hard work: mid C. 19–20. 'Equal unto us, which have borne the burden and heat of the day' (R.V., '. . . the burden of the day and the scorching heat'), *Matthew*, xx. 12.

burden of proof, the. An adaptation of the Latin legal tag, *onus probandi*, 'the burden of proving': C. 19–20; originally, legal.

burden of (the) years, the. Old age; the approach of old age; the physical debilities of old age: rather literary: late C. 19–20; slightly obsolescent.

*burn one's boats, to. Deliberately to preclude retreat: from ca. 1890. From an occasional practice of invaders.

burn one's fingers, to. To come to harm: C. 19–20. Probably from the proverb, 'Never burn your fingers to snuff another man's candle' (cf. *cat's paw* used figuratively).

burn the candle at both ends, to. To work early and late; to work hard and play hard (or to dissipate); esp. to work little and play much: mid C. 18–20. From French.

burn the midnight oil, to. To study until late at night: mid C. 19–20. There is an adumbration in Quarles's *Emblems*, 1635, in Book II, No. 2. (Benham.)

burning question, a. A subject that causes keen and general debate or discussion, esp. by the public: from ca. 1880. Used by Disraeli in 1873. The O.E.D. compares French *question brûlante* and German *brennende Frage*.

(of lights) burning far into the night. Applied to buildings where persons are studying late or are tending the sick: mid C. 19–20.

burnt to a cinder. Utterly consumed by fire: late C. 19–20.

bury the hatchet, to. To cease from quarrelling, to settle a quarrel: American from ca. 1885, English in C. 20. Red Indians bury a tomahawk when they conclude a peace.

business as usual. Despite difficulties, let us carry on as if nothing were wrong: beginning, in 1914–18, as a slogan, it became, ca. 1920, a cliché.

business, to go about one's; send (a person) **about his business.** To attend to one's own business or affairs; to dismiss abruptly or ignominiously: mid C. 18–20; C. 19–20.

'but me no *buts*.' Make no objection!: from ca. 1820; Mrs Centlivre used the phrase in 1708, but it was Scott's employment of it in *The Antiquary*, 1816, which popularized it.

'butchered to make a Roman holiday.' From Byron's *Childe Harold*, Canto IV (published in 1818), stanza 141: a cliché since ca. 1825.

*butter wouldn't (properly **would not**) **melt in her mouth;** esp., **she looks as if . . .** She looks demure and good: and is less good and demure than she looks. C. 19–20. The longer version comes from Charles Macklin's comedy, *The Man of the World*, 1781: but C. 20 users never apprehend it as a quotation.

butterfly (broken) on the wheel, a. A gay creature (usually female) broken by circumstance or ruined by the social system: C. 19–20. Pope, *Epistle to Dr Arbuthnot* (1734), 'Who breaks a butterfly upon a wheel?' (Benham.)

buxom wench, a. A sturdy, healthy, not ugly girl: C. 19–20; in C. 20, generally facetious.

*buy a pig in a poke, to. To buy without seeing what one is buying: semi-proverbial: C. 19–20. Chaucer and Sir Thomas More have *pig(ge)s in a poke* and a French proverb of 1498 runs, 'Folie est d'acheter chat en sac' (Benham).

buy for an old song, to. To buy very cheaply: from ca. 1780, although it was common by 1708, for in *The Philosophical Transactions of the Royal Society* for that year we find the significant sentence, 'An old book might be bought for an old song (as we say)', O.E.D. Old sheets of music sell very, very cheaply.

by a long chalk; not by a long chalk. By far ('by a long chalk the best'); far from it, not at all (' "That'll mean disgrace."—"Not by a long chalk, you'll find" '): mid C. 19–20. Chalk is used for scoring points.

by all means do! Please do!: late C. 19–20. *By all means* is merely an elaborated *yes*.

by fits and starts. Spasmodically; at irregular intervals: mid C. 18–20, though common since early C. 17. An elaboration of *by fits* (fitfully).

***by hook or by crook.** By any means; at all costs: C. 18–20. 'In hope her to attain by hook or crook' (Spenser, *The Faerie Queene*, III, i, st. 13). (Benham.)

by leaps and bounds; esp., **to go ahead by . . .,** to progress, or grow, very rapidly: from ca. 1880. An elaboration of *by leaps*: cf. **by fits and starts.**

by no manner of means. Interjectionally, 'No!'; adverbially, an intensive *not*: late C. 19–20.

by no means certain; esp., **it is by no . . .,** it is extremely uncertain, or, at best, uncertain: mid C. 19–20. *By no means* signifies little more than *not*.

by rule of thumb. In a rough-and-ready way; by dint of practice; empirically: late C. 18–20. Lit., by using the thumb as a linear measure: practically, not scientifically.

***by the same token.** Serves to introduce 'a corroborating circumstance, often weakened down to a mere associated fact', as in 'To receive letters from people whom they do not know, and are, by the same token, never likely to know', Phyllis

Dare, 1907 (O.E.D.): Shakespeare has it in 1606, but it is hardly a cliché before late C. 18.

by the sweat of one's brow. By hard manual labour: C. 19–20. An adaptation of 'In the sweat of thy face shalt thou eat bread' (*Genesis*, iii. 19).

by word of mouth. Orally: dating from C. 16, it was not a cliché before mid C. 18 or, at earliest, 1700.

C

cabined, cribbed . . . See **cribbed . . .**

cacoëthes scribendi. The itch to write; scripturience (on *prurience*): C. 18–20; rather literary. This phrase of Juvenal's— he was a great phrase-maker, a coiner of arresting phrases— offsets the Latin *cacoëthes loquendi* (an irresistible urge to talk).

cakes and ale. (Good food) and drink, with a connotation of merrymaking: C. 19–20. Shakespeare, *Twelfth Night*, II, iii, 'Dost thou think, because thou art virtuous, there shall be no more cakes and ale?'

call a halt, to. To cease; to desist: from ca. 1890. A weakening of the original, the correct, sense ('to decree or proclaim a halt'). 'They had been quarrelling a long time when somebody shouted, 'Hadn't we better call a halt and get some work done?'

*call a spade a spade, to. To call a thing by its right, esp. by its plain English name: current in English since C. 16 ('I cannot say the crow is white, | But needs must call a spade a spade', Humphrey Gifford, †1600); but a cliché only in C. 19–20. The prototype is in Aristophanes, but the operative original is the Latin *ficus ficus, ligonem ligonem vocat,* 'he calls figs *figs*, and a hoe a *hoe*' (Benham). Most people nowadays call it 'a bloody shovel'.

call in question, to. To dispute, or cast doubt on: mid C. 19–20. From the literary sense 'to summon for examination or trial'.

call of the wild, the. The appeal of Nature 'in the raw': C. 20. Firmly established by the immediate and long-lasting popularity of Jack London's novel, *The Call of the Wild*, which, published in 1903, became a best-seller throughout the English-speaking world and was translated into many languages.

call—esp., **not to be able to call**—**one's soul one's own, to.** (Unable) to live a (spiritually) independent life; to be in all ways a slave: mid C. 19–20.—Cf. R. L. Stevenson's 'To know what you prefer, instead of humbly saying "Amen" to what the world tells you you ought to prefer, is to have kept your soul alive' (Benham).

*calm (or lull) before the storm, the. Peace before war; quiet before an excess of noise: late C. 19–20. Much used by statesmen in 1938–39. Immediately before a storm, there is, usually, a period of silence—of suspense.

came the . . . is a literary formula-cliché, dating from ca. 1936 (though isolated instances occur earlier); esp., **came the dawn** and **came the War:** I have seen even 'came Lenin'. Perhaps on the French *vint la Révolution* (of 1789).

can safely say that . . ., I or **you.** I may assert, or affirm, that . . . : late C. 19–20.

captain of one's soul, the. Dating from ca. 1890 and arising from W. E. Henley's 'I am the master of my fate, I am the captain of my soul', in his famous poem *Invictus* ('my unconquerable soul').

*captains of industry. Men who own, manage, or control great industrial businesses: from ca. 1925: originally (and still commonly) journalistic.—Cf. **City magnate** and **Napoleon of industry:** apotheosis of Big Business.

card up one's sleeve, a; esp., **to have a . . .,** to have something in reserve, esp. to overcome an apparently victorious opponent: C. 20. From cardsharping.

care a pin (or **rap**) **for, not to.** To value very lightly, have no affection for: mid C. 19–20. In C. 17–18, the cliché was *not to care a fig for.*

cart before the horse, the; esp., **to put** (or **set**) **the . . .,** to reverse the natural—or, at worst, the usual—order; to render it, in the etymological sense, *preposterous*: already common in C. 16, but not, I think, a cliché before C. 18.

carte blanche; esp., **to give** (a person) **carte blanche,** to grant him full discretionary power: mid C. 19–20. Until mid C. 19, almost solely political. Lit., a blank sheet of paper.

cast in one's lot with, to. To join a person and share his fortunes: 1535, Coverdale; but not a cliché before mid C. 18. Originally in allusion to *Proverbs,* i. 14, where the reference is to the division of plunder by the casting of lots ('Sortem mitte nobiscum': 'tu tireras au sort ta part avec nous', Verdunoy).

cast (something) **in the teeth of** (a person). To upbraid or reproach him with it: C. 19–20; slightly obsolescent. (In C. 16–17, *cast* a person *in the teeth with* the thing.)

cast into the outer darkness, to (or **to be**). To banish; to dismiss in utter disgrace or irrevocably: mid C. 19–20. From 'Cast him into outer darkness' (R.V.: 'Cast him out into the outer darkness') (*Matthew,* xxii. 13).

cast one's bread upon the waters, to. To do good without expecting immediate recognition or reward: mid C. 18–20. From 'Cast thy bread upon the waters: for thou shalt find it after many days' (*Ecclesiastes,* xi. 1).

cast pearls before swine, to. To offer beauty to philistines ; do a kindness to the rankly ungrateful: C. 19–20. 'Neither cast ye your pearls before swine' (*Matthew,* vii. 6).

cast the first stone, to. To be the first to blame or revile a person that sins or makes mistakes: C. 18–20. From 'He that is without sin among you, let him first cast a stone at her' (*John*. viii. 7).

*castle in Spain, a, or **castles in Spain; castle in the air, a,** or **castles in the air.** Fond imaginings; a rosy dream of future wealth and happiness: semi-proverbial; but in C. 19–20, clichés. Originals: *châteaux en Espagne* and the Italian *castelli in aria* (Benham). Often **build castles in the air** (rarely *Spain*).

casual encounter, a. A chance meeting; an unsought, un-expected meeting: from ca. 1880.—Cf. the next.

casual remark, a. An undesigned remark; a remark made without ulterior motive or indeed any purpose whatsoever: 1864, D. Mitchell, 'I made some casual remark about the weather' (O.E.D.).

cause célèbre. A law-suit, a trial, that attracts much publicity; a famous case: mid C. 19–20. *Causes célèbres et intéressantes*, by F. de Petaval, 1734 (Benham).

*'caviare to the general.' (Something) unappreciated by —not suited to please—the general run of men: C. 19–20. 'The play, I remember, pleased not the million; 'twas caviare to the general.' Caviare is an acquired taste; *the general* is the generality, the mass, of mankind, the vast majority of persons.

cela va sans dire. That goes without saying; that's obvious: a French proverbial saying, from ca. 1870 an English cliché; (*it* or) *that goes without saying* is itself a cliché: from ca. 1890.

'certain lewd fellows of the baser sort.' Jocular for 'coarse, hearty fellows': late C. 19–20. 'The Jews which believed not . . . , took unto them certain lewd fellows of the baser sort . . . and set all the city on an uproar' (*Acts*, xvii. 5): οἱ Ἰουδαῖοι . . . προσλαβόμενοι τῶν ἀγοραίων τινὰς ἄνδρας πονηρούς, 'certain evil [or malicious] men from among the loungers in the *agora* (or market place)', there being in ἀγογαῖος a connotation of 'agitator', as Souter, *A Pocket Lexicon of the New Testament*, points out: Judæi, assumentesque de vulgo viros quosdam malos ('quelques méchants hommes de la populace', Verdunoy). *Lewd* here means 'ignorant'.

ceteris paribus. All other things being equal: C. 18–20. In late C. 19–20, *other things being equal* (not *all other . . .*) is also a cliché.

chacun à son goût. Each to his taste: mid C. 19–20.—Cf. **de gustibus.**

change of heart, a. A conversion, in sentiment, from evil to good: late C. 19–20.

change of scene, a. A removal from one place to another, regarded as morally and physically beneficial: late C. 19–20.

chapter of accidents, a or the. A series of misfortunes and mishaps; 'the unforeseen course of events' (O.E.D.): late C. 19–20; C. 19–20.

charmed life, a; esp., **bear a . . .,** to escape death many times; to be difficult to kill: C. 19–20. *Macbeth*, v, viii, 'I bear a charmed life', a life protected by enchantment or magic.

chasing the rainbow. Pursuing an ideal, an illusion: mid C. 19–20. From fairy-tale gold at the rainbow's end.

cheek by jowl. Side by side in intimacy: mid C. 18–20 (though current since C. 16). I.e., cheek beside cheek.

cheer to the echo, to. To applaud or cheer vociferously: late C. 19–20. So as to produce echoes. (Shakespeare has *applaud to the echo*.)

*cherchez la femme! A French dictum made by Dumas père in *Les Mohicans de Paris*, 1864, 'but apparently as an established phrase', says Benham, who compares the obsolete English proverb, 'There is no mischief done but a woman is one' (is concerned in it). Only in C. 20 an English cliché, it is often used facetiously out of its crime context. ('Look for the woman [in the case]!')

cherished belief, a; cherished beliefs, one's. A belief or opinion to which one clings and which one fosters: late C. 19–20.

chew the cud, to. To ruminate: C. 19–20. From the slow cud-chewing of cattle. Byron, in *Don Juan*, Canto XII (published in 1823), st. 43, ironically and punningly said, 'As that abominable tittle-tattle, | Which is the cud eschewed by human cattle' (Benham).

*chick or child, have no; have neither chick nor child; without chick or child. To be childless: C. 19–20. Recorded first in Cotgrave, 1611; *chick*, 'child', occurs as early as C. 14 (O.E.D.).

child of Nature, a. A person much attached to and spiritually dependent on Nature: from ca. 1840. (Wordsworth, ca. 1800, 'Dear child of nature'.)

children of this world, the. Earth-bound humanity; the worldly wise: C. 19–20. 'The children of this world are in their generation wiser than the children of light' (*Luke*, xvi. 8): the Greek original signifies 'the children of this age'.

chilled (or **frozen**) **to the marrow.** Chilled inside as well as outside: late C. 19–20.

chip of the old block, a. A son (rarely a daughter) like his father, generally in a favourable sense: C. 18–20. Used by Milton in 1642 (Benham).

chop and change, to. To change constantly: ca 1540, but not a cliché until C. 18. It means, literally, 'to barter and exchange'.

*chosen people, the; or **the C.P.** Jews or the Jews: mid C. 19–20; generally with mild facetiousness.

chronicle small beer, to. To record trifles, analyse the unimportant: C. 19–20. By many, used without reminiscence of Shakespeare's 'To suckle fools, and chronicle small beer' (*Othello*, II, i).

*circumstances over which one has (esp., **I have**) **no control.** Circumstances beyond one's power to direct or check: late C. 19–20. Sterne speaks of circumstances one cannot *govern*, Froude of circumstances to which one *is unequal* (O.E.D.).

citizen of no mean city, a. No longer apprehended as a quotation, it nevertheless comes from 'But Paul said, I am a man which am a Jew of Tarsus, a city in Cilicia, a citizen of no mean city' (*Acts*, xxi. 39): οὐκ ἀσήμου πόλεως πολίτης, 'a citizen of a not obscure city': *non ignotæ civitatis municeps*, 'citoyen d'une ville qui n'est pas sans importance' (Verdunoy). Kipling, in *The Seven Seas*, 1896, writes in the Dedication, 'Surely in toil and fray, | Under an alien sky, | Comfort it is to say: | "Of no mean city am I!" ' (Benham).

City. See **magnate.**

*city fathers, the. The town councillors: journalists' (and councillors'): from ca. 1880.

city swelters in record heat-wave. American journalists' headline: C. 20. *The city* . . . occurs frequently in the body of news reports. (Sullivan.)

civis Romanus sum. I am a Roman citizen: late C. 18–20. 'Stated by Cicero to be an ancient form of appeal which had often saved men from death and indignity in the utmost parts of the earth' (Benham). Like **pro bono publico,** it is a favourite with writers of pompous letters to the newspapers.

classes and the masses, the (?). All classes of society: from ca. 1880. The phrase was first used by Gladstone. (Benham.)

45

clean sheet, a (figurative); esp., **to start with . . .**, to begin with one's crimes or misdeeds cancelled or forgiven: late C. 19–20.—Cf. 'a *virgin* page'.

cleanse one's bosom of the (or **this** or **that**) **perilous stuff, to.** To free one's heart and mind of dangerous resentment or feelings: from ca. 1830. A reminiscence of Shakespeare's 'Canst thou not . . . Cleanse the stuff'd bosom of that perilous stuff Which weighs upon the heart' (*Macbeth*, v, iii).

cleanse (or **clean**) **the Augean stables, the.** To purge away corruption and/or immorality, esp. on a large scale: C. 19–20. Hercules purified the huge and filthy stables of King Augeas: cf. the Latin proverbial *cloacas Augiæ purgare*.

clear the decks, to (figurative). To remove obstacles and so prepare for operations: late C. 19–20. Nautical (preparing for a storm) and naval (preparing for battle).

clears (or **cleared**) **the air, that.** That has clarified the position: from ca. 1880. 'His explicit declaration . . . has cleared the air' (1885: O.E.D.).

*****clerk of the weather, the.** 'An imaginary functionary humorously supposed to control the state of the weather' (O.E.D.): from ca. 1880.

'cloistered virtue.' Virtue untested by the stress and temptations of the world: C. 19–20. From Milton's *Areopagitica*, 1644 ('a fugitive and cloistered virtue').

close finish, a (?). An exciting race or contest: horse-racing and athletics (late C. 19–20), hence general (C. 20).

close on the heels of. Only a little way behind in a pursuit, a chase (hence in a competition): mid C. 19–20.

close (or **near**) **thing, a** (colloquial). A narrow escape or a *close finish* (see above): C. 20.

*****'clothed and in his right mind'** is a jocular adoption, meaning little more than 'with changed clothes and therefore feeling refreshed or in a better humour', of *Mark*, v. 15 (ἱματισμένον καὶ σωφρονοῦντα, 'clothed and in one's senses': *vestitum, et sanæ mentis*, 'vêtu et sain d'esprit', Verdunoy).

cloud of witnesses, a. Not regarded as a quotation, it occurs verbatim in *Hebrews*, xii. 1, 'With so great a cloud of witnesses'. Obsolescent. There is a punning allusion in the title of a novel by Dorothy Sayers: *Clouds of Witness*, 1926.

cloven hoof, the; esp., **to show the . . .** The sign of the Devil; a manifestation of evil: C. 19–20. The Devil could not hide his cloven hoof.

clumsy lout, a; esp., **you clumsy lout!** A clumsy (and ill-mannered) person: late C. 19–20.

*coals of fire on a person's head, to heap. To reproach in a practical and very effective manner, esp. by repaying good for evil: C. 19–20. See *Proverbs*, xxv. 22 and *Romans*, xii. 20.

*coast is clear, the. 'The danger is over, the enemies have marched off' (Johnson), perhaps originally of pirates: C. 18–20. Also in derivative sense, 'the way is open for an operation, event, etc.' (O.E.D.): mid C. 19–20.

cock of the walk; esp., **to be . . .** (not usually *the cock . . .*). To be the best man in a given locality or at a given activity: late C. 18–20. From cock-fighting.

coign of vantage, a. A corner (French *coin*)—hence, a point—of advantage: C. 19–20. *Macbeth*, I, vi.

cold douche, a (figurative). Something that damps and chills one's enthusiasm or impulse: from ca. 1870. (A cold shower-bath.)

cold light of reason, the; esp., **in the . . .,** viewed soberly; examined intelligently, not regarded passionately or sentimentally: mid C. 19–20.

cold wave spells suffering to thousands (in headlines); **a cold wave . . .** (in articles). American journalists': C. 20. (Sullivan.)

colorful scene, a. An American cliché (not—as *colourful*—unknown in England since ca. 1919) of C. 20.

colossal undertaking, a (?). A mighty task or enterprise: C. 20. (*Colossal* itself is being overdone.)

colourable imitation, a. A specious or convincing imitation: late C. 19–20.

comb, to go through with a fine (or **with a toothcomb**). To examine or check minutely: C. 20.

come home to roost, to, 'to rebound upon the originator', is applied to curses ('Curses, like chickens, come home to roost') and mistakes: mid C. 19–20.

come into a person's life, to. To become important to a person by being made acquainted with him; generally applied to love, passion, or friendship: mid C. 19–20.

come on the scene, to. To appear; to arrive: from ca. 1830. From an actor's arrival on the stage.

come to an end, to. To end; to be concluded: late C. 19–20. (To reach the physical end.)

come to grief, to. To meet with disaster; to fail: from ca. 1860. That is, to a cause or source of grief.

come to light, to. To appear; to be revealed or disclosed: Coverdale, 1535; cliché in C. 18–19. Influenced by *Ezekiel*, xvi. 57.

come to pass, to. To happen: C. 18–20; already common in C. 16–17, the phrase being popularized by Tindale's and others' versions of *Matthew*, xxiv. 6 ('All these things must come to pass, but the end is not yet', R.V.: δεῖ γὰρ γενέσθαι, 'for they must happen': *oportet enim haec fieri*, 'car il faut que ces choses arrivent', Verdunoy).

come to stay, to have. To be generally accepted; to be permanent: from ca. 1910. The Earl of Cavan, in the House of Lords, 1928, 'Mechanization has come to stay' (O.E.D.).

come to the ears of, to. (Of a story, gossip, report, rumour) to be heard by (someone important or closely concerned): already current in C. 13; a cliché in C. 17–20.

come to the end of one's tether, to; or to have come . . ., to have reached the extreme end of one's resources, exhausted one's abilities and resources: C. 19–20. Already in C. 18 it was common. From a grazing horse.

come together again, to. (Of persons) to be reunited, to 'make it up': sentimentalists': C. 20.

comes to the same thing (in the end), it. Finally, it will make no matter or there will be no difference: late C. 19–20.

comme il faut. According to etiquette; of correct deportment; well-behaved: from ca. 1820. A Society importation; lit., 'as it is necessary'.

common herd, the. The generality of mankind; ordinary, mediocre people: mid C. 19–20.

common lot, the. The inevitable circumstances of life: C. 19–20. *Lot* = 'share' (assigned by fate), from the *lot* (or ticket, etc.) one draws. 'Utere sorte tua', Virgil; 'No man can change the common lot to rare', Hardy. (Benham.)

common or garden, adjectival phrase. Ordinary or common: colloquial: from ca. 1895. From gardening ('the Common—or Garden—Nightshade').

common understanding (?). An agreement; concord: late C. 19–20.

'compare great things with small, to' (?); often misquoted '. . . small things with great': C. 19–20. Milton, *Paradise Lost*, Book II.

[**comparisons are odious** sounds like a quotation, but is actually a proverb. **'Comparisons are odorous'**, from Shakespeare's *Much Ado about Nothing*, is almost a cliché.]

completely gutted by fire. (Of a building, a home) ruined by fire: American: late C. 19–20. (Sullivan.)

con amore. With love, zeal, delight, pleasure; with gusto ('He performed the unpleasant task *con amore*'): from ca. 1824, to judge from Lamb, 1826, 'You wrote them [poems] *with love*—to avoid the coxcombical phrase, *con amore*' (O.E.D.).

condemn (a person) **out of his own mouth, to.** To condemn him by the evidence he has himself given: late C. 19–20. With allusion to *Luke*, xix. 22, 'Out of thy own mouth will I judge thee, thou wicked servant': ἐκ τοῦ στόματός σου κρινῶ σε, where στόμα is '*the mouth*, especially as an organ of speech' (Souter): Vulgate, *de ore tuo te judico*, well rendered by Verdunoy as 'je te jugerai sur tes paroles'.

'confusion worse confounded.' Confusion added to confusion (and tumult): C. 19–20. Milton, 'With ruin upon ruin, rout on rout, | Confusion worse confounded' (*Paradise Lost*, Book ɪɪ).

considered opinion that . . ., it is my (or **his** or . . .). On careful and mature reflection, I think that . . . : late C. 19–20.

*****consign to oblivion, to.** To deliver or entrust to oblivion, i.e. to put aside and utterly forget: from ca. 1870.

*****conspicuous by one's** (or **its) absence.** Rendered conspicuous by the very fact of absence: from ca. 1860. 'Conspicuous by its absence', Lord John Russell, in an election address, April 6, 1859. A reminiscence of a passage in Tacitus's *Annals*, Book ɪɪɪ, last paragraph. (Benham.)

conspiracy of silence, a. Concerted silence; a concerted refraining to notice or acknowledge a person, a movement, a fact (of some importance): from ca. 1890; already common in the 1880's. Oscar Wilde, on being asked by Sir Lewis Morris what he should do to overcome the conspiracy of silence (among reviewers) about one of his publications, said 'Join it!'.

constant communication, in. Always in touch: C. 20. 'At opposite ends of the earth, they were nevertheless in constant communication.'

'consummation devoutly to be wished, a.' An end that is extremely desirable: C. 19–20. *Hamlet*, III, i, ' 'Tis a . . .' (concerning the peace ensured by death).

contract a chill, to. To catch a chill: mid C. 19–20. T. Hale, 1691, 'Thereby contracting dangerous colds, coughs and catarrhs' (O.E.D.).

controversial question, a (or **this** or **that**). A much disputed or a very debatable question: late C. 19–20; in the earlier half of C. 19, *a controversial point* verged on being a cliché.

cook someone's goose for him, to (colloquial). To ruin; to circumvent and put a stop to the activities of: from ca. 1860: originally (ca. 1850), slang; in C. 20, colloquial.

*cool, calm and collected. Calm (and alert, or ready to act): late C. 19–20.

cost a pretty penny, to. To cost a considerable sum: from ca. 1890. 'Armaments cost a pretty penny.' (Obsoletely, '*a fine* penny'.)

counsel of perfection, a; counsels of perfection. Advice difficult for a mere human being to take: C. 19–20. The second is an ancient theological phrase.

country cousin, a. A relative whose countrified manners and outlook tend to embarrass townspeople: mid C. 19–20. —Cf. the next.

country mouse, a; a town mouse. A country person unaccustomed to urban life; a town-dweller ill at ease in the country: from ca. 1860. From one of Æsop's fables.

coup de grâce, a. A finishing stroke, a 'settler': C. 19–20. Lit., 'a stroke of grace (kindliness, graciousness)', putting an end to a person's (or animal's) pain or misery.

51

crack of doom, to the. For ever: from ca. 1820. *Macbeth*, IV, i, 'What, will the line stretch out to the crack of doom?'

cradled in the lap of luxury. Born in affluent circumstances: mid C. 19–20. Also **to live in the lap of luxury.**

crambe repetita (?). 'I don't think you can reckon *crambe repetita* a cliché yet. It's more like what one might call an "educated noise", at present, I'd say. But that's "merely an individual contribution to the general sum of hypotheses" on the subject, as Harold Frederic put it', A. W. Stewart, in a private letter of December 27, 1939. Literally 'cabbage served up again', *crambe repetita* means 'any distasteful repetition' (Juvenal, Satire VII, 154). Hence *crambe* is used in the same way and also as an adjective: 'Nauseating crambe verities, and questions over-queried', Sir Thomas Browne, 1658; but *crambe* is obsolete, whereas *crambe repetita* is virtually a cliché, especially among scholars and writers.

crass stupidity. Gross stupidity: C. 20. (*Crass ignorance* used to be much commoner than it is now.)

cribbed, cabined and confined. Cramped and hampered; utterly restrained and constrained: mid C. 19–20. A misquotation of '(But now I am) cabined, cribbed, confined, bound in', *Macbeth*, III, iv.

cricket, as in **it's not cricket** and **is it cricket?** It is unsporting, unjust; Is it fair, honest, honourable, English (not *British*)?: recorded for 1900; a cliché since ca. 1910. W. de Morgan, 1911, 'It . . . isn't cricket, as folk say nowadays' (O.E.D.); 1940, John Gunther (an American), in the 'War Edition' of *Inside Europe*, notes, among 'many . . . forces and counter-forces . . . of English political life' and as the first of an impressive miscellany, 'cricket and the ritualistic attitude to fair play that it has produced'.—Cf. **play the game.**

*crocodile tears. Hypocritical tears, feigned weeping: C. 18–20. Bacon, *Essays*, 1612, No. 23, 'It is the wisdom

of the crocodiles, that shed tears when they would devour'
(Benham). Medieval animal-lore.

*cross the Rubicon, to. To take an irrevocable step, make
an irrevocable decision and act on it: C. 18–20. From Cæsar's
passing the Rubicon (a river dividing Cisalpine Gaul from
Italy).

cross the Styx, to. To die: C. 19–20; obsolescent. A fabled
river: Virgil, *Æneid*, vi, 425, 'irremeabilis unda' (the wave—
or stream—from which there is no return).

crown of glory, a. A victor's reward; an honourable distinction: mid C. 19–20. Perhaps, originally, in allusion to
1 *Peter*, v. 4, 'And when the chief Shepherd shall appear, ye
shall receive a crown of glory that fadeth not away': τὸν
ἀμαράντινον τῆς δόξης στέφανον, 'the unfading (or fade-
less) chaplet of glory', στέφανος being 'the Greek victor's
crown or chaplet, of perishable leaves' (Souter): Vulgate,
immarcescibilem gloriæ coronam ('la couronne incorruptible de la
gloire', Verdunoy).

crowning mercy, a or **the.** The (or a) mercy that constitutes perfection; the acme of mercies: C. 19–20. (*Crowning
folly* was fairly common in C. 19.)

crumbs from the rich man's table. Trifles given to the
poor by the rich; a slight consideration shown by the fortunate
to the unfortunate: mid C. 19–20. In allusion to *Luke*, xvi. 21,
'(A certain beggar named Lazarus) desiring to be fed with the
crumbs which fell from the rich man's table'.

cry for the moon, to. To desire, whiningly or vociferously,
the impossible: from ca. 1860. (Dickens, 1852: O.E.D.)

'cry is still, "They come", the.' (Not 'the cry is "Still
they come"'.) C. 19–20. *Macbeth*, v, v.

cry over spilt milk, to. To give way to vain regret: semi-
proverbial in form '. . . shed milk' (C. 17–18); but from ca.
1880, a cliché. (Apperson.)

*cry wolf (once) too often, to. To give a false alarm so often that one is no longer believed: from ca. 1890. Ex the proverbial saying, *to cry wolf* (recorded for 1740: Apperson).

crystal-clear. Pellucid; eminently clear; sun-clear (itself a much overused phrase at one period, but too soon discarded to qualify as a cliché): C. 20.

cudgel one's brains, to; to rack one's brains. To think hard; to try very hard to contrive some thing or end: C. 18–20; late C. 18–20. Shakespeare has *cudgel*; *rack* (put on the rack, to torture, to strain) occurs as early as ca. 1680. Earliest of all is *beat* (1530). O.E.D.

*cui bono? For whose advantage?: C. 18–20. Quoted, Benham tells us, by Cicero as 'a maxim of Lucius Cassius, whose expression was "Cui bono fuerit?" ', which might be colloquially rendered as 'Now, I wonder who got something out of *that?*'

*cum grano salis; to take with a grain of salt. The former is a Roman proverbial saying (cf. Pliny's *addito salis grano*, 'a grain of salt having been added', Benham): a cliché of C. 19–20. The latter, 'to accept with reservations', is a cliché of mid C. 19–20.

'cups that cheer but not inebriate.' In Cowper's *The Task*, 1783, the passage has *the* before *cups*. In *Siris*, 1744, Bishop Berkeley had spoken of tar-water as being 'of a nature so mild and benign . . . as to . . . cheer but not inebriate' (Benham).

curious to relate. A narrative formula, generally introductory: late C. 19–20. 'Curious to relate, the cow jumped over the moon.'

'curiouser and curiouser.' Increasingly odd (or strange): late C. 19–20. (C. L. Dodgson.)

curiously enough (?). A variant of **curious to relate:** C. 20.

curtain lecture, a; esp., **give a . . .** A reprimand or an admonitory talk delivered, generally by the wife, to spouse a-bed: mid C. 19–20. Established by Douglas Jerrold's *Mrs Caudle's Curtain Lectures*, 1846. Benham notes an adumbration in 1637 (*A Curtaine Lecture*), a parallel in 1640 (Richard Braithwaite's *A Boulster Lecture*), and a material prototype in Juvenal, Satire VI, 268–9.

cut a long story short, to. To bring a long story to an abrupt end: late C. 19–20.

cut and run, to. To decamp, or depart, hurriedly: colloquial: mid C. 19–20. Nautical: from cutting the cable and running before the wind.

cut and thrust. A mellay, a hand-to-hand struggle; a grim struggle; (in conversation) pointed remark and shrewd riposte: mid C. 19–20. Grote, 1846, 'The cut and thrust of actual life' (O.E.D.). From sword-play.

cut off one's nose to spite one's face, to. In pique, so to act as to injure oneself: mid C. 19–20.

*****cut** (a person) **off with a shilling, to.** To disinherit: C. 19–20. 'The bequest being a proof that the disinheritance was designed' (O.E.D.); such a practice is no longer valid in English Law.

cut one's coat according to one's cloth, to. To keep within one's means, or, more widely (but now less generally), to adapt oneself to circumstances: C. 19–20. From tailoring.

cut the Gordian knot, to. See **Gordian knot.**

cut the painter, to. To sever connexion: from ca. 1880. Of nautical origin, the phrase has, since the 1880's, been much used of the relations of the Empire with Great Britain.

cut to the quick, to. Wounded in one's tenderest or most delicate or profound feelings: mid C. 19–20.

cynosure of all (or **neighbouring**) **eyes, the.** A person in whom curiosity and interest are concentrated: C. 19–20. As a quotation-cliché, the precise form is 'the cynosure of neighb'ring eyes' (Milton, *L'Allegro*, 1632).

D

D.v. See **Deo volente.**

dabble in the occult, to. To interest oneself in the writings on and the practices of the occult: C. 20.

*'damn with faint praise, to.' To condemn by praise too moderate to be praise at all: applied esp. to literary critics: late C. 18–20. Pope, 'Damn with faint praise, assent with civil leer, | And, without sneering, teach the rest to sneer' (*Prologue to the Satires*, 1734).

dance attendance on, to. 'To wait upon (a person) with assiduous attention and ready obsequiousness' (O.E.D.): mid C. 18–20. Shakespeare, 'To dance attendance on their lordships' pleasures' (*Henry VIII*, v, ii, 32).

'Daniel come to judgement, a.' An exemplary judge (or a person of unerring judgement) has come to give his weighty decision: C. 19–20. Shakespeare, *The Merchant of Venice*, IV, i.

'Dark Continent, the.' Africa. It is doubtful whether this book-title (H. M. Stanley, 1878) is still apprehended as a quotation, for it has been pretty thoroughly assimilated. Stanley in 1890 varied it to 'Darkest Africa'—*Through Darkest Africa* being a very well-known book of his.

dark horse, a (colloquial). A candidate or competitor that, little known, does (or at least is expected to do) very well: C. 20. From racing slang for a horse of whose racing powers nothing, or little, is known.

darken counsel, to. To obscure the desired issue, to hinder deliberation: C. 19–20. A reminiscence of 'Who is this that darkeneth counsel by words without knowledge?' (*Job*, xxxviii. 2).

*darken one's door(s) (or **threshold**), **to; darken the door of.** To appear on (a person's) threshold as a visitor: generally in the negative: respectively C. 19–20 and C. 20.

dastardly crime (or **outrage**), **a.** A despicably cowardly crime or outrage: from ca. 1905.

dawn suddenly (up)on or **d. (up)on suddenly; or dawn suddenly (up)on** (a person's) **mind.** To begin to be perceived or understood by a person: from ca. 1870.

day after the fair, a. A mid C. 19–20 cliché based on the proverbial saying, *to come a day after the fair* (too late).

day of wrath, the (?). As *the Day of Wrath* it = *the Judgement Day*, and is certainly not a cliché; but as *the day of wrath*, 'the day on which retribution comes, or is fated to come', it is a cliché or a near-cliché of mid C. 19–20.

days are numbered, one's or **its.** One's life is near its end, illness (or injury) the cause; the usefulness of a thing is almost over: late C. 19–20.

days that are gone, the; the days that are no more. The regretted past: mid C. 19–20; the second is slightly obsolescent.

de gustibus (?). From the L. proverb, *de gustibus non est disputandum* (it's no good arguing about personal tastes). Literary: mid C. 19–20.

de mortuis nil nisi bonum (?). Of the dead, speak ever charitably: C. 19–20. An early C. 20 parody, *de mortuis nil nisi bunkum*, deserves immortality.

dead and done with. Dead and no longer important: C. 20.—Cf. the next.

dead and gone. Dead, with a connotation of 'long dead': C. 19–20. (Used by Shakespeare—and even in C. 15.) Dead, and so gone from us. 'An effigy of a dead and gone worthy, to be admired with distant respect' (R. H. Mottram, *You Can't Have It Back*, 1939).

dead certainty, a. An utter certainty: late C. 19–20; originally sporting.

dead letter, a (figurative). Something superseded or cancelled: late C. 19–20. From *dead letters*, those letters which the postal authorities have been unable to deliver or to return to the senders.

*dead men's shoes. From the proverbial *to wait for dead men's shoes*, to expect to inherit money. A cliché in C. 19–20.

dead of night, at (occasionally, **in the . . .**). At the time of the most intense darkness and stillness: mid C. 19–20 and (*in . . .*) C. 18–20.

Dead Sea fruit. Something (e.g., an anticipated joy or inheritance) that proves to be a grave disappointment: from ca. 1870. Thomas Moore, in *Lalla Rookh*, 1817, sings, 'Like Dead Sea fruits, that tempt the eye, | But turn to ashes on the lips!' (Benham); but popularized by Miss Braddon's famous novel, *Dead Sea Fruit*, 1868. In allusion to Sodom apples or mad apples (the fruit known scientifically as *Asclepias*).

deadly earnest; esp., **in . . .**, implacable; extremely serious: mid C. 19–20. Also adverbially.

deadly menace, a. A threat involving death or disaster; a potential foe, implacable and extremely dangerous: C. 20.

deadly precision (?). Unerring accuracy or precision: late C. 19–20.

death and destruction; esp., **to vow . . .,** to threaten death and ruin: mid C. 19–20; obsolescent.

death's door. See at . . .

decent, honest, (and) God-fearing (?). Respectable, honest, and reverent (or religious): late C. 19–20.

decisive effect, a (?). A conclusive or unmistakable result: C. 20.

deep calling unto deep. A literary cliché (late C. 19–20), in allusion to 'Deep calleth unto deep', *Psalms*, xlii. 7 (Vulgate, *Abyssus abyssum invocat*, 'Le flot appelle le flot', Verdunoy).

*defects of one's qualities, the. Mid C. 19–20. From the French of Bishop Dupanloup. (Benham.)

deliberate falsehood, a. An intended lie, a lie designed to mislead; a studied lie, neither hasty nor rash: mid C. 19–20.

delicate negotiations. Difficult or ticklish negotiations: late C. 19–20: originally, journalistic.

deliver the goods, to (figurative). To fulfil a promise: C. 20. This colloquialism comes from commercial phraseology.

demon rum, the. A hostile personification of rum used generically of all intoxicating liquors: late C. 19–20; originally and still mainly American.

deny ... See soft impeachment.

Deo volente and **D.v.** If God so wishes: respectively C. 18–20 and C. 19–20. Roman variants were *Deo favente* (by God's favour) and *Deo juvante* (with God's help).

*depart this life, to, corresponds to L. *decedere de vita,* itself a euphemism for *mori,* 'to die'. The English phrase began as a euphemism, became a genteelism, and is now a stupidity; a cliché in late C. 19–20.

depths of bathos, the. A signal instance of complete anti-climax; utter commonplace, the utterly bathetic: literary: late C. 19–20. *Depths* was suggested by the etymology of *bathos* itself, which is a Greek word for 'depth'.

deserving poor, the. The worthy or meritorious poor; poor people that deserve to be assisted: C. 20.

desire someone's better acquaintance, to. To wish to know someone better: late C. 19–20.

desperate situation, a (much commoner than the alternative *d. position*). An extremely dangerous, hazardous, precarious, or serious state of affairs: late C. 19–20. **Desperate case** (C. 19–20) is perhaps also a cliché.

*deus ex machina. A god most fortunately intervening' hence a person affording unexpected but opportune assistance: mid C. 18–20. With reference to those ancient dramas in which a god appears from some mechanical contrivance. A translation of the Greek θεός ἐκ μηχανῆς (Menander; Lucian). (Benham.)

devil incarnate, a. A person that is thoroughly and actively evil: mid C. 19–20. Lit., 'a devil in the flesh; the Devil in human form'.

devil's own . . . See **luck.**

devoted solely to. Used or occupied solely by; filled with: American: late C. 19–20. 'This gallery was devoted solely to Italian pictures.'

devouring element, the. Fire: journalistic: late C. 19–20; obsolescent.

devoutly hope (e.g., 'I devoutly hope . . .'); **it is devoutly to be hoped,** it is fervently or earnestly to be hoped: from ca. 1820. Scott, 1814, 'Let us devoutly hope, that . . .' (O.E.D.).

diabolical rage, a; esp., **in a . . .,** in a towering rage: late C. 19–20.

diabolical skill. Skill so great as to seem to be devilish: C. 20.

dictates of conscience, the. The monitions or urgings of conscience: C. 20. Earlier *the dictate* . . . ; cf. the next.

dictates of one's feelings (or **heart**), **the.** The commands and urgings of one's feelings: from ca. 1880. Carpenter, 1874, 'He seems to have followed the dictates of his artistic feelings' (O.E.D.).

dictatorship of the proletariat, the. Ambiguous, this political cliché; but it means '. . . by . . .' and is a product of the C. 20.

*die in harness, to. To die working: from ca. 1880. A figurative use of a horse's harness, with allusion to a draught horse's death in the shafts.

die in the last ditch, to. To die fighting to the last: from ca. 1860. Recorded in its literal sense, 'to die defending the last ditch of an entrenchment', early in C. 18 (O.E.D.).

die in the odour of sanctity, to. To die reputed a saint: mid C. 19–20; often ironically. From the French *odeur de sainteté* (see Littré) and, as to *the odour of sanctity*, recorded in England in 1756. From that balsamic odour which is said to be exhaled by eminent saints at their death: see, e.g., Freeman, *The Norman Conquest*, III, xi, 32. (O.E.D.)

*die is cast, the. The decision has been irrevocably made, for good or ill: a semi-proverbial saying (C. 17) that, ca. 1850, became a cliché. From dicing (*alea jacta est*).

die the death, to (?). To die: late C. 19–20. It is a cliché only in this loose sense; properly the phrase means 'to be put to death' and would seem to have originated as 'a solemn phrase for death inflicted by law' (Johnson: O.E.D.).

dim and distant past, from (or **in**) **the.** In the far-distant, ill-remembered past: late C. 19–20.

*'dim religious light, a.' A chiaroscuro; a poor light; dusk: C. 19–20. Milton, *Il Penseroso*, 1632.

ding-dong battle, a. A battle (or struggle, contest or competition) vigorously maintained and sustained: from ca. 1880.

discard precedent, to. To ignore—to depart from—precedent: American: C. 20.

discerning reader, the. Penetrating, intellectually most perceptive readers: late C. 19–20.—Cf. **gentle reader.**

discuss ways and means, to. To discuss the manner and the money needed: C. 20.

disjecta membra (?). 'The scattered limbs', applied metaphorically to the study-sweepings of writers, politicians, and others: C. 19–20. Allusion to Horace's *disjecti membra poetæ*, 'the remains of the dismembered poet' (*Satires*, I, iv, 63).

disrupt train schedules, to. 'Snow disrupts train schedules' (headline): American journalists': C. 20. (Sullivan.)

distance has been annihilated. The difficulties inherent in and caused by long distances have been overcome: from ca. 1920.

*'distance lends enchantment (to the view).' Mid C. 19–20. Thomas Campbell, ''Tis distance . . .' (*The Pleasures of Hope*, 1799).

*distinction without a difference, a. A discrimination or distinction 'artificially or fictitiously made in a case where no real difference exists' (O.E.D.): from ca. 1770. Used in 1688 and implied in 1579.

disturbance of mind. Mental agitation or excitement: generally pejorative: late C. 19–20.

Divine order of things, the. The pre-ordained and God-permitted social structure: mid C. 19–20; since ca. 1920, generally ironic.

divinity. See **there's . . .**

do a good turn to, to. To help—render a service or benefit to (a person): mid C. 19–20.

do good by stealth. To do good secretly: C. 19–20. Pope, *Epilogue to the Satires*, 1733, Dialogue I, 135–6, 'Let humble Allen, with an awkward shame, | Do good by stealth, and blush to find it fame'.

*do one's heart good, to. ('It does her heart good to see children at play.') To gladden, fortify, cheer, make feel better: C. 19–20.

do or die, to. To make a desperate attempt: from ca. 1820. Thomas Campbell, 'To-morrow let us do or die!' (*Gertrude of Wyoming*, 1809).—Cf. the Duke of Kent's motto, *autv incere aut mori*, 'either to conquer or to die'. (Benham.)

*dog in the manger, a. A semi-proverbial saying applied to a person that cannot do, or use, something and will allow no one else to do it or use it: as a cliché, mid C. 19–20. The saying goes back to the Latin *canis in præsæpi*.

dog's chance, a; esp., **not to have . . .,** to have no chance at all: late C. 19–20.

dog's life, a. A miserable life; a wretchedly subservient life: mid C. 19–20. It dates from C. 16.

dolce far niente. Literally, 'sweet to do nothing'; freely, 'the very pleasant state of idleness': C. 19–20. Italian proverbial saying: Benham compares Tacitus's *inertiæ dulcedo*.

done to a turn. Cooked to the required point, exquisitely cooked (esp. of baking and roasting); hence, made or manufactured exactly as required: respectively, mid C. 19–20 and C. 20.

don't you know? or **!** A tag, equivalent to 'surely you know?' or 'as you well know': from ca. 1880; in C. 20, almost meaningless, except as a vague palliative.

doom is sealed, one's. One's final ruin or death or destruction has been ensured, made certain: from ca. 1880. Green, 1874, 'Both the Cardinal and his enemies knew that the minister's doom was sealed' (O.E.D.).

dose of one's (or **his**) **own medicine, a;** esp., **to give someone a . . .,** to requite him with his own treatment of others: C. 20.

*dot one's *i*'s and cross one's *t*'s, to. To be meticulously accurate and precise; 'to particularize minutely' (O.E.D.): from ca. 1880. I.e., to avoid confusion.

double-dyed traitor, a. A thoroughly guilty and shameful traitor: late C. 19–20.

double harness; esp., **in . . .,** married: colloquial: C. 20. From horses paired abreast in harness.

doubt, one cannot justly. It would be unfair to doubt: from ca. 1910.

doubtful advantage, a. An advantage more apparent than real: mid C. 19–20.

doubtful cause, a (?). 'He is involved in a doubtful cause', an enterprise or movement or affair of which the issue is uncertain and the moral principle obscure: C. 20.

down and out (?). A colloquialism for 'penniless and homeless': C. 20.

down at (the) heel(s). Destitute or, at best, needy: C. 19–20.—Cf. **out at elbow(s).**

down to the last detail. In every detail, no matter how small; in detail, from beginning to end: from ca. 1910. 'He gave an account of his arrest, down to the last detail.'

drag into the mire, to. To besmirch: mid C. 19–20.

draw a bow at a venture, to. To take a metaphorical shot in the dark: C. 18–20. 'A certain man drew a bow at a venture' (2 *Chronicles*, xviii. 33).

draw a veil over, to. To hide, to shut away from view; to say or write no more about: mid C. 19–20. Beloved of salacity, esp. in 'Let us draw a veil over what happened next'. Also jocularly, as in 'He prefers to draw a veil over the subsequent proceedings'.

draw in one's horns, to. To become reserved, esp. less ardent, in manner; or less assertive or confident; to show reluctance and/or diffidence: C. 19–20, though dating from as early as C. 14. From the habit of snails.

draw the line at, to. To set a limit (esp. in conduct) beyond which one refuses to go: colloquial: late C. 19–20.

*draw the long bow, to. Habitually or on a specific occasion to exaggerate considerably: C. 19–20. With the *long* (as opposed to the short) bow one could shoot far.

draw to a close, to. To approach its end: mid C. 19–20. 'His life is drawing to a peaceful close.'

*dree one's weird, to. To submit to one's fate, one's lot; with a connotation of fatalism and/or fortitude: Late Middle English; revived by Scott in *The Antiquary*, 1816; classified as 'archaic' by the O.E.D. in 1897, but quite common in late C. 19, a cliché from ca. 1920.

drenched to the skin (?). With clothes wet to the skin: mid C. 19–20.

dressed up to the nines and **dressed to kill** (both colloquial). Wearing one's best and smartest clothes: respectively from ca. 1880 and 1890.

drift apart, to. To become estranged in a passive, aimless, spineless way: C. 20.

drop the pilot (figurative). To dismiss, get rid of, the statesman that has piloted the ship of state [cliché ?] for a considerable period: from ca. 1895. From a famous cartoon by J. Tenniel in *Punch*, March 20, 1890: Kaiser Wilhelm II's dismissal of Bismarck (in pilot's uniform).

drown one's sorrows in drink, to. To seek consolation or forgetfulness in drunken stupor: C. 20.

due consideration, on (or, less often, **upon**). After appropriate or proper consideration or deliberation: late C. 19–20.

*durance vile; esp., **in . . .** In prison; imprisoned: C. 19–20. It occurs first, so far as we know, in *Falstaff's Wedding*, by Wm. Kendrick († 1777).

dust and ashes. See next.

dust to dust, and ashes to ashes. A misquotation of '(Earth to earth,) ashes to ashes, dust to dust', *The Book of Common Prayer*, Burial of the Dead: mid C. 19–20. The derivative *dust and ashes* is a cliché of late C. 19–20; cf. Horace's *pulvis et umbra sumus*, 'we are but dust and shadow' (*Odes*, IV, vii, 16).

*Dutch courage. Courage produced by strong drink: mid C. 19–20. (Still, it's better than none.) From the heavy drinking of Dutch soldiers in earlier times.

dyed in the wool. Thorough-going, out-and-out: from ca. 1920 in Britain, but from ca. 1905 in U.S.A. 'He's a dyed-in-the-wool Conservative.' From colour dyed into unspun wool: *wool-dyed*.

E

each and every. All, separately and together (cf. **all and sundry** and **one and all**): late C. 19–20.

'each man kills the thing he loves.' C. 20; from Oscar Wilde's *The Ballad of Reading Gaol* (published in 1898), Part I, st. 7.

*eager for the fray.** Eager to fight or struggle, hence to participate in a game: C. 19–20. Originally a quotation from Cibber's adaptation (1700) of Shakespeare's *Richard III* (Benham). In C. 20, **ready for the fray** is equally common.

eagle eye, an (or **one's**). An eye as keen and far-seeing as that of an eagle: mid C. 19–20. John Quincy Adams, 1819, 'The eagle eyes of informers' (O.E.D.). The much older *eagle-eyed* (Bishop Barlow, 1601) is now somewhat rhetorical.

earnest consideration. Serious or careful consideration: late C. 19–20. 'I want you to give this project your earnest consideration.'

earnest desire to make the world a better place in which to live, an (or **one's**): C. 20: cf. 'an earnest longing desire to see things brought to a peaceable end', Richard Hooker, *Ecclesiastical Polity*, 1593 (O.E.D.).

'earth has not anything to show more fair.' Mid C. 19–20. Wordsworth, *Sonnet Composed upon Westminster Bridge*, Sept. 3, 1802.

Earth the Great Mother (literary); **Mother Earth** (general). Respectively C. 19–20 (obsolescent) and C. 18–20; in mid C. 19–20, the latter often, jocularly, for 'the ground'. Perhaps in reminiscence of *Terra Mater*, the Roman goddess.

'East is East and West is West (and never the twain shall meet).' C. 20; from Kipling's *The Ballad of East and West*.

*eat from** (or **out of**) **a person's hand, to.** To be subservient to, to be willingly at a person's command, or prepared to do anything for a person: late C. 19–20. From horses or birds that take food from a person's hand.

*eat humble pie, to.** To apologize humbly; to be humiliatingly submissive: from ca. 1870. In dialect (whence also *eat h.p.*), to *eat rue pie*.

eat one's heart out, to. To suffer silently in regret, remorse, or longing: late C. 19–20.—Cf. the literary *to eat one's (own) heart*, used in the same sense.

eat (a person) **out of house and home, to.** A semi-proverbial saying, recorded ca. 1388 and occurring in Shakespeare's 2 *Henry IV*; in mid C. 19–20, a cliché.

Eclipse first and the rest nowhere. Applied to a person easily first or by far the best: mid C. 19–20. Originally a race-course phrase, applied to horses, *Eclipse* being the most famous C. 18 race-horse.

*economic factor, the. The material element in human life; the place of money and supplies in civilization: C. 20. (Not a cliché in Economics contexts.)

elegant sufficiency, an. A liberal sufficiency (but not an embarrassing excess); precisely enough: from ca. 1870; obsolescent.

*eleventh hour, the; esp., **at the eleventh hour.** (Also attributively, as in 'an eleventh-hour reprieve'.) At the latest possible time: mid C. 19–20. No longer apprehended as an allusion to the parable of the labourers, of whom the last 'were hired at the eleventh hour' (*Matthew*, xx. 9).

eloquent silence, an (?). A silence that is significant with things unsaid: C. 19–20. Congreve, 'Even silence may be eloquent in love', *The Old Bachelor* (1693), II, ii.

embarras de richesses ('an embarrassment of riches'; too many riches, too wide a choice) is a misquotation of *Embarras de Richesse*, the title of a comedy (1726) by D'Allainval. The correct form is not a cliché, whereas the incorrect form is a cliché of late C. 19–20.

Emerald Isle, the. Ireland: mid C. 19–20. Apparently first used in 1795 (O.E.D.). From the greenness of the countryside.

eminently successful. Extremely or notably successful: C. 20.

emotion overcame him (etc.) or **his** (etc.) **emotion overcame him,** or **he** (etc.) **was overcome by emotion.** Late C. 19–20; esp. among fiction-writers.

end of one's tether, the. See **come to the . . .**

endowed—esp., **well endowed**—**with this world's goods** (occasionally **rich in . . .**). Possessing much property and/or money: mid C. 19–20.—Cf. 'With all my worldly goods I thee endow' (*The Book of Common Prayer*).

ends of the earth, the; esp., **to** or **from the . . .** From a far-distant point of the earth: late C. 19–20.

enemy at the gate, an. A besieging enemy, an enemy at the door of one's house or at a city's boundary: C. 19–20. In reminiscence of 'They shall speak with'—i.e., subdue or destroy—'the enemies in the gate' (*Psalms*, cxxvii. 5).

enemy in our midst, the. E.g., ostensibly friendly aliens: late C. 19–20.

enfant terrible, 'a terrifying child', often used metaphorically ('The *enfant terrible* of the theatre was Noel Coward'): mid C. 19–20. 'Origin unknown. (Goethe uses the expression, 1809)'. (Benham.)

engage (a person) **in conversation, to.** To begin talking with; to occupy his time by talking to him: C. 20. Generally with a connotation of ulterior motive.

engaged in work of national importance. See **work of . . .**

*****enough to make one turn in one's grave; and somebody must be turning in his grave.** 'Such waste is enough to make a miser turn in his grave.'—'He must have turned in his grave.' Mid C. 19–20.

enter the lists, to. To arrive as a combatant, a rival, a competitor, an opponent: from ca. 1830. Originally, to arrive on the field of combat, but used figuratively as early as 1647 (O.E.D.).

entertain an angel unawares, to. To have converse with, to meet, a virtual saint or a very kind person: late C. 19–20. From 'Thereby some have entertained angels unawares' (*Hebrews*, xiii. 2).

entertain (high) hopes, to. To be optimistic in respect of some plan or approaching event: mid C. 19–20. Browning plays thus on the phrase: 'Who knows most, doubts not; entertaining hope | Means recognizing fear' (*Two Poets of Croisic*, 1878).

entre nous. Just between you and me; confidentially: mid C. 19–20. '*Entre nous*, she's no chicken.'

eppur si muove (?). 'Yet it does move', as Galileo is said to have exclaimed in 1615 'after being induced to abjure the theory of the earth's motion' (Benham): literary and philosophical: C. 19–20.

errand of mercy, an. A going with a kindly message or commission: late C. 19–20.

error in (or of) taste, an (?). An infringement of good taste: late C. 19–20.

***escape by the skin of one's teeth, to.** To have a very narrow escape: almost colloquial: mid C. 19–20. In C. 16–18, the form was *with*: see, e.g., *Job*, xix. 20, 'I am escaped with the skin of my teeth'.

escape unscathed, to. To get away unharmed: American: C. 20. 'The gangster escaped unscathed from the "bulls".'

(et) hoc genus omne. Literally, as in Horace, *Satires*, I, ii, 2, it means 'all this sort of people', but it is often used of things: C. 19–20.

et in Arcadia ego vixi; (2) *et in Arcadia ego.* And once (or long ago, or at one period) I too was idyllically happy; lit., 'and *I* lived in Arcadia' (fabled for rural peace and felicity): late C. 19–20. This, if my faulty memory serves me aright, is an adaptation of several Classical references to Arcadia, perhaps with a glance at B. Schidoni's 'I, too, was born in Arcadia' (ca. 1600). A variant is *et in Arcadia ego fui,* understood by some as the effective origin of (2); in certain references, *fui pastor* (I have been a shepherd), or some such phrase, is presumed. (2) *et in Arcadia ego,* 'and in Arcadia I (or, even I)', is the more familiar form: C. 19–20. See *La Gazette des Beaux-Arts,* Dec. 1937 and May 1938, for a discussion of the meaning and origin of the phrase. This is the title of a famous painting by Poussin. (With thanks to J. Isaacs, Esq.) Arcadia is the Greek Switzerland, as *Lewis & Short* phrases it.

*'et tu, Brute.' And you too, Brutus: C. 19–20. In full, *et tu, Brute fili* ('you also, O son Brutus'); variant, *tu quoque, Brute.* 'Suetonius says that Cæsar's words, on seeing Brutus [who stabbed him], were "καὶ σὺ τέκνον"—"You also, my son?"' (Properly, τέκνον = 'child' and υἱός = 'son'.) Often punningly, *You too, you brute!*

eternal feminine, the (?). Since ca. 1860. From *l'éternel féminin,* which occurs in Blaze de Bury's translation, 1847, of Part II of Goethe's *Faust.* (Benham.)

*eternal triangle, the. Two men and one woman, or two women and one man; a married couple and a male or female third party, in a tragi-comedy of love and/or passion: from ca. 1910. (The O.E.D. records it for 1907.) *Eternal* = constantly recurring.

eternal verities, the. The immutable truths or principles that govern or at least are concerned in life viewed spiritually: literary: late C. 19–20.

*eve of great events, the; esp., **on the . . .,** immediately before: from ca. 1880. At any time since August, 1938, it has been permissible to say, 'We are on the eve of great events'.

even if the worst happens (or **happened**). Late C. 19–20. 'Even if the worst happens, there is still hope—or death.'

*even tenor of one's way, the; esp., **pursue the . . .** To go quietly and steadily on: mid C. 19–20. Gray, 'They kept the noiseless tenor of their way' (*Elegy Written in a Country Churchyard*, 1751).

event. See **more than.**

ever and anon. Continually, though not at very short intervals; every now and then: C. 18–20, though common in C. 17 and though Shakespeare uses it in *Love's Labour's Lost* (1588), v, ii, 102.

ever so nice. Extremely pleasant or agreeable: colloquial: a cliché only since ca. 1930. ' "I think it's ever so nice," said Molly, whose vocabulary appeared somewhat limited ', Grierson Dickson, *Design for Treason*, 1937.—' "What do I think of marriage?" said the newly wed, prim old maid. "Why, it's ever so nice, but it's ever so rude!" ', a story going the rounds late in 1939.

every canon of international law. A C. 20 political and journalistic cliché. (Stuart Chase, *The Tyranny of Words*, 1938.)

every effort is being made (or **was made** or **will be made**). A C. 20 panacea and appeasement.

every inch a king. In every respect, a king: C. 19–20. Shakespeare, *King Lear*, IV, vi, 109, 'I, every inch a king': but the phrase is no longer thought of as a quotation.

every last one. All; every one or everyone, according to the context: American: C. 20. Michael Roberts, *A Rabble in Arms*, (English edition) 1939, '. . . Every last one of them howling a dolorous farewell'.

*'every man has his price.' Mid C. 18–20. Attributed to Sir Robert Walpole († 1745); his son Horace, in 1785, said it was a maxim ascribed to him 'by his enemies',—which is probably true. It was, in 1734, mentioned, verbatim, as 'an old maxim'. (Benham.)

every man Jack (colloquial); **'every mother's son'.** Every man: respectively from ca. 1860; C. 19–20. The latter comes in Shakespeare, and in 1583 an annalist wrote, 'The Spaniards murdered every mother's son of them' (O.E.D.).

every principle of decency and humanity. Journalistic: C. 20. *Decency* rather lessens the dignity of the phrase: it is made to carry too wide a meaning.

ex pede Herculem. 'By his foot [you know] Hercules'; hence, by a certain trait you know (or recognize) a person: mid C. 19–20. From the Roman proverbial saying.

expense of blood and treasure, an (?). A loss of men and money (or, lit., treasures): literary: late C. 19–20; obsolescent.

*experto crede! Late C. 19–20: literary. From *experto crede Roberto*, 'believe the experienced Robert'. Antonius de Avena († 1544) and Robert Burton in 1621 (Benham). In slang, 'You're telling *me*!' or 'I've had some!'

*explore every avenue, to. To try everybody and everything to gain one's end: political and journalistic: from ca. 1925. An absurd phrase, which, in 1935, A. P. Herbert (*What a Word!*) oddly thought was disappearing.

express concern, to. To give utterance to anxiety or solicitude: late C. 19–20.

express one's appreciation, to. To state, make clear, one's favourable opinion or reception of something: late C. 19–20.

extra precautions; esp., **to take . . .** To take additional measures of protection or to be more careful than usual: from ca. 1910.

*eye for an eye, (and a tooth for a tooth), an. A misquotation of 'Eye for eye, tooth for tooth', which continues: 'hand for hand, foot for foot', *Deuteronomy*, xix. 21. A cliché not until ca. 1860.

eye to (now often **on**) **the main chance, an;** esp.' **with an eye to . . .** and **to have . . .** To keep in mind (and view) the pecuniary, political, social or occupational advantage to be gained from an enterprise or a situation: mid C. 19–20. 'Probably from the game called hazard, in which the first throw of the dice is called the *main*' (Brewer).

eyes of faith, the; esp., **with the . . .** Late C. 19–20. From 'We walk by faith, not by sight', 2 *Corinthians*, v. 7 (διὰ πίστεως γὰρ περιπατοῦμεν, οὐ διὰ εἴδους).

F

face the music, to (colloquial). To confront an enemy, stand up to trouble: C. 20. From a singer's facing the orchestra as he sings in public.

faced with ruin. See **ruin . . .**

*'facilis descensus Averni' (but not the better '. . . Averno'). Easy is the descent to Hell: C. 19–20. *Avernus* (*lacus*), 'the birdless lake', gave off a stench that killed birds flying over it; hence, it was metaphorically used for Hell. 'Facilis descensus Averno | Noctes atque dies patet atri janua Ditis' (*Æneid*, VI, 126–7).

*fact of the matter is . . ., the. The fact is: from ca. 1880. An introductory formula, with which cf. **as a matter of fact.**

fair and square (colloquial). Adjective and adverb, 'honest(ly)', 'straightforward(ly)': C. 19–20. Recorded for as early as 1604 (O.E.D.).

fair, fat, and forty. A facetious cliché of mid C. 19–20; applied to women.

*fair sex, the. Women in general: C. 18–20; slightly obsolescent. A translation of French *le beau sexe* (the *beautiful* sex). Popularized by Addison.

'fair women and brave men.' Since ca. 1820. Byron.

fait accompli, a or **the.** The accomplished fact, as in 'He confronted his leader with a *fait accompli*': mid C. 19–20.

*fall between two stools, to. To fail because of hesitation between alternatives: C. 19–20. From the proverb *between two stools you fall to the ground*.

fall from grace, to. To suffer a moral decline or disgrace: C. 19–20, though recorded for 1643.

fall head over heels in love with, to. To fall very much in love with, to become infatuated with: late C. 19–20.

fall on deaf ears, to. To be unheard; or rather, to be heard but ignored: mid C. 19–20.

fall on stony ground, to. Despite the ruling (1939) of the British Broadcasting Corporation, this phrase from the Parable of the Sower has been thoroughly assimilated; C. 20.

fall to with a will, to. To work, or eat, with vigour or gusto: mid C. 19–20.

far and away; esp., **far and away the best.** Much the best: late C. 19–20.

far and wide. Reaching to many quarters or parts of the world; far abroad; so as to affect many persons or places in various quarters: mid C. 18–20. (Current since C. 10.)

far as in me lies. See *as far* . . .

*far be it from me to . . . A (sometimes falsely) modest disclaimer, often in speeches: late C. 18–20. It dates from late C. 14; cf. *Genesis*, xliv. 17.

far cry, a; esp., **it is a far cry from** (something) **to** (something else). A long way; there is a great interval of time or space, a great difference: mid C. 19–20.

far-flung Empire, our. A British cliché, dating from the stridently imperialistic last twenty years of C. 19.

far from accurate. (Very) inaccurate: late C. 19–20.

'far from the madding crowd.' Far from the insane turmoil of crowds: since ca. 1880; an adoption of Hardy's title (1874), itself based on Gray's 'far from the madding crowd's ignoble strife' (*Elegy*, 1751).

far-reaching effects; esp., (something) **has** . . . 'A great financier's death has far-reaching effects.' Late C. 19–20.

far-reaching policy, a. A policy of many immediate ramifications and much influence upon future events: C. 20.

*fast and furious; esp., **the fun was fast and furious.** Applied also to games. Late C. 19–20.

fasten the blame on, to. To fix or attach the blame on or to: mid C. 19–20.

fatal deed, (generally) **the.** A deed that, intentionally or unwittingly committed, causes death: mid C. 19–20.

fatal scene, (always) **the.** The scene of death: late C. 19–20. Originally journalistic.

*fate worse than death, a; esp., **to suffer** . . . (Of a woman) to be raped: mid C. 19–20; since ca. 1918, usually jocular.

*Father Time. Time personified: C. 19–20. Shakespeare, 'The plain bald pate of Father Time himself' (*A Comedy of Errors*, II, ii, 71).—Cf. **Time with his sickle.**

fatted calf. See **kill the . . .**

faute de mieux. For lack of something better: mid C. 19–20. '*Faute de mieux*, he went to an art-gallery.'

'fearfully and wonderfully made.' Applied properly to the human body; hence, allusively, to intricate things: C. 19–20. *Psalms*, cxxxix. 14, 'I am fearfully and wonderfully made'.

feather in one's cap, a; esp., it (or **this** or **that**) **is a . . .,** it is something to be proud of; a notable achievement; a mark of distinction or honour: mid C. 18–20.

feather one's nest, to. To enrich oneself slyly, secretly, or with prescient deliberation and at every opportunity: C. 18–20.

feel a different person to. To feel oneself to be a different person; i.e., to feel much better, to be 'one's own man again' —almost 'on top of the world'. Late C. 19–20.

feel in one's bones that . . ., to; to feel it in one's bones. Without proof or definite information, to be convinced that . . .; to have a deep-seated premonition or intuition; to know it intuitively: C. 20.

feel like a giant refreshed, to. See **like a . . .**

feel one's age, to (?). To be conscious of one's advancing age and to betray the diminution of one's powers: late C. 19–20.

feet of clay. The weak and human, the immoral, evil, or wicked part of a great, admired, or beloved person's character: C. 19–20. In allusion to the composition of many ancient idols (cf. *Daniel*, ii. 33, 34, 42, and 45).

feline amenities. Catty remarks and actions made or performed by women: from ca. 1910.

'fellow of infinite jest, a' (?). See **alas . . .**

female of the species, the. Woman; women generically: from ca. 1912. 'The female of the species is more deadly than the male', Rudyard Kipling, Oct. 20, 1911. (Benham.)

festive board, the. A laden table at, or as if at, a feast: mid C. 19–20. Praed, ca. 1839, 'Around the festive board' (O.E.D.).

festive occasion, a. A feast, a dinner, a party: late C. 19–20. Often **on this festive occasion**—a favourite with public speakers. Perhaps also **the festive season:** Christmastide: from ca. 1870.

*few and far between. Very few; few and at long intervals (in space or **time**): C. 20. 'His visits have become few and far between.'

'fiat justitia, ruat cælum.' Let justice be done, even though the heavens fall: C. 17–20. A Roman semi-proverbial saying; cf. Augustine's *fiat jus et pereat mundus,* 'let right be done, and let the world perish' (Benham).

fiddle while Rome burns, to. To amuse oneself, to be engaged in trivial activities, while a war, a crisis, a disaster, or something otherwise important is in progress: C. 19–20. G. Daniel, 1649, 'Let Nero fiddle out Rome's obsequies'.

'fierce light which beats upon a throne, that.' Late C. 19–20; in reference to Royalty's lack of privacy. From Tennyson, *Idylls of the King,* 'Dedication', 1861.

fight tooth and nail, to. I.e., with tooth and nail; hence, with the utmost ferocity or vigour: mid C. 19–20, though recorded so early as for C. 16.

filled to capacity. See **taxed . . .**

filthy lucre. Literally 'sordid gain, base profit', it came to mean 'dirty money', then 'any money, but esp. cash': only in this last sense is it a cliché (mid. C. 19–20). 'Not greedy of filthy lucre' (ἀφιλάργυρον, 1 *Timothy*, iii. 3; μὴ αἰσχροκερδεῖς, *ibid.*, verse 8) and 'for filthy lucre's sake' (αἰσχροῦ κέρδους χάριν, *Titus*. i, 11) constitute the Biblical origin. The Vulgate equivalent for the *Titus* phrase is *turpis lucri gratia*, where *turpe lucrum* = 'disgraceful profit'. (See my *A New Testament Word-Book*.) In slang, 'filthy lucre' is *the filthy* (Blackmore, 1877), mostly an upper-class (esp. Regular Army officers') term.

fin de siècle, noun and adjective; applied esp. to a tired literature or a sophisticated society: from ca. 1890. From the title of a comedy (1888) by F. de Jouvenot and H. Micard. (Benham.)

final and unalterable. Ineluctable; decisively final: mid C. 19–20; slightly obsolescent. 'His decision is final and unalterable.'

find it in one's heart to do something, to; esp., **to be unable to find it . . .,** to find oneself mentally or morally unable to do something one has intended to do: mid C. 19–20.

find (or **get**) **one's bearings, to** (figurative). To learn, discover or determine one's position in relation to what one has to do or to experience: C. 20. Nautical.

fine feather, to be in. To be in good health and/or spirits: mid C. 19–20; slightly obsolescent.

fingers itch (or **are itching**) **to** (do something), **one's.** One is eager or impatient to do something: C. 19–20.

finishing touch, the. That final touch (as of a painter's brush) which ensures perfection or a satisfactory completeness: mid C. 19–20.

firm footing, a (figurative) (?). An established place or position: C. 20.

first and foremost. Most notable, remarkable, or outstanding; best; principal: mid C. 19–20, though recorded for 1483

(Caxton: O.E.D.). As an adverb, it = before anything else happens, takes place, is done: late C. 19–20.

first and last. All the time; in all; what with one thing and another: C. 19–20.

'first fine careless rapture, the.' Mid C. 19–20. From Browning's *Home thoughts from Abroad*, 1845, concerning a thrush's song.

first magnitude, the. See **of the . . .**

first robin, the. As an index of Spring: American: from ca. 1880. (The American robin is the red-breasted thrush.)— Cf. the English *the first cuckoo*.

*first saw the light of day, he. He was born: mid C. 19–20. 'This famous man first saw the light of day on a cross-Channel steamer.' An elaboration of *to see the light*, applied to babes and books.

first water, the. See **of the first water.**

fish in troubled waters, to. To profit by disturbance, political or financial; to turn the troubles of others to one's own advantage: C. 18–20. From angling.

*fish out of water, a. A person in circumstances to which he is strange or to which he fails to adapt himself: mid C. 19–20.

fit for a king. Of the best quality: C. 18–20. ('Wasn't that a dainty dish to set before a king?')

fit to hold a candle to, not. Not to be compared with, much inferior to: C. 19–20. Byron, 'Others aver that he to Handel, | Is hardly fit to hold a candle'.

flash in the pan, a. 'An abortive effort or outburst (O.E.D.): late C. 19–20. But, from ca. 1920, generally 'an unsustained effort or a momentary success, a sole, unrepeatable success'. From the C. 17 firelocks (flint-locks).

flashed through (e.g., **my**) **mind, it.** It occurred to me: late C. 19–20.

flat denial, a. A blunt or unqualified denial: late C. 18–20. Swift, 1713, 'She gave no flat denial'.

flat, stale and improfitable (or **unprofitable**) is the usual form—a misquotation-cliché (mid C. 19–20) formed from 'How weary, stale, flat, and unprofitable | Seems to me all the uses of this world' (*Hamlet*, I, ii, 133–4).

flatter but (or **only**) **to deceive, to.** To flatter, or make fair promises, in order to, or, in the event, to mislead: late C. 19–20. 'A fine morning often flatters only to deceive.'

*****flesh and blood;** esp. in **a creature of . . .** and **one's own . . .** Human nature ('Flesh and blood can't bear it', John Byrom, † 1763); a human being (mid C. 19–20); a relative (C. 19–20).

flesh-pots of Egypt, the. Luxurious living, prosperity, comforts and privileges, regretted—or regarded enviously: C. 18–20. In allusion to *Exodus*, xvi. 3, 'Would that we had died . . . in the land of Egypt, when we sat by the flesh-pots, when we did eat bread to the full': Vulgate, *super ollas carnium*. *Flesh-pot* is a pot in which flesh is boiled.

flight of fancy, a (?). A fanciful sally; an imaginative excursion; a poetical or rhetorical extravagance: mid C. 19–20. The phrase is not subject to the literary discrimination between fancy and imagination.

flood-gates of (affection, grief, etc.**), to open** (or **loose) the.** To give free vent to affection, tears, etc.: mid C. 19–20.

*****flotsam and jetsam.** Ruinous remains; human wreckage; odds and ends: from ca. 1870. 'On the Embankment we saw the flotsam and jetsam of humanity.' Lit., floating goods and ship-parts from a wreck.

flourish like a (or **the**) **green bay-tree, to.** To prosper exceedingly: C. 19–20. From 'The ungodly . . . flourishing like a green bay-tree' (*The Psalter*, xxxvii, 36).

flowers of speech. Choice phrases; figures of speech and/or other stylistic embellishments: from ca. 1880. In C. 16–18, it was *flowers of rhetoric*.

flowing bowl, the. 'Lashings of liquor', as the slangy have it: mid C. 19–20. 'Seek consolation in the flowing bowl' is alluded to in *Artemus Ward His Book*, published in the 1860's.

fly in the face of Providence, to. To ignore timely warnings, excellent advice, clear evidence: C. 19–20.

fly in the ointment, a. Some small object or trifling circumstance that lessens one's enjoyment of a thing and detracts from its attractiveness or agreeableness: C. 20. In allusion to *Ecclesiastes*, x. 1, 'Dead flies cause the ointment of the perfumer to send forth a stinking savour': *Muscae morientes perdunt suavitatem unguenti.*

fly off at a tangent, to. To leave, abruptly, one course of action—one thought or subject—to pursue another: from ca. 1870.

foam at the mouth, to (?). To be in a violent rage, to be extremely angry: mid C. 19–20.

*foeman worthy of one's steel, a. A worthy opponent: mid C. 19–20. Scott, *The Lady of the Lake*, 1810, 'Foemen worthy of their steel' (swords), cited by Benham.

follow in the footsteps of (esp., a great man), **to.** To accept him as a master or a guide, and act upon that acceptance: late C. 19–20. Earlier, *follow the steps of*: cf. 1 *Peter*, ii. 21.

fons et origo. The fount and origin: literary: C. 18–20. The original is the semi-proverbial *fons et origo mali* ('. . . of the evil', Benham).

fool (a person) **to the top of one's bent, to.** To dupe or impose upon him to the limit of one's endurance or forbearance: C. 19–20. *Hamlet*, III ii, 401, 'They fool me to the top of my bent'. *Bent* = bendableness.

*fool's paradise, a; esp., **to live in . . .** Bliss based on a blind trust: C. 19–20: George Colman the Elder († 1794), 'A fool's paradise is better than a wiseacre's purgatory' (Benham); cf. 'Where ignorance is bliss, 'tis folly to be wise'.

for all (or **aught,** obsolescent) **I know.** So far as I know: mid C. 19–20.

*for auld lang syne and the synonymous **for old time's sake.** C. 19–20; mid C. 19–20. The oldest version of *Auld Lang Syne* (Burns, 1789) is recorded in 1711 (Benham).

*for better or (for) worse. A misquotation of 'for better, for worse' in the marriage service (*The Book of Common Prayer*): mid C. 19–20.

for good and all. For always; finally: C. 18–20; fairly common in C. 17. 'She left him for good and all.'

for love or money, not to be able to (e.g., **get**). To be unable to (e.g., obtain) at any price or by any means: recorded in 1590 (O.E.D.), but a cliché only in C. 18–20.

for many a long day. For a long time: late C. 19–20. An elaboration of *for many a day*.

for the life of me, I cannot (or **could not**) **. . .** Even to save one's life; even if I gave my life: mid C. 19–20. 'I could not resist a smile for the life of me', 1843 (O.E.D.).

'for this relief much thanks.' C. 19–20. (*Hamlet*, I, i.) In C. 20, often jocularly. In allusion to military relief.

for very shame; esp., **not to (be able to) do** something **for . . .,** to be precluded, by a sense of shame, from doing it: C. 19–20. Earlier, *for shame*.

for what it is worth. See **my opinion.**

forbidden fruit. A forbidden pleasure; something stolen: late C. 19–20. From *forbidden fruit is sweetest,* a proverb (cf. *chose défendue est la plus désirée*) recorded in 1498 (Benham).

force to be reckoned with, a. A formidable person, organization, power: late C. 19–20.

*foregone conclusion, a. A conclusion (or end) already known; hence, a conclusion or result taken for granted: C. 19–20. From Shakespeare's 'But this denoted a foregone conclusion' (*Othello,* III, iii).

forlorn hope, a. An enterprise that is very unlikely to succeed; something done in sheer desperation: mid C. 19–20.

formulate a plan, to. This C. 20 cliché, originally American, has been English since ca. 1925. Often used loosely for 'to *form* a plan'.

fortune of war, the. A chance, esp. a mischance, to be expected from the nature of the enterprise or undertaking: mid C. 19–20.

foul one's own nest, to. To commit a sin, a fault, that will ruin one's reputation at one's home, one's lodging, one's place of business: mid C. 19–20. From an old proverb about a bird.

four corners of the earth, the; esp., **from the,** from the remotest parts: mid C. 19–20. In C. 16–18, generally . . . *world.* Perhaps originally in allusion to *Psalms,* xciv. 4, and *Isaiah,* xi. 12.

Fourth Estate, the. The Newspaper Press: C. 19–20; coined ca. 1790, perhaps by Burke. The three estates, proper, of the realm are the Peers, the Bishops, the Commons.

frame an excuse, to. To devise or invent an excuse: C. 19–20. Bishop Hall, 1608, 'He is witty in nothing but framing excuses to sit still' (*Characters,* 'Slothful'). O.E.D.

fraught with danger (or **peril**); esp., **the situation is ...,** attended with much risk and/or danger; bound to produce danger: mid C. 19–20. Lit., '(heavily) laden ...'

free and easy. (Of persons) unaffected, unconstrained; (of manner) natural; (of things) careless or slipshod: mid C. 19–20, though very common too in C. 18.

*free, gratis and for nothing. Free; without cost, without payment: C. 20; now mostly jocular. An elaboration of *free, gratis,* itself an elaboration of *free*.

*fresh fields and pastures new. A new activity or scene of operations: C. 19–20. A misquotation of Milton's 'fresh woods, and pastures new' (*Lycidas,* 1637).

fret and fume, to; esp., **fretting and fuming,** vexing oneself, worrying, generally with a connotation of angry, querulous, or peevish complaint at the cause of the vexation or distress: mid C. 19–20 or perhaps C. 19–20, the phrase already existing in C. 17. Probably at first an alliterative intensification of 'to *fret*'.

*friend at court, (to have) a. To have an influential friend where he can be of service: C. 19–20. From the proverb, *a friend in court makes a process* [law-suit] *short.*

friend in need, a. A dependable friend: C. 19–20. From the proverb, 'A friend in need | Is a friend indeed' (? originally *in deed*). Adumbrated in a Latin saying by Ennius.

friend of man, the. The dog: from ca. 1840; obsolescent.

frightened out of one's wits. Panic-stricken: late C. 19–20. '[Corris Morgan] was far too frightened to think. Panic numbed him. He was in the grip of a terror which would certainly have been quite incomprehensible to Mr Mulliner, who had often been frightened, but never out of his wits': thus allusively by Margaret Kennedy, *The Midas Touch,* 1938.

from A to Z. From beginning to end; throughout; thoroughly: mid C. 19–20, though in current use as early as C. 17.

from bad to worse; esp., **things went from . . .,** became still worse: C. 18–20. Recorded for 1579 (Spenser). O.E.D.

'from Dan to Bersheeba.' From one end of the kingdom —a country—to the other: C. 19–20. Dan was the most northerly, Bersheeba the most southerly city of the Holy Land. See *Judges*, xx. 1; 1 *Samuel*, iii. 20; 2 *Samuel*, iii. 10; etc.

from head to heels; from top to toe. From head to foot—of which these two key-phrases are variants: mid C. 19–20.

*from pillar to post. (Hunted) from one place to another: C. 18–20. The phrase is as early as C. 16; *from post to pillar* in C. 15–16.

from start to finish (?). From beginning to end: colloquial (originally, sporting): C. 20.

from the bottom of one's heart; esp., **to thank . . .** To thank very gratefully, in a heartfelt manner: mid C. 19–20.

from the cradle to the grave. From birth to death; throughout one's life: C. 19–20. (Steele, 1709) 'From the cradle to the grave, he never had a day's illness'.

*from time immemorial. Synonymous with (and rather literary for) **time out of mind:** mid C. 19–20. Earlier *for time immemorial* or simply *time immemorial*.

from top to toe. See **from head to heels.**

'from whose bourn no traveller returns.' C. 19–20. Shakespeare, *Hamlet*, III, i, in reference to death. *Bourn* here = 'frontier of a country' (O.E.D.).

frozen to the marrow. See **chilled . . .**

fulfil a long-felt want, to. See **long-felt want.**

full and hearty co-operation; esp., **promise one's.**
One's entire help and good-will: C. 20.

fulsome flattery (or **flatteries**). Gross flattery; excessive
or extravagant flatteries: 1692, Bentley, 'Puffed up with the
fulsome flatteries' (O.E.D.); but not a cliché until C. 19.

further the interests of (a person; less often, a cause), **to.**
To promote the interests of: C. 20.

G

G.O.M., the. See **Grand Old Man.**

gain ground, to (?). To advance (figuratively), to progress:
C. 19–20, though common throughout C. 17–18. From the
literal military sense, 'to conquer ground from the enemy'.

gala occasion, a. A special occasion, marked by gala:
American: late C. 19–20. (Sullivan.)

gall and wormwood. A source of much bitterness of spirit;
rancour and asperity: C. 19–20. Both *gall* (bile) and *wormwood* are very bitter. An allusion to *Lamentations*, iii. 5 ('gall
and travail'); iii. 19, 'Mine affliction and my misery, the wormwood and the gall' (Vulgate, *absinthii et fellis*); and *Acts*, viii.
23, 'Thou art in the gall of bitterness, and in the bond of
iniquity'.

*gay Lothario, a. A merry male heart-breaker or woman-
chaser: C. 19–20. 'Is this that haughty, gallant, gay Lothario?'
(Nicholas Rowe, *The Fair Penitent*, 1703, Act v, sc. i).

gay Paree (colloquial). Paris (*la Ville Lumière*), city of pleasure (and art and intellect and . . .): from ca. 1870. Since
ca. 1920, regarded as rather 'cheap'.

general exodus, a. A general movement of people, as of
immigrants, refugees, holiday-makers: late C. 19–20.

generous to a fault; good-natured to a fault. Almost excessively generous or good-natured: late C. 19–20. I.e., to the extent of falling into the fault of excess.

gentle reader (vocative); **the gentle reader.** The former, very common in C. 19 (e.g., in the button-holing Thackeray), is obsolescent; so is the latter, always less frequent.

germane to the matter (or **subject**). Relevant: C. 19–20. Shakespeare ('The phrase would be more germane to the matter', *Hamlet*, v, ii, 165) and Scott (in 1816), have '. . . matter'; Mrs. Trollope in 1840 and J. G. Holland in 1863 have '. . . subject'. *Germane to the case* also occurs, but not so frequently as to amount to a cliché.

get down to bed-rock; colloquially (originally, slangily) **to get down to brass tacks** (rhyming *hard facts*). To examine essentials; to be practical: respectively late C. 19–20 and C. 20.

*****get more than one bargained for, to.** To receive pejoratively more than one arranged for or asked for or expected: late C. 19–20.

get one's second wind, to (figurative). To recover after a difficult period: C. 20. From athletics (long-distance running).

get one's teeth into, to. To become fairly embarked on (an enterprise); to tackle in earnest: from ca. 1910.

get up on the wrong side of the bed, or **get out of bed on the wrong side, to.** To rise in a bad humour: late C. 19–20. 'Oh, he's got out of bed on the wrong side!'

giant refreshed, a. See **like a . . .**

giddy vortex, the. A constant round of gaiety, pleasure, excitement: mid C. 19–20; slightly obsolescent.

gift from the gods, a. A notable or extremely welcome gift; hence, something very easily acquired: late C. 19–20.— Cf. Lucan's *o munera nondum intellecta Deum*, 'O gifts of the gods, not yet understood' (Benham).

gift of tongues, the. The being a good linguist; a (esp. spoken) knowledge of many languages: mid. C. 19–20.—Cf. *the tongues,* 'foreign languages', a literarism.

gild refinèd gold, to; gilding the lily (properly: **painting**), indulging in excessive embellishment: C. 19–20; late C. 19–20. Shakespeare, *King John*, IV, ii, 'To gild refinèd gold, to paint the lily, | To throw a perfume on the violet . . . | Is Wasteful and ridiculous excess'.

gild the pill, to. To soften the harsh, or tone down the unpleasant: mid C. 19–20. (Fairly common ca. 1670–1850.) To encase a bitter pill in a coating of, e.g., sugar.

gilded youth. Youths of fashion; esp. aristocratic (and rich) young men-about-town: from ca. 1840; obsolescent, as are the youths. On French *la jeunesse dorée.*

gilding the lily. See **gild refinèd gold.**

*gird (up) one's loins, to, the longer form being now the commoner. To adjust one's figurative belt for freer and vigorous action: C. 19–20. First in Coverdale (*gird up*). In allusion to 1 *Kings*, xviii. 46—2 *Kings*, iv. 29 ('Gird up thy loins': cf. *Job*, xxxviii. 3 and xl. 7; *Jeremiah*, i. 17)—1 *Peter*, i. 13, 'Wherefore gird up the loins of your mind' (*Διὸ ἀναζωσάμενοι τὰς ὀσφύας τῆς διανοίας ὑμῶν,* 'wherefore bracing up the loins of your mind': *succinti lumbos mentis vestræ*), 'Let your minds be intent upon, ready, and prepared for your spiritual work' (Cruden).

give a bad mark to, to. To condemn, think less of a person, in a certain matter: late C. 19–20. From a school system of marking.

*give a dog a bad name, to. To give a man a bad name and thus damage, for years, his reputation: C. 19–20. From the proverbial *to give . . . and hang him.*

give a wide berth to, to. To avoid sedulously; to keep well away from (a person, a practice): from ca. 1870. Nautical.

give and take, n. and v. (To make) mutual concessions: mid C. 19–20. By 1816 (see O.E.D.) it was already 'a familiar phrase'.

give carte blanche to, to. See **carte blanche.**

give chapter and verse, to. To give the exact authority (for a statement), the precise reference: from ca. 1860. (Recorded for 1711: O.E.D.) Originally of a passage of Scripture.

give oneself airs, to. To put on 'side'; to assume an air of superiority: mid C. 19–20, though current since early C. 18.

give pause to, to. 'To check the progress or course of' (O.E.D.); to abate the assurance or confidence of (a person): mid C. 19–20. Originally, in allusion to Shakespeare's 'In that sleep of death, what dreams may come, | . . . Must give us pause'—cause us to hesitate.

give short shrift to, to. To despatch, make short work of: from ca. 1880. From the Confessional.

*give (a person) **the cold shoulder, to.** To treat (a person) with studied and ostentatious coldness or indifference: mid C. 19–20. Culinary.

give the Devil his due, to. To admit an enemy's merits: C. 19–20. A sense-adaptation of the proverbial saying.

give the lie to, to. To refute (a person) vigorously; to prove the falsity of (allegations, appearances): C. 19–20. Originally, to contradict flatly.

*glorious uncertainty (e.g., **of cricket), the.** As applied to cricket: C. 20. As applied to the law, since ca. 1770; *to the glorious uncertainty of the law* was a C. 18 legal toast (Benham).

glorious victory, a. A notable and/or famous victory: C. 19–20.—Cf. Southey's ironic 'It was a famous victory' (*The Battle of Blenheim*, 1798).

go about . . . See **business.**

go at it hammer and tongs, to. To engage very vigorously in combat, contest, or work: mid C. 19–20. From the smithy.

go by the board, to. To be lost, abandoned, finally or definitely: from ca. 1870. Lit., 'to fall overboard'.

go down to the sea in ships, to. To sail the seas, to be a sailor, mid C. 19–20. 'They that go down to the sea in ships, that do business in great waters' (*Psalms*, cvii. 23).

go from strength to strength, to. To improve one's work, increase one's reputation, at every new attempt: mid C. 19–20. From 'They go from strength to strength' (*Psalms*, lxxxiv. 7).

go further and fare worse, to. Not content with something available or offered, to pass on and experience bad fortune or inferior treatment: mid C. 19–20. Adumbrated in 1614 (O.E.D.).

go hat in hand, to (?). To go obsequiously (to plead, to intercede, etc.): mid C. 19–20. With head uncovered, to show respect.

go in at one ear and out of the other, to. (Of a warning, a discourse) to make no impression: C. 18–20. 'The professor's lecture went in at . . .'

go off with one's tail between one's legs, to. (Of persons) to depart, take one's dismissal, with cowed or dejected mien: late C. 19–20. Like a whipped dog.

go on the war-path, to. To seek trouble, look for a person that one regards as foe, opponent, insulter: late C. 19–20. From Red Indian warfare.

*go the whole hog, to (colloquial). To make every effort, regardless of cost: late C. 19–20; originally American and recorded much earlier.

go through fire and water for (a person), **to.** To face, *to* undergo, great dangers and risks: mid C. 19–20.

go through with ... See **comb.**

go to one's account, to. To die: mid C. 19–20; slightly obsolescent. In C. 18–early 19, it was regarded as slangy ; later as colloquial.

go to the dogs, to. (Of an institution) to go to ruin; (of a person) to become thoroughly dissipated and neglectful of business: from ca. 1840. That it was a very common phrase even earlier in the century appears from Dickens's 'He has gone to the demnition bow-wows' (*Nicholas Nickleby*, ch. lxiv, 1838).

go to the other extreme, to. To pendulum-swing to the opposite side in an opinion or, esp., a course of behaviour: late C. 19–20.

God and Mammon. God and personified possessions and riches (regarded as anti-Divine forces and influences): C. 19–20.—Cf. **Mammon of unrighteousness,** q.v.

goes without saying, it (or **that**). See **cela va sans dire,** of which it is a translation.

Golden Age (or **g. a.**), **the.** An ideal age (originally, the first age of the world) of perfection and happiness; Utopia realized: C. 18–20. With reminiscence of passages in Horace, Ovid, Virgil. In Kenneth Grahame's story, *The Golden Age*, 1895, it is childhood.

*golden mean, the. The ideal average; ideal moderation; avoidance of excess in either direction: C. 18–20. Horace's *aurea mediocritas* (Odes, II, x, 5).

Golden West, the. California (*The Golden State*, 1847): American: from ca. 1880.

gone (before) but not forgotten. Dead but unforgotten: late C. 19–20.

*good, bad, and (or or) indifferent. Good, bad, and of medium quality: C. 20. 'Let's have them all—good, bad, and indifferent!'

good cheer, to be of. To be cheerful (and to show one's cheerfulness): C. 19–20. The locution (a rendering of Fr. *faire bonne chère*), literally 'to be of good face', was consecrated by its use in *Matthew*, ix. 2, and xiv. 27.

good clean fun. Harmless fun, activities, jokes: from ca. 1930.—Cf. the catch-phrase, *keep the party clean!*, cut out dirty stories and innuendoes!

good for nothing. Worthless (person): C. 19–20; fairly common also throughout C. 18.

good general education, a. An education that, unspecialized, is soundly instructive and formative: C. 20.

*good in parts; or, as a battered simile, good in parts— like the curate's egg. Of mixed character: from ca. 1910. In *Punch*, Nov. 9, 1895, there is a drawing of a meek young curate that, eating a bad egg, said that 'parts of it' were 'excellent'. (O.E.D.)

*good men and true; (of a jury) twelve good men and true. Current from C. 17, but a cliché only in C. 19–20.

good-natured to a fault. See generous . . .

*good Queen Bess. Queen Elizabeth of England: Protestants': C. 19–20. From the good she did for her country.— Cf. spacious times and contrast *bloody Mary*.

*good Samaritan, a. One who helps another in distress: C. 19–20. The phrase occurs nowhere in the New Testament: not even in the source of the phrase, the parable of the priest, the Levite, and the Samaritan (*Luke*, x. 30–5).

'good time was had by all, a.' All present, all the guests, enjoyed themselves: literary and/or high-brow: from a month or two after the appearance, in 1937, of Stevie Smith's book of verses so titled.

good woman's love, a; or the love of a good woman. Regarded as a safeguard and a comfort: from ca. 1870.

*goods and chattels. (All one's) personal property: C. 18–20, though common since late C. 16. Originally, it would seem, a legal phrase.

Gordian knot; esp., to cut a (or **the**) **...** To solve, by force or by evasion, a very difficult problem, a grave difficulty: C. 19–20. (Shakespeare *unlooses* this knot in *Henry V*, first scene.) The allusion is to that intricate knot which, tied by Gordius (a Phrygian king), should ensure dominion over Asia to the *unlooser*; Alexander the Great *cut* through it with his sword.

gorge rises at, one's. One feels extremely disgusted at or resentful of: C. 19–20. *Hamlet* v, i, 207, 'How abhorred my Imagination is, my gorge rises at it'.

gorgeous East, the. A mid C. 19–20 cliché; now obsolescent, and always rather literary—with an allusion to 'Once did she'—Venice—'hold the gorgeous East in fee' (Wordsworth, 1802).

grain or chaff; to separate the grain from the chaff. The genuine or valuable on the one hand, the spurious or worthless on the other: C. 19–20.

grand finale, the. The glorious end: C. 20. From concert programmes.

*Grand Old Man (e.g., **of English politics**), **the.** Applied first to Gladstone; then to W. G. Grace (*the G.O.M. of English cricket*). Originated by Labouchère, 1881.

grapes of wrath, the. An American cliché, rather literary, from ca. 1870. In 1939, for instance, John Steinbeck used it as the title of a powerful novel. It is in the first stanza of *The*

Battle Hymn of the Republic, which, though written earlier, occurs, in 1866, in *Later Lyrics*, and in 1899 ushers-in *From Sunset Ridge*, by Julia Ward Howe (1819–1910):

Thine eyes have seen the coming of the Lord;
He is trampling out the vintage where the grapes of wrath are
    stored;
He hath loosed the fateful lightning of His terrible, swift
    sword;
       His truth is marching on.

From the Biblical turn of the language, I suspect a Biblical reminiscence—and find it in *Revelation*, xiv. 19–20: 'And the angel . . . gathered the vine of the earth, and cast it into the great winepress of the wrath of God. And the winepress was trodden without the city, and blood came out of the winepress, even unto the horse bridles, by the space of a thousand and six hundred furlongs' (with which eloquence, neither the New Testament Greek nor the Vulgate Latin can justly be compared).—Cf. *Revelation*, xv. 7, 'And one of the four beasts gave unto the seven angels seven golden vials full of the wrath of God', on which Blount in his *Glossographia*, 1656, furnishes the pertinent gloss, 'Vials of wrath, mentioned in the Apocalipse, signifie Gods readiness to be fully revenged on sinners'.

graphic description, a; graphic descriptions. Vivid description: mid C. 19–20; perhaps originally journalistic, despite Swift's 'a description graphic' (ca. 1745).

grasp the nettle, to. 'To attack a difficulty boldly' (O.E.D.), like a man of mettle (as in folk-lore): from ca. 1880. Re-popularized by Mr Neville Chamberlain, late in 1939.

grateful acknowledgements. A thankful admission of help or favour: C. 20. Generally *with g.a.* or *to make g.a.*

grave concern. 'Grave concern was felt.' 'It caused grave concern.' The meaning is simply 'much concern' or 'deep anxiety': late C. 19–20.

---

*grave international situation, a or **the.** A political and journalistic cliché, dating from ca. 1910. (In 1938–40, hardly a cliché: unless life be one.)—Cf. the next.

grave issue, a. A serious or dangerous situation: from ca. 1920. *Grave Issues* is pilloried by A. P. Herbert in *What a Word!*, 1935; common too is the tautological *grave issues at stake.*

grave miscarriage of justice. See **miscarriage** . . .

great fleas . . . See **big fleas** . . .

great majority, the (the dead); esp., **join the** . . ., to die. A C. 20 euphemism.

*great open spaces, the; occasionally *the wide open spaces.* The open spaces of the country; esp. of such less populous countries as Australia, Canada, South Africa: from ca. 1910.

great ovation, a or **the.** Much applause; a warm, public reception or welcome: mid C. 19–20.

(great) strapping wench, a. A big, strong, stoutly built girl: mid C. 18–20 for the shorter, mid C. 19–20 for the longer phrase.

great unwashed, the. The proletariat: from ca. 1840. Already a well-known phrase when Theodore Hook used it in 1833. Its snobbishness has caused it to become obsolescent.

'greater love hath no man than this (that a man lay down his life for his friends'—often misquoted as 'for his friend'). Mid C. 19–20. *John*, xv. 13.

Greek kalends, the; esp., **to put off to the** . . . A literary cliché of C. 18–20; from a reputed phrase (*ad Kalendas Græcas*) of Augustus Cæsar's. There being no Greek kalends, *to the G.k.* means 'indefinitely' and *G.k.* = never.

green-eyed monster, the. Jealousy: C. 19–20. It occurs, with quotation-marks, in *The Sporting Magazine*, 1804, and comes from *Othello*, 'Oh, beware, my lord, of jealousy, | It is the green-eyed monster'; cf. 'green-eyed jealousy' in *The Merchant of Venice*. (O.E.D.)

grievous error, a. A flagrant, obvious mistake: late C. 19–20. On the analogy of *grievous sin*, a stock phrase of late C. 14–17.

*grim death, in *to hang* (or *hold*) *on like grim death* and *to look like grim death*. Respectively mid C. 19–20 and late C. 19–20. To hang on grimly; to look exceedingly grim.

grin and bear it, to. To submit with a grin (and without lament or recrimination) to one's fate: from ca. 1880. In late C. 18–mid 19, it was *to grin and abide* (see O.E.D.).

grind the faces of the poor, to. To oppress, with taxes and/or injustice, the poor: C. 19–20. A Hebraism: 'What mean ye that ye beat my people to pieces, and grind the faces of the poor? saith the Lord God of hosts', *Isaiah*, iii. 15 (A.V.; Wyclif, 1388, has 'grynden togidere the faces of pore men'). (O.E.D.)

gross exaggeration ('Guilty of gross exaggeration'; 'It is a g.e.'); **gross overstatement, a** ('It is a g.o.'). A glaring or flagrant exaggeration: late C. 19–20.

ground floor. See **in on the . . .**

grow no younger, to; esp., **to be growing . . .** To have reached the midway of life: late C. 19–20.

'guide, philosopher and friend', a or **one's.** Belonging to C. 19–20 and drawn from 'Thou wert my guide, philosopher, and friend' in Epistle 4 (published in 1734) of Pope's *An Essay on Man*.

guiding light, a; a guiding principle (?). A means of determining one's life or actions: mid C. 19–20; late C. 19–20.

H

hair, as in **without turning a hair** and **he** (etc.) **did not turn a hair.** To be unruffled, unexcited, unafraid, unaffected: late C. 19–20. Originally of horses: not to show sweat by a roughening of the hair (O.E.D.).

hair like (or **of**) **spun gold.** Female hair that looks like spun gold (silk thread wound with gold): C. 20, esp. among writers of fiction.

*halcyon days. Days that are calm and quiet, or peaceful and undisturbed: mid C. 19–20, though recorded so early as 1578. Literally, 'kingfishers' days'—the fourteen days of calm weather commemorated in classical mythology: ἀλκυονίδες ἡμέραι: alcyonei dies. (O.E.D.)

hale and hearty. Robust: mid C. 19–20. A reduplication of *hale,* 'healthy'.

half the battle; esp., **it's . . .** Something contributing largely to success: from ca. 1860: Marryat, 1849, 'Youth . . . is half the battle' (O.E.D.).

hallmark(s) of truth (or **sincerity**), **the.** A quality that constitutes a distinctive token of truth or sincerity: late C. 19–20.

hammer and tongs. See **go at it . . .**

hand against every man, (with) one's. Applied to outcasts and outlaws: mid C. 19–20. 'In a way they'—six hardened criminals—'were like wolves, their hand against every man's' (a not unusual variant), Hugh Clevely, *The Wrong Murderer,* ca. 1938. From *Genesis,* xvi. 12, concerning Ishmael, 'He will be a wild man; his hand will be against every man, and every man's hand against him'.

*hand and foot, bound (or **tied**). Bound or tied—controlled—utterly by (a superior authority): C. 20. Government officials are bound hand and foot, by rules and regulations and by tradition.

hand has lost its cunning, one's. One has become less skilful, adroit, familiar with a mastered art or craft: C.19–20. In allusion to 'If I forget thee, O Jerusalem, let my right hand forget her cunning' (*Psalms*, cxxxvii. 5: Vulgate, *oblivioni detur dextera mea*).

*hand in glove (with a person), **to be.** To be on very intimate terms or in constant contact with him: from ca. 1870. In C. 17–18, *hand and glove*.

hand on the torch, to. To hand to the next in office, to the next or younger generation, the tradition (of freedom, right living, intellectual possessions, and esp. enlightenment): from the 1880's. A rendering of λαμπάδα παραδιδόναι, the reference being to the Greek torch-race, a glorified relay-race, in which one handed on, not a baton, but a torch.

hand-to-mouth, adjective; **to live from hand to mouth.** Improvident; to live improvidently, thriftlessly: respectively mid C. 19–20 and late C. 18–20. 'I subsist, as the poor are vulgarly said to do, from hand to mouth', Cowper, in a letter, Feb. 5, 1790 (O.E.D.).

handle with kid gloves, to. To handle or treat (too) delicately or gently or genteelly; to treat or handle gingerly: late C. 19–20. Instead of spitting on one's hands and getting to work.

hands across the sea. Friendship with people, or nations, abroad: C. 20. From a poem entitled *Hands across the Sea*, by Byron Webber (fl. 1886–94). (Benham.)

hang by a thread, to. To depend on something very easily destroyed or upset; (of a life) that may continue, may be extinguished; (of negotiations) to be extremely delicate: C. 19–20. With reference, originally, to the **sword of Damocles.**—Cf. also **hanging in the balance.**

hang on . . . See **grim death.**

hang on by one's eyelids, to. To retain a military, occupational, or sentimental position, post, standing, status, in a desperate proximity to failure or defeat: colloquial: C. 20.

hanging in the balance. Quite undecided or in dubious suspense: C. 15–20; but not a cliché until C. 19.

happiest moment of one's life, the; esp., this is the happiest moment of my life (I was never so happy); also **that was . . . of his** (or **her**) **life.** Late C. 19–20.

happy couple, the, in reference (mid C. 19–20) to a bridal or a golden-wedded pair of whom we have already been told something. (*A happy couple*, as in 'Mr and Mrs X. are a happy couple', is obviously not a cliché.)

happy despatch. Hara-kiri (the Japanese ceremonial self-disembowelling): from ca. 1880; obsolescent.

happy ending, a. In reference to a story, whether told or played or printed: virtue rewarded, lovers united, penury no longer existent. C. 19–20.

happy event, a or **the.** The birth of a child; esp. the first in a family: mostly lower-middle class: from ca. 1880.

happy ever after; esp., to live . . ., 'for the rest of their lives' (after getting married): C. 18–20.

happy hunting-ground, one's; the Happy Hunting-Grounds. One's favourite place for collecting or acquiring (information, objects): from ca. 1895.—(2) The future life or state: C. 20. From the Red Indian conception of heaven.

happy pair, the. A bridal couple. Journalistic: late C. 19–20.—Cf. **happy couple.**

happy solution, a. A solution that pleases either the people concerned or the mind of the critic or onlooker: C. 20.

hard and fast line, a; esp., **to draw a . . .,** to lay down rigidly and as rigidly adhere to a figurative dividing line: from ca. 1870: originally political. **A hard and fast rule** is rapidly qualifying to become a cliché.

hard facts. Facts, which are hard enough without that insistent *hard* in front of them: mid C. 19–20.

hastily summoned (doctor, fire-brigade). C. 20: mostly journalistic.

hat in hand. See **go hat in hand.**

hated rival, one's; esp. in a love-affair or **a** courtship: late C. 19–20. Often jocular.

*have a bone to pick with (someone), **to.** To have something to decide or settle with, or to be explained by, him: mid C. 19–20. Canine.

have a finger in every pie, to (generic or habitual); **have a finger in the pie** (particular). To participate—or have a financial interest—in an affair, a business: mid C. 19–20, though current since mid C. 17.

have a great mind to (do something), **to.** To feel much inclined, or well-disposed, to do it; to have almost made up one's mind . . .: C. 18–20, though current since ca. 1400.

have a shot at something, to (colloquial). To attempt it; to attempt to do it: colloquial: from ca. 1910.

have a wholesome respect for, to. To respect profoundly and with something of fear; to respect deeply, in a manner salutary to the respecter: late C. 19–20.

have and to hold, to. To possess and to retain; to possess continuously: C. 19–20. (In respect of a man 'possessing' **a** wife, there is a connotation of 'to cherish'.)

have at one's finger-tips, to. See at **to the finger-tips.**

have no truck with, to. To have no dealings—to avoid association—with (persons, institutions): late C. 19–20.

have one's cake and eat it, to, incorrect for **to eat one's cake and have it** (i.e., still have it). To have it both ways: C. 19–20. From a proverb.

have one's heart . . . See the **heart** entries.

have other fish to fry, to. To have something better to do: mid C. 18–20. Swift used it at the beginning of C. 18 (Benham).

have sold one's birthright for a mess of pottage, to. To barter one's inheritance or heritage for a trifle: C. 18–20. In allusion to *Genesis*, xxv. 29–34.

have something up one's sleeve, to. See **ace . . .**

have the whip-hand (of someone), **to.** To control, with an implication of imperiousness, brutality, callousness; to have the upper hand of; to have at a disadvantage: C. 19–20, though current centuries earlier.

*****have too many irons in the fire, to.** To be engaged in too much work; to have too many monetary interests: mid C. 18–20; current since ca. 1550. From smithy or armoury.

have too much of a good thing, to. 'I had had too much of a good thing.'—'One can have too much of a good thing.' C. 20.

*****have two strings to one's bow, to.** Not to depend on one person or thing; often applied to a girl with two suitors: a proverbial saying (1546) that, in C. 19–20, is a cliché.

head and front of (e.g., **it), the.** The most important part or feature; the essential: from ca. 1820. 'The head and front of your offence is that . . .' In allusion to *Othello*, I, iii, 81–82.

head and shoulders above. Far above; much superior to: mid C. 19–20. 'Shakespeare is—or, stands—head and shoulders above the rest.' From stature.

heap . . . See **coals of fire.**

*heard a pin drop, one (or **you) could have.** The silence was complete or intense: late C. 19–20.

*heart and soul; esp., **with all one's . . .,** often shortened to **with all one's heart.** With complete sincerity, utter devotion, or much earnestness: C. 19–20.

heart bleeds for (someone), **one's.** One is poignantly sorry or grieved for the misfortunes of someone: late C. 19–20.

heart in one's mouth, with one's; or **to have one's . . .,** to feel, in fear or alarm, the apparent jumping of the heart: C. 18–20; common since mid C. 16.

heart in the right place, to have one's. To mean well; to sympathize with the right person, side, or cause: from ca. 1870.

*heart of gold, a; esp., **to have a . . .** To be very kind-hearted and considerate of others: mid C. 19–20.

heart of hearts, in one's. Secretly; inwardly: C. 19–20. 'In her heart of hearts, she feared him.'—Cf. *Hamlet,* III, ii, 78–79.

heart of stone, to have a. To be very hard-hearted: mid C. 19–20.—Cf. the Biblical *to harden one's heart.*

heart of the matter, the. The most important or significant part or aspect of the matter: from ca. 1880.

heart-to-heart talk, a (slangily: *a heart-to-heart*). A very intimate, frank, friendly talk: late C. 19–20.

hearts of oak. Stout hearts: 1717, Mrs Centlivre, 'Where are the rough brave Britons to be found | With hearts of oak, so much of old renowned?' (cited by Benham).

hearty applause; a hearty British cheer. Vigorous applause; typically British cheering: respectively late C. 19–20 and C. 20.

hearty congratulations. Heart-felt, or sincere and affably expressed, congratulations: from ca. 1880.

heated argument, a. An angry, impassioned, or very warmly conducted argument: late C. 19–20. 'The heated arguments he had heard in Simon's rooms' (at Cambridge), Somerset Maugham, *Christmas Holiday*, 1939.

heated retort, a; esp., **to make a . . .,** to reply angrily or passionately: from ca. 1905.

heathen Chinee, the. The Chinese: 1870, Bret Harte, *Plain Language from Truthful James*, 'The Heathen Chinee is peculiar'; slightly obsolescent.

*****heave a sigh of relief, to.** To sigh with relief: late C. 19–20.

heaven on earth, a. No longer apprehended as a quotation (Milton, *Paradise Lost*, IV, 208): C. 19–20.

heavy responsibilities; esp., **to assume . . .,** to undertake grave or important obligations: C. 20.

height of absurdity, the. The acme of absurdity; extreme absurdity: C. 20.

*****hell for leather** (adverb). At great speed; in urgent or desperate haste: late C. 19–20. Kipling, 1892, 'When we rode Hell-for-leather | Both squadrons together' (O.E.D.). The origin of the phrase is obscure.

Hell has no fury like a woman scorned is an adaptation of Congreve's 'Heaven has no rage like love to hatred turn'd | Nor hell a fury like a woman scorned' (*The Mourning Bride*, 1697, at III, viii): C. 19–20. Congreve may have drawn the idea from personal experience, but probably it came either from Fletcher's 'The wages of scorn'd love is baneful hate' (*The Knight of Malta*, ca. 1625, at I, i) or from Cibber's 'We shall find no fiend in hell can match the fury of a disappointed woman' (*Love's Last Shift*, 1696, at IV, i).

*Hell is paved with good intentions. A proverb of C. 17–18; a cliché of C. 19–20. Perhaps the effective origin is Dr Johnson's 'Sir, Hell is paved with good intentions' (1775). It occurs in many languages: see, esp., Benham, 832b–833a.

*help a lame dog over a stile, to. To help a needy or unfortunate person: mid C. 18–20. From the proverbial saying, *help the . . .*

*helping hand, a. Assistance, help: from C. 15; a cliché in C. 18–20.

'here is God's plenty.' Here is abundance: mid C. 19–20.

here, there, and everywhere. Everywhere; 'in every place, indicated or not indicated' (O.E.D.): from ca. 1870. An elaboration of *here and everywhere*.

here to-day and gone to-morrow is applied, predicatively, to a person constantly on the move: late C. 19–20.—Cf. **bird of passage.**

*'hewers of wood and drawers of water.' Humble labourers; drudges: mid C. 19–20. Much used by Mr Neville Chamberlain. *Deuteronomy*, xxix. 11 and esp. *Joshua*, ix. 21, 'Let them live; but let them be hewers of wood and drawers [= carriers] of water unto all the congregation': Vulgate, *Sed sic vivant, ut in usus universæ multitudinis ligna cædant, aquasque comportent*, 'Qu'ils vivent donc; mais ils seront employés à fendre le bois et à puiser l'eau pour toute la communauté' (Verdunoy).

*hide one's light under a bushel, to. To conceal one's merit, one's abilities; be modest and retiring: mid C. 19–20. In allusion to *Matthew*, v. 15, 'Neither do men light a candle, and put it under a bushel, but on a candlestick'.

high and dry (figurative). Stranded, abandoned; out of the course of progress or the current of events: from ca. 1860. From a vessel beached out of the water.

high days and holidays. Solemn days and holidays; holidays, whether joyous (Christmas) or solemn (Good Friday): mid C. 19–20.

high hopes. Optimism; well-based expectation or hopes: late C. 19–20.

high in the heavens; esp., the sun was . . . The day was well advanced: late C. 19–20.

high moral tone, a. A very moral tone: C. 20. In Somerset Maugham's *Christmas Holiday*, 1939, a 'special correspondent', referring to his own newspaper, says, 'You know what our newspaper is, bloody patriotic as long as it helps our circulation, all the dirt we can get, and a high moral tone'.

highly confidential information. Extremely confidential information; secret information: from ca. 1915.

*highly improbable. Extremely unlikely: late C. 19–20.—Cf. **height of absurdity.**

highly respected; a highly respected member of the community. (A) much respected (citizen or resident): journalists' and public speakers': C. 20.

historic occasion; esp., that h. o. and on this h. o. (On) that important occasion, (at the time of this) important event: late C. 19–20.

hit below the belt, to (figurative). To take an unfair advantage: colloquial: late C. 19–20. From boxing.

hit or miss, n. and adj. Haphazard; (a) trusting to luck: C. 20. 'Hit or miss; luck is all', Dykes, *Moral Reflections*, 1708 (Benham).

*hit the nail on the head, to. To hit the mark; to guess or state correctly or accurately: current from C. 16; cliché in C. 19–20.

hitch one's wag(g)on to a star, to. To have, and act on, a lofty ideal; to be nobly or ethically ambitious: late C. 19–20;

more American than English. Emerson, 'Hitch your wagon to a star', in 'Civilization', *Society and Solitude*, 1870. *Sic itur ad astra.*

hither and yon. Hither and thither; to and fro; in various directions: C. 19–20. 'The wan characters of Chekov's stories drifted hither and yon at the breath of circumstance like dead leaves before the wind' (Somerset Maugham, *Christmas Holiday*, 1939).

hive of industry, a. An extremely busy place (factory, town, etc.): from ca. 1870. P. Barry, *Dockyard Economy*, 1863, 'A private dockyard is a hive of industry' (O.E.D.).

Hobson's choice. No choice at all; an enforced decision: C. 18–20. Of unascertained origin: see Weekley, *An Etymological Dictionary of Modern English*.

hoi polloi, the. The multitude; the populace: C. 19–20. Greek οἱ πολλοί, 'the [many' (as opposed to the few, the governing classes).

hoist on (properly, **with**) **one's own petard, to be.** To be caught in one's own trap: C. 19–20. From Shakespeare's 'For 'tis the sport, to have the engineer | Hoist with his own petard' (*Hamlet*, III, iv).

hold forth, to. To orate; to speak pompously: from ca. 1830 as a cliché with this pejorative connotation. Originally, to speak publicly, or to preach.

hold (a person) **in suspense, to.** To keep in suspense: C. 20. 'He deliberately held the poor devil in suspense!'

*hold no brief for, to. To be far from supporting or being an advocate of: late C. 19–20. 'Tolstoy held no brief for Shakespeare.' From barristers' briefs.

hold one's head high, to (?). To be decently proud in the face of misfortune or disgrace: mid C. 19–20.

hold one's own, to; generally, **to be holding . . .,** to stand, successfully, against either opposition, rivalry, or competition: current since C. 16; cliché in C. 19–20.

hole(-)and(-)corner (adjective). Clandestine, secret; underhand: pejorative (the opposite of 'public' and 'open'): mid C. 19–20.

holiday exodus, a. Departure of people, on holiday, from a great city: American: C. 20. (Sullivan.) With reference to the Biblical *Exodus.*—Cf. **general exodus.**

hollow tones. Sepulchral tones; in tones that lack body: from ca. 1880.

***holy matrimony; the bonds of h.m.** Marriage, matrimony. Although the phrase has been in common use since C. 16, it was not a cliché before C. 19. Used seriously and correctly, it is obviously not a cliché.

home comforts (?). Such comforts as, those comforts which, one expects at home; esp. as viewed from abroad, in absence, on active service: from ca. 1915.

***'home of lost causes, the.'** Oxford: late C. 19–20. Matthew Arnold, in the preface to *Essays in Criticism,* First Series, speaks of Oxford as 'home of lost causes, and forsaken beliefs, and unpopular names, and impossible loyalties!'

home of one's own, a. A home one owns: late C. 19–20. 'He longs to have a home of his own.'

Homeric laughter. Loud, hearty laughter: from the 1880's.

honest penny, an; esp., **to turn an . . .,** to earn an honest living; to make honest money at some specific piece of work: mid C. 19–20.

honest truth, the. The complete truth; truth without reservation: late C. 19–20. 'The honest truth is: I don't know *what* to do.'

'**honour rooted in dishonour.**' See **rooted in dishonour.**

***hope against hope, to.** 'He was hoping against hope that no one would see the boat', Michael Annesley, *The Missing Agent*, 1938: i.e., against (reasonable) expectation, against probability: mid C. 19–20.

hope deferred (with an ensuing pause). Short for the proverb, *hope deferred maketh the heart sick*: mid C. 19–20.

'**hope springs eternal (in the human breast).**' Late C. 18–20. Pope, *An Essay for Man*, Epistle I (1733), line 95.

hopeless despair. Blank despair: despair without a gleam of hope: mid C. 19–20.

horns of a dilemma, the. See **on the horns . . .**

horny-handed. See **son of the soil.**

horse of another colour, a; esp., **that's a . . .** A very different matter: from ca. 1860.—Cf. Shakespeare's 'My purpose is indeed a horse of that colour' (*Twelfth Night*, II, iii, 181).

host of friends, a; very often, **to have a . . .,** to have many friends: late C. 19–20.

hotly contested. Keenly contested or fought out: C. 20; esp. of contests and games.

hour of need; esp., **in one's . . .,** in or at one's time of danger or (great) trouble: C. 19–20.

***house and home** (Scottish **hame**). See **eat out of house and home.** But *house and home* has an independent existence and has been a cliché throughout C. 18–20. 'It looks as though they'll lose house and home.'

how the world wags. How the world goes; what is happening in the world: C. 19–20. 'Well, tell me how the world wags; I have been long away.' Originally a reminiscence of

'Thus may we see . . . how the world wags' (*As You Like It* II, vii).

how time flies! See **march of time.**

howling wilderness, a. An utter wilderness; a dreary, savage wilderness: mid C. 19–20. *Deuteronomy,* xxxii. 10, 'He found him in a desert land, and in the waste howling wilderness' (Vulgate, *Invenit eum in terra deserta, in loco horroris et vastae solitudinis,* rendered by Verdunoy as 'Il l'a trouvé dans une contrée déserte, dans un lieu informe, dans le rugissement des steppes'). The *howling* is that of wild beasts and/or the wind (O.E.D.).

*hub of the universe, the. The business centre of the world (London): mid C. 19–20. Oliver Wendell Holmes, in *The Autocrat of the Breakfast Table,* 1857–8, was ironically allusive in 'Boston State-house is the hub of the Solar System' (cited by Benham).

hue and cry (figurative). A clamour of assault, a shouting of pursuers, an outcry (in alarm or opposition): mid C. 19–20. Originally, a legal phrase.

hum and haw, to. To make vague sounds expressive of hesitation or beating about the bush: mid C. 18–20. Echoic.

human—all too human. With all a human being's weaknesses: late C. 19–20. I should guess that it is a Victorianism.

human interest. 'A newspaper story must have human interest.' This journalistic cliché arose from—and dates from —Lord Northcliffe's '*do*'s for journalists'.

humanum nihil a me alienum puto. I am interested in everything that concerns mankind; everything that is of men and women and children; human nature: C. 19–20. Terence, who prefaces it with *homo sum* (I am a man).

hundred-to-one chance, a (non-literally). A very small chance indeed (the odds being 100 to 1 *against*): late C. 19–20. From horse-racing.

I

'**I am no orator, as Brutus is.**' C. 19–20. Shakespeare, *Julius Cæsar*, III, ii, Antony *loquitur*.

*I am not my brother's keeper; 'am I my brother's keeper?' I am not morally responsible for this person. The former (C. 19–20) derives from the latter, which occurs in *Genesis*, iv. 9.

I could hardly believe my eyes (—yet it was true). See **believe one's eyes.**

I hate to mention it—but (e.g., I think you ought to know). The scandalmonger's self-exculpation: late C. 19–20.

I have no hesitation in saying. I say frankly: C. 20. Not unheard in the House of Commons.

*I mean to say; often preceded by *well!* What I really mean is this; I wish to make my meaning clearer: a conversational formula, common in C. 19, and in C. 20 a cliché.

I shall not die happy unless (or **until**) . . . : late C. 19–20.

I should be the last to say (**it,** or **that** . . .). I do not think (or say) that: late C. 19–20.

I think I ought to tell you that . . . mid C. 19–20.—Cf. **I hate to mention it,** than which it is less objectionable.

I would not touch (**it,** etc.) **with a barge-pole.** I should have nothing to do with it: colloquial: late C. 19–20.

idle rich, the. Rich persons that do no work: socialistic (from ca. 1880), become, since ca. 1910, general and, usually, jocular.—Cf. **bloated plutocrat.**

. . . if ever there was one. 'He's a brave man if ever there was one', he is pre-eminently brave. C. 19–20.

'if the mountain won't come (properly, **will not go**) **to Mahomet, Mahomet must go to the mountain.'** C. 18–20. See Bacon, *Essays* (edition of 1612), No. 12, 'Of Boldness'; Ray's *Proverbs* (late C. 17).

if the truth were known —something or somebody would be seen to be very different from what it (or he) appears to be: mid C. 19–20.

*if the worst comes (occasionally **came**) **to the worst,** one could or would do something: late C. 19–20.

ignominious retreat, an; esp., **to beat an . . .,** to depart in an undignified or discreditable manner: C. 20. Weakened sense of *ignominious; retreat* used loosely.

ilk. See **of that ilk.**

*ill-gotten gains. Money (or other advantage or benefit) obtained illegally, illicitly, or disgracefully: C. 19–20. Macaulay used it; cf. Shakespeare's 'Didst thou never hear | That things ill got had ever bad success [result]?' (*King Henry VI*, Part 3, II, ii).

ills that flesh is heir to, the (thousand). A misquotation of Shakespeare's 'the thousand natural shocks that flesh . . .' (*Hamlet*, III, i): C. 19–20.

illustrious dead, our or **the.** The illustrious persons of one's nation: C. 19–20. The O.E.D. shows that it was a familiar phrase in 1809 (*illustrious,* 3).

*imagination runs riot; esp., **to let one's imagination run riot,** to let imagination have free play: from ca. 1840 (see *run riot* in the O.E.D., at *riot*).

*immaculate attire; immaculate evening dress. Spotless clothes, evening dress. Whereas the former (late C. 19–20) is obsolescent, the latter (from ca. 1920) is a pest.

immeasurably superior. Strikingly better or superior; better by far: C. 20. 'A.'s plan is immeasurably superior to B.'s.'

'immemorial elms' (?). Tennyson, *The Princess*, 1847, Canto VII, 206, 'The moan of doves in immemorial elms': mid C. 19–20.

impenetrable darkness. Utter darkness: C. 20.

implicit confidence; esp., **to have** (or **place**) i.c. **in** (a person), to trust him unquestioningly and unreservedly: mid C. 19–20. *Implicit confidence*, used (with *place*) by Washington Irving, is fast superseding *implicit faith* (except in its ecclesiastical and theological sense).

important inside information, e.g., from the War Office: C. 20. Often a cheap attribution (of importance) to oneself.

improve each (or **the**) **shining hour, to.** To make good use of, to profit by, an action or an event, a period or an occasion: C. 19–20; slightly obsolescent. The *the* form is an adaptation of the other, which comes from Watts's *Divine Songs* (No. xx), 1720, 'How doth the little busy bee | Improve each shining hour!'

*in a certain condition; in an interesting condition. Pregnant. These two euphemistic clichés date from the mid-Nineteenth Century, though isolated instances may be found earlier.

in a cleft stick. In a dilemma or predicament: from the 1780's. Cowper, 1782, 'That sort of alternative which is commonly called a cleft stick' (O.E.D.). From the catching of reptiles with a cleft stick.

*in a nutshell. Very briefly: mid C. 19–20. (In a very small space; compactly.)

in a Pickwickian sense. 'In a technical, constructive, or conveniently idiosyncratic or esoteric sense; usually in reference to language . . . compromising in its natural [or everyday] sense' (O.E.D.): from ca. 1860. The source is 'He had used the word in its Pickwickian sense . . . he had merely considered him a humbug in a Pickwickian point of view' (Dickens, *The Pickwick Papers*, 1836, ch. 1).

in a trice. In an instant; instantly, without delay: late C. 18–20. Lit., in one pull (e.g., of a bell).

in a word. In short, briefly : 1591, Shakespeare; but not a cliché until late C. 19. Margaret Ernst & James Thurber, *In a Word*, 1939 (delightful drawings and entertaining etymologies).

*in all conscience. A modificatory tag; e.g., 'little enough, in all conscience' = 'extremely little, by all that is reasonable': C. 18–20.

in apple-pie order. In thorough order; admirably tidy: mid C. 19–20. Origin obscure.

in at one ear and out of the other. See go in at . . .

in at the death. Present at an arrest, a person's ruin, at the completion of an investigation or of a difficult and/or important task or enterprise: late C. 19–20. From fox-hunting.

in character, esp., **not to be in character,** (to) be inappropriate, unsuitable, out of harmony: incipient cliché: has been very common, in this metaphorical sense, since mid C. 19. From the theatre.

in cold blood. See act . . .

in durance vile. See **durance vile.**

*in flagrante delicto. (Caught) unmistakably in the crime —'in flagrant delight', as Mr A. P. Herbert phrased it in *Unholy Matrimony*; C. 19–20. The Latin original seems to have been *flagrante delicto* ('while the crime is blazing').

in full cry. In hot pursuit; in keen pursuit: late C. 19–20. From fox-hunting.

in good set terms. Roundly; with frank severity: mid C. 19–20. *As You Like It*, II, vii, 18–19, 'Rail'd on Lady Fortune in good terms, | In good set terms'.

in high dudgeon. In a huff; ill-humouredly; resentfully: from ca. 1880. 'He went off in high dudgeon.' Earliest as *in great dudgeon*; also, in C. 19, *in deep dudgeon*.

in hot water (figurative). In trouble; in a scrape: mid C. 19–20. In C. 18, it meant 'in a state of ferment'.

in less than no time. 'Immediately—if not sooner'; very rapidly or expeditiously; very soon: late C. 19–20. 'Oh! I'll have it ready for you in less than no time.'

*in medias res. Into the midst (of business, affairs); esp., into the middle of a story, a narration (generally *plunge in medias res*): C. 19–20. Horace's *Ars Poetica*, 148.

in more senses than one. With favourable implication or unpleasant innuendo: mid C. 19–20. 'He is the father of his people, in more senses than one.'

in my opinion. A modifying tag overdone by the modest, for, after all, everything we say is, philosophically and necessarily, an opinion: from C. 15; a cliché in C. 19–20.

in no uncertain manner (or **terms** or **voice**). Clearly, unequivocally, firmly: late C. 19–20.

in on the ground floor (colloquial); esp., **to let** or **be let in . . .**, to admit (a person) into a transaction, company, etc., before it is made known, or thrown open, to the public: C. 20. I.e., to give a metaphorical office on the ground floor of a new building.

in round numbers. Approximately; properly, to the nearest ten (763, in round numbers is 760); often to the nearest hundred (763 becomes 800): mid C. 18–20. This round-number enumeration is typical of Biblical computations.

in some mysterious way. In some unexplainable way; mysteriously: C. 20. 'In some mysterious way, he contrived to escape.'

in the affirmative (or **negative); the answer is ...**
See **reply in ...**

***in the arms of Morpheus.** Asleep: from ca. 1870.
Morpheus, god of dreams, is commonly taken to be the
god of sleep; even Chaucer, in *The Book of the Duchess*, has
'Morpheus, | Thou knowest him well, the god of sleep'.

in the event of (an) emergency. Should a great need, a
crisis, arise: from ca. 1920. Verbose for *in (an) emergency*.

in the extreme. 'It was difficult in the extreme'—extremely
difficult. Late C. 18–20. (Shakespeare, 'Perplex'd in the extreme', *Othello*, v, ii, 347.)

in the heat of the moment. Impetuously; in the anger
or excitement natural at a time of anger or excitement: late
C. 19–20.

in the land of the living. Alive: C. 19–20, but a cliché
only in late C. 18–20. *Jeremiah*, xi. 19, 'Let us cut him off from
the land of the living, that his name may be no more remem-
bered', the phrase being a Hebraism (O.E.D.).

***in the last resort.** As a last measure or expedient; finally:
mid C. 19–20. Originally, a legal phrase, translated from
French *en dernier ressort*.

in the light of recent (or **subsequent**) **events.** To judge
by recent events: from ca. 1914.

in the mind's eye. Either of the past: in remembrance
(C. 19–20); or of something never seen: in imagination, in
one's mental vision (late C. 19–20).

in the nick (or **the very nick**) **of time.** At the critical
moment; only just in time: late C. 19–20. An elaboration of
in the (very) nick.

in the public eye. Prominent; (much) publicized: late C.
19–20. 'Recently, he has not been very much in the public
eye.'

*in the same boat (colloquial). In the same circumstances, position, affair, enterprise: mid C. 19–20.

in the toils; esp., **taken in . . .,** entrapped (figuratively): C. 19–20.—Cf. *Julius Cæsar*, II, i, 206–8. From wild beasts snared in nets.

in the twinkling of an eye. In an instant: C. 19–20, though current since C. 14. In the time it takes an eye to twinkle.

in the very nick of time. See **in the nick . . .**

in the whole wide world (or **the wide, wide world**). Anywhere; anywhere on earth: from ca. 1870.

in the world to-day. To-day; on earth to-day: late C. 19–20. 'In the world to-day, there is more chivalry than is generally supposed.'

in the wrong box. Not where one is supposed, or has intended, to be: mid C. 19–20. (In C. 16–18, *in a . . .*)

in these hard times, one cannot spend as one would wish: from ca. 1915.

in this year of grace, this year; *in . . . grace,* [e.g.] 1940, in 1940: clichés in late C. 19–20. From *anno gratiæ*: cf. *anno Domini*: both referring to *Christian* chronology.

incident is (or **was**) **closed, the; the incident passed without further comment** (journalistic). The former is of late C. 19–20; the latter, C. 20.

incontrovertible fact, an. A certain fact; a proved fact: from ca. 1880. *Incontrovertible evidence* is in danger of becoming a cliché.

indistinguishably mixed. Hopelessly mixed or mingled: C. 20.

*ineffable contempt (or **scorn**). 'She gave him a glance of ineffable contempt',—a contempt beyond the power of words to express: late C. 19–20. Very common among writers of fiction.

inevitable conclusion is . . ., the. One must conclude that . . . : from ca. 1870. Tyndall, 1860, 'The conclusion seems inevitable that . . .' (O.E.D.).

inevitable consequences, the. Ineluctable or unavoidable consequences; certain results: late C. 19–20.

inevitable surrender, an (or **one's**). Surrender enforced by circumstances: C. 20.

inferiority complex, an (or **one's**). A pronounced and constant feeling of inferiority: from ca. 1930. *Complex* is here misused—as is often the way of psychological words and phrases that become popular.

inferno, a blazing (or **raging**). A conflagration: late C. 19–20. Originally, journalistic.

infinite capacity for taking pains, an, whether as a definition of genius or as a plodding virtue, is an adaptation or a misquotation of Carlyle's 'Genius, which means the transcendent capacity of taking trouble, first of all' (how often that 'first of all' is forgotten), perhaps in allusion to Buffon's 'Le génie n'est autre chose qu'une grande aptitude à la patience'. (Benham.)

initial (or **the initial**) **steps have been taken.** A beginning has been made; it has been begun: mostly journalistic: C. 20.

*inner man, the. One's stomach as the receptacle of food: colloquial: from ca. 1860. From the original sense ('the soul'): 'To be strengthened . . . by his Spirit in the inner man' (*Ephesians*, iii. 16)—Vulgate, *in interiorem hominem*—Greek Testament, εἰς τὸν ἔσω ἄνθρωπον, in 'that part of man which is spiritual' (Souter).

ins and outs; esp., **the ins and outs of the case,** the intricacies, the subtle ramifications and implications: from ca. 1880.

instant destruction. (Almost) immediate death: mid C. 19–20.

insubstantial pageant, an or **the.** A pageant seen by imagination; a seeming pageant: C. 19–20. 'Like this insubstantial pageant faded, | Leave not a rack behind' (Shakespeare, *The Tempest*, IV, i).

intents. See **to all . . .**

iota. See **not one iota.**

Iron Duke, the. The Duke of Wellington: from ca. 1830; slightly obsolescent. Fonblanque, 1850, 'The Duke of Wellington, the "Iron Duke", the "hero of a hundred fights" ' (O.E.D.).

iron entered his soul, the (and in other tenses and persons). As given, it is now an unconscious quotation of a passage in *The Psalter*, cv, 18—a passage based on the Vulgate mistranslation of the Hebrew (lit., 'his person entered into the iron', rendered in the *Psalms* as 'He was laid in iron'), with the sense, 'He became much embittered': mid C. 19–20.

*iron hand in the velvet glove, the. Mercilessness or despotism or extreme severity beneath suavity and/or courtesy: from ca. 1880.

irons in the fire. See **have too many . . .**

irreducible minimum, an. An ultimate minimum; or rather, a minimum beyond which one is not prepared to go: from ca. 1920.

irreparable loss; an irreparable loss. 'A sense of irreparable loss.'—'They felt it to be an irreparable loss.' C. 19–20 (in C. 20, esp., *a sense of irreparable loss*), though fairly common in early C. 17.

islands (or **isles**) **of the blest, the** (better with capitals). The Hesperides, 'the Fortunate Isles', 'the Sunset Land': literary: C. 19–20. Greek *αἱ μακάρων νῆσοι*.

it all came out. Everything transpired or was divulged or discovered: late C. 19–20.

it gives furiously to think. A translation of the French *cela donne furieusement à penser*. From ca. 1870; slightly obsolescent.

it goes without saying. See **goes without saying.**

it hurts me more than it does you. Late C. 19–20; esp. from punitive parent to erring child. If it were always true, *Sadism* would be unknown to the dictionaries.

'it is a far, far better thing that I do (not, as so often quoted, **now**) **than I have ever done** (not **done before**). Late C. 19–20. Sydney Carton in Dickens's *A Tale of Two Cities*, 1859, Book III, ch. 15; cf. **nothing in his life . . .**

' 'tis better to have loved and lost than never to have loved at all.' Almost immediately on the publication of *In Memoriam* in 1850: Canto 27.

it is notorious that . . . It is well known that . . . , generally of something unpleasant or, to the auditor, unexpected: from ca. 1870.

it may interest (generally **you**) **to know that . . .** Late C. 19–20. An introductory formula.

*it may well be that . . . It is possible—it is not unlikely—that . . . : C. 20. Always a polite and, since ca. 1920, mainly a literary formula.

it might be (or **have been**) **worse,** often prefaced by **well!** and often followed by *I suppose*, there being a suppressed 'but not much!': mid C. 19–20.

it stands to reason that . . . It is quite reasonable to suppose that; it is natural or evident or even apparently certain that . . . : current (and very common) since ca. 1600, but perhaps not a cliché before C. 19.

it (generally **but it**) **was not to be.** Fate determined otherwise; it did not fall out thus: from ca. 1870.

***it would ill become me to . . .** It is not for me (to say or do something): introductory formula: mid C. 19–20.

it's an old (adjective) **custom;** esp.—and earliest—**it's an old Spanish custom.** In *The Times Literary Supplement*, Jan. 27, 1940, is a review of *It's an Old Scottish Custom* (folklore). In explanation or, often, in palliation; C. 20. Originally American.

itching palm, an; esp., **to have . . .,** to be grasping, mercenary: C. 19–20. Shakespeare, 'You yourself | Are much condemned to have'—blamed for having—'an itching palm' (*Julius Cæsar*, IV, iii).

J

je ne sais quoi, a. Something one is too lazy to define exactly: from ca. 1890; slightly obsolescent. Originally a term in literary criticism for that which defies analysis.

Job's comforter, a; Job's comforters. One who, pretending to comfort, aggravates the distress of somebody: mid C. 18–20. Swift, 1738, has the latter form. *Job*, xvi. 2. (O.E.D.)

John Bull; John Bull's other island. The typical Englishman; Ireland. The former arose in 1712; the latter, much later. Clichés in late C. 18–20, late C. 19–20.

join issue, to. 'To take up the opposite side of a case, or a contrary view *on* a question' (O.E.D.): from ca. 1770. Originally (and still) a legal phrase. Often misapprehended to mean 'to come to an agreement'.

jot or tittle, a; esp., not a jot . . . Not even a tiny bit; nothing; not at all: C. 19–20. With a reminiscence of *Matthew*, v. 18, 'One jot or tittle shall in no wise pass from the law': ἰῶτα ἓν ἢ μία κεραία, 'one iota or one little hook', with reference to *yod*, the smallest letter in the Aramaic alphabet.—Cf. **not one iota.**

joy and a delight, a. (Something that brings) lasting joy and immediate pleasure: late C. 19–20.

'joy cometh in the morning.' Mid C. 19–20. *Psalms*, xxx, 5, 'But joy . . .', which becomes 'But joy shall come with early light' in *Blessed Are They That Mourn*, a poem by Wm. Cullen Bryant († 1878): cited by Benham.

*jump from the frying-pan into the fire, to. C. 18–20. On a proverbial saying that occurs in various forms and many languages, including Latin (*de fumo in flammam*): see esp. Benham, 871*b*–872*a*.

*Jupiter Pluvius. Rain (properly, the dispenser of rain), as in 'Jupiter Pluvius permitting'. Dating from ca. 1860, this cliché, which is also a genteelism, is slightly obsolescent. The phrase occurs in Tibullus, I, vii, 26 (Benham).

justly famous (?). Deservedly famous: late C. 19–20. 'Stonehenge is justly famous for its ruins.'

K

keep a civil tongue in one's head (originally **mouth**), **to.** To be civilly spoken, to speak politely: colloquial: late C. 19–20.

keep a stiff upper lip, to. To be firm against adversity: American, since ca. 1850; English since ca. 1880. To prevent one's lips from trembling.

keep (a person) **at arm's length, to.** To keep him at a respectful distance, to prevent him from becoming familiar: mid C. 19–20. Originally, *at arm's end.*

*keep body and soul together, to. To live at semi-starvation level: C. 19–20. Recorded for 1753 (O.E.D.).

keep in watertight compartments, to. To keep things (e.g., beliefs, social and Society activities) separate and, thus, free from contamination: C. 20. From the watertight compartmenting of ships, to keep them from sinking in a collision.

keep one's end up, to. To maintain equality with others in competition, conversation, business: colloquial: C. 20.

keep one's head above water, to. To remain financially above ruin-level by virtue of persevering struggle: C. 19–20.

keep one's mouth shut, to. To be silent: mid C. 19–20.— Cf. the Scottish proverb, *keep your gab* (mouth) *steeket* (shut) *when ye kenna* (know not) *your company.*

keep (one's own or someone else's) **nose to the grindstone, to.** To be—or force another to be—continually engaged in hard and monotonous work: from ca. 1830. From the earlier sense (C. 16–18), 'to grind down; to oppress'. (O.E.D.)

keep one's weather-eye open, to. To be on the alert: from ca. 1880. Originally nautical, 'to watch for stormy weather'.

keep the ball rolling, to. To continue to do something, esp. to maintain social talk: colloquial: from ca. 1890. From football.

*keep the pot boiling (or **the wolf from the door**), **to.** To do something that brings in money and keeps one alive: mid C. 19–20. Adumbrated by 'Peter Pindar', ca. 1790 (Benham).

keep to oneself, to (?). To be of reserved demeanour: C. 20. Perhaps = *keep oneself to oneself.*

keep watch and ward, to. To keep watch and guard; or rather, merely to act as (metaphorical) guard: C. 19–20. Originally, to perform—as a feudal obligation—the duty of sentinel and/or guard (see O.E.D.).

key of the mystery, the. The *open Sesame* that unlocks the doors of mystery: late C. 19–20.

kick against the pricks, to. To resist hard facts; to resist irresistible authority: late C. 18–20. Applied to C. 14–17 to oxen that kick against the goad. We owe the figurative sense to the influence of *Acts*, ix. 5; cf. Terence's *Inscitia est | Adversum stimulum calces*, where *stimulus* is a spur.

kill or cure; esp., it's (a case of) kill or cure. Drastic action or treatment that will ruin or set all right: mid C. 19–20. From medicines that will cure—or prove fatal.

*kill the fatted calf, to. To prepare a warm home-coming for a prodigal (hence for a relative, esp. a son or daughter) long absent: C. 19–20. In allusion to *Luke*, xv (parable of the prodigal son).

kill the goose that lays the golden eggs, to. Wantonly or thoughtlessly to put an end to a profitable source of income; a proverbial saying (C. 15 onwards) that has, in mid C. 19–20, been worked to death.

*kill two birds with one stone, to. To contrive to effect two desired purposes: this proverbial saying (recorded in 1611 and coming from Latin) may fairly be classified as a cliché of C. 19–20.

kindred spirit, a. A person like another in character and temperament: late C. 19–20.

King Charles's head. An obsession from which one cannot escape; an *idée fixe*: a cliché only from ca. 1910. With reference to Mr Dick's obsession in Dickens's *David Copperfield*, ch. xiv.

'**king is dead, long live the king,—the.'** One powerful man, one acknowledged authority, is dead: welcome to his successor! C. 20; rather literary. From the literal sense—which is a translation of *le roi est mort: vive le roi.*

king's (or **King's**) **English, the.** English; *to speak the k.e.* is 'to speak English with fair accuracy, tolerably well, both in pronunciation and in idiom': C. 17–20. (Recorded in 1560; adumbrated by Chaucer, ca. 1380.) Very generally used—though then usually with a small *k*—even in the reigns of queens: see, esp., Apperson's *English Proverbs and Proverbial Sayings*, 1931, at p. 342.

kith and kin. Kinsfolk, family connexions: mid C. 19–20. From the sense 'one's friends and relatives' (in C. 14–15, 'country and kinsfolk': see O.E.D.).

knit one's brows, to. To draw them close together: late C. 19–20.

knock the bottom out of, to (colloquial). To render ineffective or invalid: from ca. 1880. E.g., 'to knock the bottom out of a theory'.

knotty point, a. Some difficulty or problem very hard to solve or unravel: C. 19–20. Pope, 1702, 'The knotty point was urg'd on either side' (O.E.D.).

know chalk from cheese, esp. in the negative, which = 'to be very ignorant, to have very little worldly knowledge': mid C. 19–20. (Originally proverbial.)

know (something) **for a fact, to.** To know to be true: C. 20. Often the over-emphasis of a person in doubt.

know (a person) **from Adam, not to** (colloquial). Applied to a complete stranger or a person wholly unknown to one: mid C. 19–20. There is very little opportunity of getting to know Adam.

know full well, to. To know; to be well aware: C. 19–20; slightly obsolescent.

*know on which side one's bread is buttered, to. To know what is to one's advantage, or where one's monetary interest lies: a proverbial saying; in C. 19–20 a cliché.

know the ropes, to (colloquial). To be well informed; esp., to be worldly-wise: from ca. 1890. Either nautical or circus slang in origin.

know where one stands, to (?). To know one's social or monetary position: from ca. 1870.

know where the shoe pinches, to. To know monetary difficulties, or where the lack of money hampers one the most: from C. 14; but a cliché only in C. 18–20.

know whether one is standing on one's head or one's heels, not to. 'To be in a state of utter bewilderment' (O.E.D.): from ca. 1820.

L

labour of love, a. Work undertaken from affection for, or from a desire to please, another: mid C. 19–20. No longer apprehended as a reminiscence of 1 *Thessalonians*, i. 3 and *Hebrews*, vi. 10.

'labourer is worthy of his hire, the.' A workman is entitled to the money that his work brings him: C. 19–20. *Luke*, x. 7.

lady of the house, the. The mistress of a household: late C. 19–20. An elaboration of the earliest sense of *lady* (C. 9–mid 18).

land of milk and honey, a; and its original, **'a land flowing with m. and h.'** A land rich in natural food: C. 19–20. 'Palestine is often referred to in the Bible as a land flowing with milk and honey' (Dr C. H. Irwin's *Cruden's Concordance*); e.g., *Exodus*, iii. 8.

land of the living, the. See **in the land . . .**

lap of luxury, the; esp., **to live in the . . ., be cradled in the . . .** See **cradled.**

lapse from virtue, a (or **one's**). A moral fall, slip, act of weakness: mid C. 19–20.—Cf. the theological *lapse of Adam.*

*Lares and Penates. Household goods; hence, hearth and home, or, esp., home and household goods: late C. 18–20. In Latin, both *Lares* and *Penates* are household gods, metaphorically home or hearth.

*last but not least. C. 19–20. An adaptation (perhaps originally a misquotation) of Spenser's 'though last, not least' (*Colin Clout,* 1595).

last extremity, the. The final state of illness, grief, destitution, etc.; the last stage; hence, *in the last extremity* means also **in the last resort:** late C. 19–20.

last gasp, at one's (or **the**). See **at one's last gasp.**

last legs; esp., **to be on one's . . .,** very frail, near death; hence, of things, extremely dilapidated or worn: C. 20.

last straw, the. From the proverb, 'It's the last straw that breaks the camel's back'. The cliché is of C. 19–20.

late in the day; esp., **it's rather late in the day to . . .,** it is too late to do something if you wish to succeed or profit: C. 20.

late in the field (?). 'He was rather late in the field: many applicants had been interviewed days before he appeared.' Late C. 19–20.

latest intelligence, the. The latest information or news: mid C. 19–20; slightly obsolescent, owing to the obsolescent (but not moribund) state of that excellent word *intelligence.*

laudator temporis acti. One who is constantly praising 'the good old days': C. 19–20. Horace, 'Difficilis, querulus, laudator temporis acti, | Se puero' (*De Arte Poetico*, 173).

laugh in (now often **up**) **one's sleeve, to.** To laugh to oneself; to be inwardly amused: late C. 18–20.

laugh on the wrong side of one's mouth, to. From glad to become sad—from confident, vexed or abashed—from exultant, depressed: late C. 19–20. In C. 18–mid 19, one laughed on the *other* side.

laugh out of court, to. To render (a person, a project) ridiculous by derisive laughter: from ca. 1880; originally, legal.

laugh to scorn, to. To deride; so to laugh at a person as to induce scorn in others: C. 19–20. Recorded for C. 15 and common in Bible: e.g., *Psalms*, xxii. 7; *Matthew*, ix. 24.

law-abiding citizen, a; law-abiding citizens, persons submitting to (and upholding) the law: late C. 19–20.

law and order; esp., **to be on the side of law and order,** to range oneself with those who enforce and maintain the laws and by-laws: mid C. 19–20.

law is an ass, the, is the usual form of ' "If the law supposes that," said Mr Bumble . . . "the law is a ass—a idiot" ' (Dickens, *Oliver Twist*, Part III, 1839). Mid C. 19–20.

law of the Medes and Persians, the. See **Medes and Persians.**

law to (obsolescently, **unto**) **oneself, to be a.** To be self-willed *and* in some way remarkable; to have one's own way of doing things: late C. 19–20.

*lawful occasions; esp., **to go about one's,** to attend to one's business or affairs, whether official, occupational, or social: very common in C. 17–mid 19; uncommon in late C. 19–early 20; extremely common—a cliché—from ca. 1915.

lay down the law, to. To make arrogant or dogmatic statements, esp. in discussion or argument: colloquial: from the 1880's.

lay (esp., **laying**) **heretical hands on our imperishable constitution.** An American political cliché of late C. 19–20. (Recorded by Stuart Chase.)

lay it on with a trowel, to. To flatter (or eulogize) excessively and/or unsubtly, grossly: mid C. 19–20. Shakespeare, *As You Like It*, I, ii, 112, 'Well said, that was laid on with a trowel'.

'lay on, Macduff.' Strike vigorously!; attack vigorously! C. 19–20. *Macbeth*, v, viii, 33.

lay one's cards on the table, to; to show one's hand. To say frankly what one intends to do; to disclose one's resources, confess one's weaknesses: C. 20. From cardplaying.

lay the flattering unction to one's soul, to. To be fatuously pleased with praise: mid C. 19–20. From 'Lay not that flattering unction to your soul' (*Hamlet*, III, iv).

lead a cat and dog life, to. (Of relatives, married couples, associates) to be constantly quarrelling: from ca. 1880. (In C. 16–18, *to agree like cat and dog*.)—Cf. **lead a dog's life.**

lead (someone) **a dance, to.** To hurry a person from place to place; hence, to force or induce him to do a number of troublesome things: from C. 16; a cliché in C. 18–20.

lead a dog's life, to. To cause a person distress and constant trouble; to be caused . . .: late C. 19–20.

leading light, (to be) a. To be a conspicuous or prominent person, a (figurative) guiding light: late C. 19–20. Nautical: a light on a buoy, etc.

'lean and hungry look, a.' C. 19–20. 'Yond' Cassius has a lean and hungry look; | He thinks too much; such men are dangerous' (Shakespeare, *Julius Cæsar*, I, ii).

learn something to one's advantage, to. To hear of something advantageous: late C. 19–20. From the legal formula concerning an inheritance or a legacy.

leather and prunella. A misquotation of Pope's 'leather or prunella', but a cliché (from ca. 1820) in its own right, with the meaning 'something to which one is quite indifferent'.

leave a door open, to. Not to settle a questionable point; not to do something that cannot be undone: political, esp. since early September, 1938.

leave an aching void, to. See **aching void**

leave in the lurch, to. See **left . . .**

leave much to be desired, to. 'That book leaves much to be desired', is very unsatisfactory; applied to a process, a method, the phrase means that it is imperfect: from ca. 1880; originally, journalistic. From the French *laisser à désirer* (O.E.D.).

leave (a person) **no option, to.** To give a person no choice, no alternative: from ca. 1910.

*leave no stone unturned, to. To make every effort; to try all means: C. 18–20. Recognized as a proverbial saying in C. 16.—Cf. Euripides's πάντα κινῆσαι πέτρον, 'to move every stone'.

leave out in the cold, to (?); to leave severely alone. To neglect a person; (latter phrase only) to avoid utterly: late C. 19–20.

leeway to make up. Much yet to do, be done: from ca. 1880. *Leeway* is 'the lateral drift of a ship to leeward of her course' (O.E.D.).

left-handed compliment, a. An ambiguous compliment; esp. a compliment that is, on consideration, an aspersion: from ca. 1890.

left in the lurch, to be. To have been abandoned (by someone): late C. 18–20, though in fairly common use for some two hundred years before that.

*left to one's own devices, to be. To be left alone; properly, to follow one's inclinations: from ca. 1880. 'Wagstaffe, left to his own devices, wandered about the garden for a while' (Anthony Webb, *Mr Pendlebury Makes a Catch*, 1939). —Cf. *The Book of Common Prayer*, 'the devices and desires of our own hearts'.

leg to stand on, not to have a. To be entirely wrong to have no case; (of a theory, a supposition) to have no basis in fact, nothing to support it: from ca. 1885.

legal light (or **luminary**), **a.** A prominent barrister, solicitor, or judge: late C. 19–20; mainly journalistic.

legible hand, a. Handwriting easily read; clear writing: C. 19–20. Middleton, 1620, 'A fair, fast, legible hand' (O.E.D.).

lend a (helping) hand to, to. To render assistance to, to help, a person: C. 19–20; recorded for 1632. An elaboration of *lend a hand* (1598). (O.E.D.)

lend an ear, to; 'lend me your ears'. To pay attention: C. 19–20. The quotation is from *Julius Cæsar*, III, ii, 78.

length and breadth of the land, through (or **throughout) the.** Over the whole area or extent of a country; in all directions, in every part: C. 19–20.—Cf. *Genesis*, xiii. 17, 'Arise, walk through the land in the length of it and in the breadth of it'.

leonine locks. Hair like the mane of a lion: C. 20.

let loose the dogs of war, to; to unleash or **let slip . . .,** to declare war (and wage it): mid C. 19–20 (*loose*), late C. 19–20 (*unleash*), C. 19–20 (*let slip*: after Shakespeare, *Julius Cæsar*, III, i, 273–6).

let one's imagination . . . See **imagination.**

let slip through one's fingers, to. To miss, slackly or inadvertently, e.g. an opportunity; to allow something to escape: late C. 19–20.

let the cat out of the bag, to. (Unthinkingly, carelessly) to disclose a secret, divulge secret information, important news: C. 19–20.

*let the grass grow under one's feet, (not) to. To lose no time; to set promptly to work (and keep at it): anticipated in 1550; recorded for 1707; a cliché since ca. 1860. (Apperson.)

let the sun go down on one's wrath, (not) to. An adaptation of 'Be ye angry, and sin not: let not the sun go down upon your wrath' (*Ephesians*, iv. 26): ὁ ἥλιος μὴ ἐπιδυέτω ἐπὶ παροργισμῷ ὑμῶν, 'let not the sun set upon your angry resentment'.

let us return to our muttons! See **revenons . . .**

lethal weapon, a. A deadly—a death-dealing—weapon: late C. 19–20.

'letting ".' dare not" wait upon "I would" ', where *would* = 'wish': C. 19–20. Lady Macbeth in her urging Macbeth to murder Duncan (i, vii).

*lick into shape, to. To make (a person) capable or presentable, to render (a thing) presentable: current since C. 17; cliché in C. 19–20.

lick one's chops, to. To relish something keenly, to anticipate with delight a 'dainty morsel': current since ca. 1650, a cliché since ca. 1850.

life and soul of the party, (to be) the. To be so lively as to make a party a success: late C. 19–20; cf. Serjeant Ballantine, 1882, 'He was the soul of the table' (O.E.D.). (Often an objectionable person.)

life-blood of industry, the. That which vitalizes industry; money circulating freely; fair wages and efficient management: journalistic: from ca. 1910.

life in the raw. Rough existence away from civilization; life at its crudest: from ca. 1910.

life is (or **was** or **will be**) **not worth living without her** (or **him**). Late C. 19–20.

light and leading; esp., **men of . . .,** leaders and thinkers: mid C. 19–20. Used by Burke in 1790.

light fantastic (toe), the; 'trip it on the light fantastic toe', to. Dancing; to dance: from ca. 1870. Milton, *L'Allegro*, 1632, 'Come, and trip it as you go, | On the light fantastic toe'.

*light on the subject; esp., **to shed more** (or **a little**) **light on** (or **upon**), to explain a subject; to make it clear: late C. 19–20.

'light that never was on sea or land, the.' Mid C. 19–20. 'The light . . . land, | The consecration, and the poet's dream' (Wordsworth, *Elegiac Stanzas*, 1805).

lighten one's darkness, to. To cheer; encourage and comfort (a person); jocularly, to give light to: late C. 19–20. From 'Lighten our darkness' in *The Book of Common Prayer*.

like a giant refreshed; esp., **to feel . . .,** to feel strong and refreshed: late C. 19–20. Psalm 78, v. 66, in *Prayer Book*.

like the curate's egg. See **good in parts.**

'lilies and languors (of virtue), the.' From ca. 1870. 'The lilies and languors of virtue, | The roses and raptures of vice' (Swinburne, 'Dolores', in *Poems and Ballads*, 1865).

limpid glance, a (or **her**). A pure, clear glance: C. 20.

link in the chain of progress, a. Late C. 19–20. From the theory of Evolution.

'lion shall lie down with the lamb, (and) the.' C.
19–20. A version of *Isaiah*, lxv. 25 (concerning the New
Jerusalem).

*lion's share, the. The principal (or the largest) share or
portion: mid C. 19–20. Burke, 1790. Phædrus, *Fables*, I, v, 7,
'Ego primam tollo, nominor quia Leo'.

*lips are (or **were**) **sealed, one's** (esp., **my**). I am bound
to keep silence: C. 20; esp., from late 1937, when Lord Baldwin
said, more than once, 'My lips are sealed'.

*little bird told me, a. I have heard (but do not wish to
name the speaker): C. 19–20. 'I heard the little bird say so',
Swift to Stella, May 23, 1711 (Benham).

'Little Corporal, the.' Napoleon (*le Petit Caporal*): C.
19–20; slightly obsolescent, except among historians. With
reference to his size and the strict discipline he exacted.

little dreaming (or **thinking**) **that . . .** Not at all dreaming or thinking that . . .: late C. 19–20. Meiosis.

little Latin and less Greek is a misquotation-cliché of
C. 19–20. Ben Jonson, addressing the dead Shakespeare in
the Preface to the First Folio, 1623, said, 'And though thou
hadst small Latin and less Greek'.

little thin on top, to be a; less often **to be thin on top.**
To be going bald: C. 20. From the barbers' stock remark
(since when?) to customers to whom they wish to sell a hair-
oil or other 'preparation'.

live from hand to mouth, to. See **hand to mouth.**

live in clover (or **like pigs in clover**), **to.** To live
luxuriously: mid C. 19–20. The shorter phrase has been
common since ca. 1700. Clover, as Dr Johnson remarked,
being extremely delicious and fattening to cattle.

live in the past, to. To draw, for one's interest and entertainment, far more on memory than on expectation and
realization: late C. 19–20.

livery of shame, the. Disgrace about one as a garment: C. 19–20; slightly obsolescent.—Cf. 'White (the livery of innocence)', Boyle, 1661 (O.E.D.).

living rock, the; esp., **sculptured in the . . .,** carved in rock in the open air: late C. 19–20.

loaves and fishes. 'Pecuniary advantages as a motive for religious profession' or 'for display of public spirit': C. 19–20. See *John*, vi. 26. (O.E.D.)

'local habitation and a name, a.' A home and a name; definiteness, physical existence, as in 'The poet's pen . . . gives to airy nothing | A local habitation and a name' (*A Midsummer Night's Dream*, v, i): mid C. 19–20.

*lock, stock and barrel. Entirely, completely: from ca. 1820. From the lock, the stock, and the barrel of a blunder-buss.

*lock the stable door after the horse is stolen, to. A proverbial saying (= to take measures after the harm has been done), which may fairly be classified as a cliché in its C. 20 use, if not indeed in its use since ca. 1880.

lone wolf, a. A person that works alone or is conspicuously self-dependent and independent: C. 20; originally American.

lonely furrow, the. A lonely life; also **to plough a lonely furrow,** to play a lone hand, plan and work independently and/or in solitude: late C. 19–20.

long and (the) short of it, the. The substance, the essence, the most important part or aspect of a thing; the upshot: late C. 18–20. (Recorded first in 1690; and as *the short and (the) long* in C. 16–17.)—2. Applied jocularly to a tall and a short person walking side by side: late C. 19–20.

long arm of the law, the. The Law, whose influence stretches far; the police, who are everywhere: late C. 19–20.

long-drawn sigh, a. A long, a lingering, sigh: mid C. 19–20.

*long-felt want, a; esp., **to fulfil a . . .,** to fill a big gap, esp., to invent something, write a book, much needed: C. 20.

long pull and a strong pull, a. Consistent, determined effort: late C. 19–20. From rowing.

longo intervallo (pronounced as English words), 'at a far remove', hence 'in a more modest way': literary: C. 19–20. 'I have always preferred to follow, "longo intervallo", the system of . . . Montaigne' (Ernest Weekley, *Jack and Jill*, 1939). From Virgil's *longo intervallo insequi*.

look daggers, to. To look extremely angry or hostile; to look fiercely or savagely: from ca. 1830. Gleam of eyes: gleam of daggers.

look facts in the face, to. To be realistic and practical: late C. 19–20.—Cf. *look a person in the face*, 'to look straight at him'.

look for a needle in a haystack, to. See **needle in a haystack.**

look on the wine when it is (or **it's**) **red, to.** To drink much wine (or even other liquor), to drink wine often, to yield to the desire to drink wine: C. 19–20. From 'Look not thou upon the wine when it is red' (*Proverbs*, xxiii. 31).

lords of Creation, the. Men: mostly women's (ironically; men use it jocularly): late C. 19–20. One would think that they had created the world and ruled it entirely.

lose the thread of one's discourse, to. To forget where one is in speech or conversation: mid C. 19–20.—Cf. **pick up the threads.**

lost to view. Lost from sight, gone from the view; disappeared: C. 20.

loud enough to waken the dead. Very loud indeed: applied esp. to noises made by persons at night: from ca. 1870

love in a cottage. Love in humble circumstances; idyllic love in the country: late C. 19–20. Originally in reference, perhaps, to Keats's 'Love in a hut, with water and a crust, | Is—Love, forgive us!—cinders, ashes, dust' (*Lamia*, 1819, at II, 1).

love of . . . See **good woman.**

luck of the Devil, the; the Devil's own luck. Extreme or excessive or most remarkable luck: colloquial: mid C. 19–20.

Lucullan (properly, **Lucullean** or **-ian**) **banquet, a.** A sumptuous and exquisite feast: mid C. 19–20; obsolescent. Licinius Lucullus (115–48 B.C.), a Roman famed for his luxurious feasts.

lucus a non lucendo. It must be so because the opposite seems to be true; it is clear because of its very obscurity ('. . . presumably on the principle of *lucus a non lucendo*', an acerb reference to a disputed etymology): literary, philological, and philosophical: C. 19–20. Lucus, 'a grove', is 'so called from non lucendo (not admitting light [*lux*])', an etymology 'referred to by Quintilian . . . and by numerous ancient authors and commentators' (Benham).

lull. See **calm.**

lulled to a false sense of security. Deluded into a sense of security: late C. 19–20. Politicians, please note!

M

Machine Age, the. The 20th Century: from ca. 1921. 'Those are the clichés of this decade. It was Babbitts'—a vogue word, not a cliché—'and the machine age in the twenties' (Edwin Lanham, *Banner at Daybreak*, 1937); it still is.

*magnate, as in **a City magnate** and **a newspaper magnate.** A rich and powerful man in finance or in the newspaper world: from ca. 1910.

magnificent figure of a woman, a. 'A magnificent figure of a woman, as they say' (Rupert Penny, *Policeman's Holiday*, 1938). From ca. 1860; obsolescent; as is the figure.

magnitude. See **of the . . .**

*mailed fist, the. Brute military force: C. 20. *The Times* December 17, 1897 (O.E.D.).

main chance, the. See **eye to . . .**

*maintain the status quo, to. To preserve the present order of society and condition of things: late C. 19–20; journalistic.

major phenomenon, a. A phenomenon of great importance: from ca. 1910; scientific and journalistic.

make a clean breast of it, to. To confess or disclose everything relevant to a crime, an accident, etc.: from ca. 1860.—Cf. **cleanse one's bosom . . .**

*make a mountain (out) of a mole-hill, to. To exaggerate; esp., to exaggerate greatly the importance of a trifle (e.g., a difficulty, a grievance): late C. 18–20. Current since mid C. 16. (O.E.D.)

make a virtue out of necessity, to. To profit by a misfortune, set-back, compulsion: C. 19–20.. 'Found in Chaucer and Shakespeare' (Benham); and in Dutch, French, Italian.

make assurance doubly sure, to. To take additional precautions: C. 19–20. From 'But yet I'll make assurance double sure, | And take a bond of fate' (*Macbeth*, IV, i).

make bricks without straw, to (be asked to). To be obliged or expected to do or make something without the tools or means usually held to be required for the work or task: C. 19–20. In misapprehensive allusion to *Exodus*, v.

*make ends meet, to.** To succeed in paying one's way (esp., by living within one's income): C. 19–20. (B.E.'s *Dictionary*, 1690.) From the French *joindre les deux bouts* (O.E.D.).

make glad the heart of man, to. Mid C. 19–20. From 'Wine that maketh glad the heart of man' (*Psalms*, civ. 15).

make good, to (?). To succeed, to prosper: U.S.A., C. 20; English, from ca. 1919.

*make hay, to.** An adaptation of the proverb, *make hay while the sun shines*: mid C. 19–20.—Cf. the German *Mann muss Heu machen, weil die Sonne scheint* (quoted by Benham).

make no bones about it, to. To make no fuss about it; expend no scruples on: mid C. 18–20. From bones found in stew or pottage.

*make on the swings what one loses on the round-abouts, to.** To recoup in one activity or department what one loses in another: C. 20. From fairs.

make one's blood boil, to. To cause one to become very angry or indignant: mid C. 19–20.

*make one's hair stand on end, to.** To terrify (a person): C. 19–20.—Cf. More, 1534, 'He made my own hair stand up upon my head' (O.E.D.).

*make one's mouth water, to.** To cause one to wish earnestly or enviously to possess or enjoy something: mid C. 18–20. From the saliva that flows at the sight, or in anticipation, of appetizing food.

make oneself scarce, to. To go away (and stay away): colloquial: from ca. 1830.

make or mar, to; now often **to make or break.** To cause (a person or a thing) to succeed completely or to be completely ruined: from ca. 1830, though common since mid C. 16.

*make the best of a bad bargain (or **job**), **to.** To adapt oneself resignedly (and resourcefully) to adverse circumstances: mid C. 19–20. Boswell, in 1790, alludes to it as 'the vulgar phrase' (O.E.D.).

make the punishment fit the crime, to, is an adaptation of W. S. Gilbert's 'To let the punishment fit the crime' (*The Mikado*, 1885): late C. 19–20.

make the supreme sacrifice, to. To die (for a cause, a king, a friend): late C. 19–20, but esp. in 1914–18 and 1939–?.

make the welkin ring, to. To cheer or shout very loudly: C. 19–20. Charles Wesley († 1788) begins his *Christmas Hymn* thus, 'Hark how all the welkin rings, | Glory to the King of kings!'

make the world a better place, to. See **earnest desire.**

make the worse appear the better cause, to, is a misquotation (C. 19–20) of 'His tongue | Dropp'd manna, and could make the worse appear | The better reason' (Milton, *Paradise Lost*, II, 112–14), after Diogenes Laertius (concerning Socrates).

malignant fate, a. A hostile influence or power that is, or appears to be, that of fate; extreme ill-fortune: late C. 19–20. 'It seemed that a malignant fate was dogging him with relentless persistence' (Van Wyck Mason, *The Washington Legation Murders*, 1937).—Cf. Shakespeare's 'malignant and ill-boding stars' (1 *Henry VI*, IV, v, 6).

Mammon of unrighteousness, the. Wealth as a god, an idol: C. 19–20. No longer apprehended as a quotation of 'Make to yourselves friends of the mammon of unrighteousness', *Luke*, xvi. 9 (ποιήσατε ἑαυτοῖς φίλους ἐκ τοῦ μαμωνᾶ τῆς ἀδικίας, where μαμωνᾶς is the transliteration of an Aramaic word for 'riches' or 'possessions, property').

*man after his (or **my** or . . .) **own heart, a.** This, too, is no longer apprehended as a quotation (1 *Samuel*, xiii. 14): in mid C. 19–20, a cliché.

man and a brother, a. A fellow human being: late C. 19–20. Perhaps cf. Campbell's 'Ye are brothers! Ye are men!' in *The Battle of the Baltic*, 1801. Cf. also the Slave Trade.

*man in the street, the (English); **the man in the car** (American). Respectively since ca. 1870 (though a common race-course phrase as early as 1830) and since ca. 1900. The ordinary citizen.

man of parts, a. A talented or a highly intellectual man: mid C. 18–20; slightly obsolescent and, in C. 20, literary.

man of straw, a. An imaginary adversary: C. 19–20; obsolescent.—A man of no substance: from ca. 1830. Contrast the next.

man of means or **substance, a.** (*Means*) a man of good income and a certain amount of property or capital; (*substance*) a wealthy man. Both: C. 19–20.

man to man. See **as man to man.**

manner. See **to the manner . . .**

'manners makyth man' (?). Manners and morals make the person: C. 19–20. This was the motto of William of Wykeham († 1404); cf. *mores cuique sui fingunt fortunam*, 'everyone's manners make his fortune' (Benham), from Cornelius Nepos.

many a time and oft. Often: mid C. 18–20; recorded for 1560 (O.E.D.). *Many a time* is also a cliché: C. 18–20. 'Many a time (and oft) he played the fool.'

many are called (but few are chosen) is a cliché in mid C. 19–20. *Matthew*, xxii. 14, 'For many are called, but few are chosen' (cf. xx. 16).

march of time, the; time marches on; how time flies! The passing of time, the course of history; time goes on; how quickly time flies: C. 20. Lamb uses the first, in 1833 (O.E.D.).

*mare's nest, a. A false alarm, a great disappointment, something worthless, something quite other than one has expected; often *to find a mare's nest*: C. 18–20.

mark my words! See you mark . . .

mark of recognition, a; esp., as a . . ., as a token of gratitude, admiration, respect: late C. 19–20.

mark of the beast (or B.), the. A sign or indication of evil or corruption: mid C. 19–20. *Revelation*, xix. 20, with reference to the great whore of Babylon: τὸ χάραγμα τοῦ θηρίον, 'the stamp of the wild beast'.

mark time, to (figurative) (?). To remain, for a time, where one is; to stand still, make no progress: late C. 19–20. Macaulay, 1837, 'The human mind, accordingly, instead of marching, merely marked time' (O.E.D.).

maroon thousands, to. 'Snow maroons thousands of commuters' (American journalists' headline): from ca. 1910. (Sullivan.)

marriage terminated in divorce, the. American (esp. journalists'): from ca. 1905. (Sullivan.)

martial tread. (The sound of) soldierly steps or warlike marching: mid C. 19–20; slightly obsolescent.

marvels of science, the. The wonders of science: late C. 19–20.

master mind, the. The mind of the great man; the most notable expert: C. 20; often jocular. Abused in advertisements.—Cf. Shakespeare's 'the choice and master spirits of this age', *Julius Cæsar*, III, i.

master of one's fate, the. From Henley's verses. See captain of one's soul.

*masterly inactivity. Coined by Sir James Mackintosh, *Vindiciae*, 1791, though perhaps with a glance at Horace's *strenua inertia* (as Benham notes), it became a cliché in the 1880's.

material interests. Non-spiritual matters; affairs of money, monetary well-being: late C. 19–20. Used by Mark Pattison in 1861: 'community of material interests' (O.E.D.).

matter is receiving the closest attention, the. Official and commercial: C. 20. Often it means that it has been pigeon-holed and forgotten.

matter of form, a. See **as a matter of form.**

*****matter of life and death, a.** A matter of vital importance: mid C. 19–20. Originally (and still properly) applied to something of which the omission entails death.

Mayor fears milk shortage. An American journalists' cliché-headline: C. 20. (One of the numerous clichés delightfully satirized by Frank Sullivan in 'The Cliché Expert', published in *The New Yorker*, June 20, 1936, and reprinted in 1939.)

mean 'maybe', not to; esp., and I don't mean 'maybe'. See **and I don't . . .**

mean well, to (?). To have good intentions; to be a kindly person: C. 19–20. 'Oh, he means well—but that's as far as he goes.' Hell is paved with good intentions.

meat and drink; esp., (something) is meat and drink to (someone), is a source of much enjoyment to him: C. 18–20. Used by Shakespeare, and even earlier. (*Meat* = food.)

Medes and Persians, the; esp., (according to) the law of the . . . , (according to) unalterable law or custom: mid C. 19–20. *Daniel*, vi. 12, 'The thing is true, according to the law of the Medes and Persians, which altereth not' (King Darius's sentence against Daniel); cf. verse 8.

meet with an untimely end, to. To die (hence of things, to end) before one's due time: late C. 19–20.

*mention in a connexion, to; esp., **I may mention in this** (or **that**) **connexion.** A C. 20 cliché.

mercury continues to soar. American journalists': C. 20; esp. as a headline in reference to increasing temperature of the weather. (Sullivan.)

merest conjecture, the; mere conjecture. Guess-work: from ca. 1890. 'Yes; but, after all, it's mere conjecture.'

***Merry Monarch, the.** Charles II: C. 19–20; slightly obsolescent. The Earl of Rochester (1647–80) in his poem *On the King*, spoke of him as 'A merry monarch, scandalous and poor' (Benham).

meum et tuum. (The rights of) private property: mid C. 18–20. 'He has no sense of *meum et tuum*.' Literally, 'mine and thine'.

midsummer madness. Extreme folly; the height of madness: C. 19–20. Shakespeare, 'Why, this is very midsummer madness' (*Twelfth Night*, III, iv, 61); at the midsummer moon (*luna*), madness, it was formerly supposed, is prevalent.

***might and main;** esp., **with (all one's) might and main,** with all one's strength, forcibly, very vigorously: C. 19–20; used as early as C. 14.

'mighty hunter before the Lord, a.' A great hunter: C. 19–20. *Genesis*, x. 9, in respect of Nimrod.

milk and water (figurative), as adjective. 'Wishy-washy'; weakly amiable: mid C. 19–20. From the noun (= milk diluted with water). O.E.D.

milk of human kindness, the. Kindliness: C. 19–20. Lady Macbeth says that Macbeth's nature is 'too full of the milk of human kindness to catch the nearest way' (I, iv).

milling crowd. See **roar a welcome.**

mills of God, the (C. 19–20); and perhaps also its original, 'the mills of God grind slowly, but they grind exceeding small' (or, as a proverb recorded in 1639, 'God's mill grinds slow but sure'. Benham records the Greek ὀψὲ θεῶν ἀλέουσι μύλοι, ἀλέουσι δὲ λεπτά (the mills of the gods grind tardily, but they grind small).

mince matters, not to. To speak plainly and frankly: mid C. 19–20, though fairly common since late C. 16; cf. Shakespeare's 'Thy honesty and love doth mince this matter' (*Othello*, ii, iii).

*mind one's P's and Q's, to. A proverbial saying that, in C. 19–20, is a cliché. Origin dubious: see the O.E.D. and Benham.

mine host. A landlord of an inn, a tavern: mid C. 19–20; mercifully, it is obsolescent, like the synonymous *Boniface*.

minion of fortune, a. A favourite of fortune, one of fortune's darlings: C. 19–20. Shakespeare, 'A son ... | Who is sweet fortune's minion, and her pride' (1 *Henry IV*, i, i, 83–4).

minions of the law. Policemen (and detectives): from ca. 1870.

'minister to a mind diseased', to. ('Canst thou not minister to a mind diseased?', Shakespeare, *Macbeth*, v, iii.) To heal—to do something towards healing—mental derangement: C. 19–20.

minor matters. (Comparatively) unimportant matters: late C. 19–20. 'Most of us have to spend most of our time dealing with minor matters.'

mint of money, a. Much money; wealth: C. 19–20. Fuller, 1655, 'A mass, a mint, a mine of money could easily be advanced to defray the expenses thereby' (O.E.D.)

mirabile dictu. Marvellous (or very strange) to relate: an introductory tag: C. 19–20. From its occurrence in Virgil (*Georgics*, ii, 30).

miraculous escape, a (or **one's**). A marvellous escape: mid C. 19–20. (Hyperbolical.)

miscarriage of justice, a, not by itself (a legal phrase) but in **a grave miscarriage of justice,** which is a mainly journalistic cliché of late C. 19–20.

missing link, a or **the.** 'Something lacking to complete a series' (O.E.D.): from ca. 1870. Jowett, 1875, 'The missing link between words and things'. As a technicality of Evolution, the phrase is derivative.

modern classic, a. A literary work of considerable merit and apparently enduring fame: book-reviewers': C. 20.

moment of victory, the; esp., **in the moment of victory.** C. 19–20.

momentary aberration, a. A mere, passing—or merely transitory—wandering of the intellect (such as an act of forgetfulness, a swift, mild brain-storm): C. 20.

momentous decision, a (or **one's** or **the**). A (very) important decision: late C. 19–20.

*****monarch of all one surveys, to be** (less often **to be the ——**). C. 19–20. From Cowper's 'I am monarch of all I survey, | My right there is none to dispute' (verses supposed to be written by Alexander Selkirk).

monumental effort, a; a monumental work. A work (esp. a book) that has required years of strenuous or patient labour: late C. 19–20.

monumentum aere perennius. A literary cliché (C. 19–20); from Horace's *Exegi monumentum aere perennius*, 'I raised a monument more enduring than brass'.

*****moot point, a.** An arguable, debatable, or doubtful point: from ca. 1730. Originally a point or case chosen for discussion by a moot of law students (O.E.D.).

moral victory, a. A result that, despite its adverse physical bearing, is ethically a gain: late C. 19–20.

more and more (adverbial). Increasingly: C. 19–20. Recorded, by O.E.D., for ca. 1200.

more anon. See *of which* . . .

more dead than alive. Half dead; in a low physical condition; emaciated and/or utterly exhausted: mid C. 19–20.

more frightened than hurt. A proverbial saying (in C. 16: *more frayd then hurt*) so overworked, so hackneyed that it has, in C. 20 at least, become a cliché.

*'**more honoured in the breach than the observance.**' Applied, as in Shakespeare's *Hamlet*, I, iv, to a custom more generally neglected than observed: C. 19–20.

***more in sorrow than in anger** is used adverbially—a cliché of mid C. 19–20—whereas Shakespeare's phrase is '**a** countenance more in sorrow than in anger' (*Hamlet*, I, ii).

more or less. Approximately or (very) roughly; in a greater or less degree, to a greater or less extent; to some extent: late C. 17–20. (The O.E.D. records it for ca. 1225.)

*'**more sinned against than sinning.**' More wronged than sinful: C. 19–20. In Shakespeare's *Lear*, III, ii, the King cries, 'I am a man | More sinned against than sinning'.

more than a languid interest; esp., **to betray or show** . . ., to be enthusiastic or in love: from ca. 1880; slightly obsolescent.

***more than meets the eye;** esp., **there is more in it than meets the eye.** More than is at first visible or deducible: late C. 19–20. ' "There's more here, sir," says the Inspector over the dead body, "than meets the eye" ' (John Galsworthy, *The Man of Property*, 1906).

more than ordinary importance; esp., **an event of** . . ., a very important event: C. 20; originally, journalistic.

more than pleased. Delighted; (very) grateful: late C. 19–20. Elliptic for 'more than merely pleased'.

more (or **perhaps more**) **than you realize** (or **may realize**). More than you suppose, believe, perceive: from ca. 1910.

more the merrier, the. A proverbial saying so bandied about and hackneyed in C. 19–20 as to be a cliché of that period. In Ray's *Proverbs*, there is the variant, 'The more the merrier, the fewer the better cheer'.

more's (or **the more's**) **the pity.** Unfortunately; 'worse luck!': mid C. 19–20. An 'historical survival' (O.E.D.).

'most unkindest cut ...' See **unkindest cut ...**

Mother Earth. See **Earth the ...**

Mother of Parliaments, the. The British Parliament; properly, England: from ca. 1870. 'England, the mother of Parliaments', John Bright, in a speech at Rochdale, Jan. 18, 1865 (Benham).

move and have one's being, to. To live and work (or play) at (some specified place); to exist in the material world: C. 19–20. *Acts*, xvii. 28, 'For in him [God] we live, and move, and have our being': ἐν αὐτῷ γὰρ ζῶμεν καὶ κινούμεθα καί ἐσμεν, 'for in him we live and are moved and *are* (or, exist)': Vulgate, 'In ipso enim vivimus, et movemus, et sumus' ('car en lui nous avons la vie, le mouvement et l'être', Verdunoy).

*move heaven and earth, to. To make every effort, to do all one can, to achieve a purpose: from ca. 1870. Trollope, 1862, 'Papa ... would move heaven and earth for her if he could' (O.E.D.).

'moving finger writes, and having writ moves on,— the.' Fate is inexorable: from ca. 1880. FitzGerald's *Rubáiyát of Omar Khayyám*, basic edition (4th), 1879.

*much ado about nothing. A fuss about a trifle: C. 18–20; perhaps, C. 17–20, for it was a common phrase even in Shakespeare's day.

much as I hate to do it (or **say it** or **say so**). A gossip's introductory formula: mid C. 19–20.

much in evidence. Prominent; conspicuous: late C. 19–20. 'His pedantry was much in evidence.' An elaboration of *in evidence*.

*much of a muchness (n. and adj.). Similarity or sameness; very much alike, of much the same value, importance, significance: colloquial: from ca. 1840.

*much water has flowed under the bridge since then (or **that time**). A long time has passed and/or much has happened since then: late C. 19–20. An allusion to the stream of time: 'Assiduo labuntur tempora motu, | Non secus ad flumen', Ovid, *Metamorphoses*, XV, 180–1 ('Time glides past with constant movement, rather like a stream').

muffled report. 'Of that fatal shot, nothing was heard but a muffled report.' This detective-story writer's phrase became a cliché only ca. 1925.

multum in parvo. Much in little; a short book or article that is full of matter; a 'compactum': C. 19–20.

murder most foul. A horrible and/or remarkable murder: from ca. 1830. No longer—except by scholars—apprehended as a quotation from *Hamlet*, I, v.

murdered in cold blood. See **act . . .**

*must of necessity. Must necessarily: C. 19–20, as a cliché, although recorded as early as 1577. 'It must of necessity be discovered.'

mutatis mutandis. Necessary changes having been made: mid C. 19–20. In Roman Law it means 'Those things being exchanged which the sense requires should be changed' (Benham).

---

mutual attraction of opposites, the. 'Contrasting personalities (characters and temperaments) attract each other', applied esp. to love and friendship: late C. 19–20. From the laws of magnetism?

my dear Watson! See **simple . . .**

my opinion—for what it is worth—is that . . . *For what it is worth* (worth little) is itself a cliché of C. 19–20; the longer one is of C. 20.

N

nail one's colours (loosely **flag**) **to the mast, to.** To be intransigent or unyielding in one's attitude: mid C. 19–20. From an old naval practice that precluded surrender.

nail to the counter is a cliché only in **to nail a lie to the counter,** to expose a falsehood: from ca. 1860 in U.S.A. and from ca. 1890 in Britain. (Shopkeepers used to nail spurious coins to the counter.)

naked truth, the. The plain truth (Latin *nuda veritas*): mid C. 19–20; obsolescent.

*name is Legion, their. They are very numerous: mid C. 19–20. An adaptation (and originally a misapprehension) of 'My name is Legion: for we are many', *Mark*, v. 9: Λεγεὼν ὄνομά μοι, ὅτι πολλοί ἐσμεν.

name to conjure with, a. A famous name—the name of a (very) famous person—a name that works wonders: late C. 19–20. Originally, a name that one may worthily swear by.

nameless orgies. Abominable orgies: late C. 19–20. 'Facetious' Tom Brown speaks, in 1704, of 'nameless vices'.

Napoleon of finance, a. A brilliant financier on a very large scale: C. 20.

nasty spill, a. A severe fall, literal and figurative: colloquial: late C. 19–20. From horse-riding.

nation of shopkeepers, a. The English: C. 19–20, though used non-specifically by Adam Smith in *The Wealth of Nations* in 1775 and specifically in the French National Convention in 1794. 'Attributed, without authority, to Napoleon I' (Benham).

nation speaks to nation or **(and) nation shall speak to nation.** There is—there shall be—international goodwill: late C. 19–20. From a poem (? Tennyson's) on the laying of the Transatlantic cable.

naughty Nineties, the. The 1890's: C. 20.

*ne plus ultra. '(Let there) be no (passing) beyond a certain point', used to mean 'the acme'—'the point of highest possible attainment': mid C. 18–20. The variant (rapidly gaining ground), *nec plus ultra*, was formerly much more common in French than in English; it is less logical than *ne . . .*

near thing, a. See **close thing.**

neck and crop. Bodily; hence, altogether, entirely: from ca. 1870. Dickens, 1865, 'We're going in neck and crop for fashion' (O.E.D.); *to throw* (a person) *out, neck and crop.*

neck and neck (?). In close competition; level in a fierce competition or rivalry: colloquial: C. 20. From horse-racing.

neck or nothing is applied to 'determination and readiness to venture everything or to take all risks' (O.E.D.): C. 19–20; used earlier by Swift and Cowper.

*needle in a haystack, a. Something (small and) extremely difficult to find: C. 19–20. From the proverbial saying *to look for a needle in a haystack*, which derives from the Medieval Latin *acum in meta fœni quaerere* (Benham).

*needs no introduction. 'Mr H. needs no introduction to this audience.' Public speakers' and chairmen's: late C. 19–20.

*neither fish, flesh, nor good red herring. This proverbial saying (recorded in 1546) is, in C. 20 (if not in C. 19–20) a cliché. Neither one thing nor the other.

neither here nor there; esp., **it's . . .,** it's of no consequence: late C. 19–20.

*neither rhyme nor reason; more often **without rhyme or reason.** Nonsense; senseless: C. 19–20. Bacon has the former.

Nemesis pursues one; a nemesis pursues one, 'retribution is at hand': late C. 19–20. Nemesis is the goddess of retribution, esp. of retributive justice.

nethermost pit, the; esp., **condemn to the . . .,** condemn to hell or to severe punishment, unrelenting remorse, etc.: mid C. 19–20. In allusion to *Psalms*, lxxxvi. 13.

'never the time and the place and the loved one all together!' From ca. 1890. This comes in Browning's 'Never the Time and the Place' in *Jocoseria*, 1883.

nevertheless and notwithstanding. Nevertheless: late C. 19–20.

*new broom, a. Formed from the proverb, 'a new broom sweeps clean', it means 'a newly appointed official is full of energy and reform': mid C. 19–20.

*new lease of life, a. A renewed life or (of things) existence: mid C. 19–20. Seeley, 1878, 'Wherever Estates still existed, they seemed to have gained a new lease of life' (O.E.D.). From the renewing of leases.

new wine in old bottles. Something new in an old frame, case, cadre, system: C. 19–20. *Matthew*, ix. 17, 'Neither do men put new wine into old bottles': οὐδὲ βάλλουσιν οἶνον νέον εἰς ἀσκοὺς παλαιούς (into old wine-skins).

newspaper magnate, a. See **magnate.**

nice distinction, a; nice distinctions. Delicately discriminated or slight differences (or rather, distinctions): late C. 19–20.

night out, a; esp., **to have a . . .** (colloquial). To have a riotous time away from home: from ca. 1910.

'nihil tetigit quod non ornavit.' He dealt with nothing without adorning it: literary: C. 19–20. Applied to writers; originally to Goldsmith.

*nine days' wonder, a. A newspaper sensation lasting a week and then dropped completely: Chaucer, Shakespeare; but a cliché only in C. 19–20 (Byron, Hughes).—Cf. Livy, Book I, 31.

*nip in the bud, to. To put an early stop to something, before it becomes important or dangerous: mid C. 18–20, though fairly common throughout C. 17.

no balm. See **balm.**

no better than she should be; esp., **she's (or she was) . . .,** she is somewhat immoral: mid C. 19–20.

no chicken. See **she is . . .**

no expense has (or had) been—or will be—spared. Money has (etc.) been spent freely (to attain a specified object): late C. 19–20.

*no love lost between them, there is (or there's) or there was. There is (was) no affection, indeed there is enmity, between them: mid C. 19–20.

no mean; esp., **no mean city** (q.v. at **citizen**). Considerable; great: C. 19–20. *No Mean City* is the title of a documentary novel (1935) on Glasgow.

no (e.g., mistakes) **of any sort or kind.** None at all: late C. 19–20.

no respecter of persons, to be. To make no distinctions of rank or wealth: C. 19–20. *Acts*, x. 34 (St. Peter *loquitur*) 'I perceive that God is no respecter of persons': καταλαμβάνομαι ὅτι οὐκ ἔστι προσωπολήπτης ὁ Θεός (God is not a favourer [of persons]).

*no sinecure, it (or **this**) **is** (or **was**). It is a difficult position (post, job): late C. 19–20. A sinecure is a position in which there is no work but a stipend.

no small; esp., **of no small value,** of considerable value: mid C. 19–20.—Cf. **no mean.**

no uncertain. See **in no . . .**

*noblesse oblige. Good breeding (*noblesse*, 'noble birth and/or rank') demands or expects it: from ca. 1880. Semi-proverbial in French, it is indubitably a cliché (in C. 20, often jocular) in English. Littré, 'Quiconque prétend être noble, doit se bien conduire'.

nodding acquaintance, a. A person to whom one merely nods, a slight acquaintance: from ca. 1870.

noise abroad, to. To rumour or report widely: late C. 19–20; obsolescent.—Cf. **bruit about.**

*non compos mentis. Insane; temporarily insane; distraught: in C. 17 (and after), a legal phrase; in C. 18–20, a general cliché. Lit., 'not master of one's mind'.

nose to the grindstone. See **keep nose . . .**

not a breath of air; esp., **there is** (or **was**) **not . . .,** it is stifling (the air being without perceptible movement): late C. 19–20.

not a shadow of doubt. No doubt at all: late C. 19–20. —Cf. **beyond a shadow of doubt,** q.v.

not a whit. Not at all; in no degree, to no extent: C. 19–20; now regarded as something of an elegancy or genteelism—and slightly archaic.

not all beer . . . See **beer and skittles.**

not an iota. See **not one iota.**

not by a long chalk. See **by a long chalk.**

not enough room to swing a cat, with or **there is.** Space is cramped: applied to a room, a compartment: colloquial: C. 20.

not for me to say, it's (or **that's**). A formula, often indicative of false modesty: C. 19–20.

not impossibly. Possibly; perhaps: C. 20.

'not in our stars.' Not in predestination, but from negligence or slackness: mid C. 19–20. Shakespeare, 'The fault, dear Brutus, is not in our stars, | But in ourselves, that we are underlings' (*Julius Cæsar*, I, ii).

not lost but gone before. From ca. 1830; often in reference to a friend lost by death. It was the title of a song current in 1829. An ancient parallel is Seneca's *non amittuntur sed praemittuntur*, 'they are not lost but sent before' (Benham).

not one (or **an**) **iota; not a single iota,** esp., **not by a single iota,** not by the smallest particle, in no degree—to no extent—at all. Late C. 18–20. The iota is the smallest letter in the Greek alphabet; cf. **jot or tittle,** q.v.

not the only pebble on the beach, one is. There are others (e.g., suitors, candidates): colloquial: late C. 19–20.

'not theirs to reason why.' It is for them to obey, not to argue: from 1855. Tennyson, *The Charge of the Light Brigade*, published Dec. 9, 1854 (Benham).

*****not to put too fine a point upon it,** 'to speak bluntly', is an introductory or a modifying formula: mid C. 19–20.

not what you would call . . . 'He is not what you would call robust.'—'It was not what you would have called easy to do.' Mid C. 19–20.

not wisely but too well. Applied to loving and, esp., to drinking: late C. 19-20. *Othello*, v, vii.

not without reason. With some show of reason; reasonably, sensibly: C. 20.

not worth powder and shot. Not worth the effort or the money expended (or to be expended): late C. 18-20. (Recorded for C. 17.)

not worth the paper it's written on. Worthless, as applied to a cheque, a promissory note, a guarantee, a pact ('a mere scrap of paper'): C. 20.

'nothing in his life became him like the leaving it.' Applied to a man that, like Dickens's Sydney Carton, dies better than he has lived: C. 19-20. Shakespeare, *Macbeth*, I, iv.

nothing in it; esp., **there's nothing ...** (there is no appreciable—or important—difference): C. 20.

nothing to boast about. Not remarkable; quite ordinary: colloquial: late C. 19-20.

*****'nous avons changé tout cela.'** We have changed all that: mid C. 19-20. Molière, *Le Médecin malgré lui*, II, vi.

now and then. Occasionally: C. 18-20. Common since C. 16.

now or never (?). This is the last, or the only, chance: C. 18-20. Common since late C. 16.

null and void. Null; cancelled; no longer operative or valid; without binding force: C. 19-20. Originally, a legal and political phrase.

nuptial knot, the. Marriage; *tie the nuptial knot*, to marry two persons: mid C. 19-20; obsolescent.

O

'o tempora! o mores!' Lit., 'oh, the times! oh, the manners!' From Cicero's Catiline Orations. A cliché since ca. 1770.

'observed of all observers, the.' The most important or prominent man in the state (or at a gathering): C. 19–20. Said of the Prince, in *Hamlet*, III, i.

obvious to even the meanest intelligence. 'It was obvious . . . that something unpleasant had happened.' Late C. 19–20. Often ironic: cf. **as every schoolboy knows.**

ocean greyhound, an. A swift steamship or other liner: from ca. 1890; originally, journalistic.

ocular proof. Proof addressed to, or conveyed by, the eye: mid C. 19–20. Shakespeare, 'Give me the ocular proof' (*Othello*, III, iii, 360).

*odds and ends. Oddments, odd remnants; miscellaneous articles, miscellanea: from ca. 1840. Recorded for 1746 (O.E.D.).

odour of sanctity, the. See **die in the odour . . .**

of a certain age. See **woman of a certain age.**

of course. Obviously; naturally (in the natural course or order of things); (*of course!*), yes: mid C. 19–20. Especially when tautological or meaningless.

of no avail. Ineffectual, useless, in vain: from ca. 1820. Here, *of avail* = 'of assistance or of advantage'.

of no value to anyone but the owner. Of sentimental value only: C. 20. Frequent in advertisements for lost articles.

(of) one flesh, to be. To be married: C. 19–20; now only literary. Cf. 1 *Corinthians*, vi. 16, 'For two, saith he, shall be one flesh': "Ἔσονται γάρ, φησιν, οἱ δύο εἰς σάρκα μίαν, 'for two . . . shall result in one flesh'.

of pith and moment, 'Of great importance; weighty; grave', is a cliché of mid C. 19–20. The original—Shakespeare's '(enterprises) of great pith and moment' (*Hamlet*, III, i, 86)—is almost a cliché: C. 19–20.

*of that ilk, when used incorrectly, i.e. as 'of that family, class, set or "lot"' (O.E.D.): from ca. 1880; originally and still frequently journalistic. *Guthrie of that ilk* properly = Guthrie of Guthrie (a landed-family title).

*'of the earth, earthy.' Earth-bound; material (without imagination or holiness): C. 19–20. 1 *Corinthians*, xv. 47, 'The first man is of the earth, earthy': ἐκ γῆς, χοϊκός, 'of earth, made of earth'.

of the first magnitude. 'Of the utmost greatness [or size] or importance': mid C. 19–20. From *stars of the first magnitude*, 'the most brilliant stars'; *a star of the first magnitude*, a theatrical or cinematic 'star of stars' is itself a cliché: from ca. 1920.

of the first water. Of the finest quality; (of persons) thorough, thorough-paced, out-and-out: from ca. 1825. Scott, 1826, 'A . . . swindler of the first water' (O.E.D.). From *diamonds of the first water*, the best diamonds (in a superseded grading).

*of the same kidney. (Of persons) of like character: C. 19–20. Shakespeare, 'A man of my kidney' (*The Merry Wives of Windsor*, III, v).

of which (or whom) more anon. Concerning . . . I shall say more, soon—in due course and soon: late C. 19–20.

off and on. Intermittently or at intervals; occasionally: mid C. 19–20.

*off the beaten track. Unusual; a by-path; not on the well-beaten highway of life or things: late C. 19–20. 'His chemical experiments are off the beaten track.'

officer and a gentleman, an. A gentleman-officer in the Army: ruling classes' and Regular Army's: C. 20.

*official capacity; esp., **in one's . . .,** as an official: C. 20.
'The affair did not touch him in his official capacity'; 'In his
official capacity, he is a dry old stick, but in his home he is
delightful.'

'oh! to be in England now that April's there.' Late
C. 19–20. Browning, *Home Thoughts from Abroad*, 1845.
'There' is often misquoted 'here' as if the sense were 'now
that April's arrived'.

oil and water. Incompatible; incompatibles: C. 19–20. Oil
and water do not mix.

old Adam, the. Human (as opposed to Divine) nature in
men; unregenerateness; often, men's sexuality: mid C. 19–20.
Cf. *Romans*, vi. 6, 'Our old man is crucified with him, that
the body of sin might be destroyed', where 'our old man' signifies 'the Adam in us' and renders the Greek ὁ παλαιὸς ἡμῶν
ἄνθρωπος ('our former character').

old head on young shoulders, an; esp., **to have an . . .,**
to be wiser (or more notably prudent) than one's youth would
lead others to expect: mid C. 19–20.

'old order changeth, the.' It continues, 'yielding place to
new': Tennyson, *Morte d'Arthur*, 1842, and in *The Passing of
Arthur*, 1869: a cliché from ca. 1880.

old school tie, the. A phrase applied to Public School
associations, influences, importance, memories: from ca. 1920.

oldest inhabitant, the. The oldest resident; the oldest
villager: late C. 19–20. A stock figure in *Punch, The Humorist,
The Passing Show*, etc.

olive branch, an; esp., **to hold out an . . .,** to propose or
suggest peace, to make overtures of peace: from ca. 1830. An
olive branch being the symbol of peace.

Olympian calm (or **indifference**); **Olympian pride** (or
scorn). Godlike calm or pride: mid C. 19–20; slightly
obsolescent. Olympus: the Greek heaven.

on . . . there can be no two opinions. There is no room for doubt; the matter is perfectly clear: late C. 19–20.

on bended knee; to thank God on bended knee(s), to pray thankfully, kneeling: C. 19–20. *On bended knee* is often used in contexts other than that of prayer.

*on his (or my or your) own head be it! He must suffer the consequences: mid C. 19–20.

on more than one occasion. More than once, several times; rather often: late C. 19–20.

on one's lawful occasions. See **lawful occasions.**

on one's mettle, to be or **to put.** To be stirred or persuaded—to stir or persuade someone—to do one's utmost, one's best: mid C. 19–20.

on one's native heath. In one's birthplace, one's village or town or district; where one is known: C. 20. 'A cricketer or footballer generally plays better on his native heath than away.'

*on pins and needles. Extremely uneasy: C. 20. 'He was on pins and needles: he did not know what to do nor could he guess what the enemy would do.'

on pleasure bent. Seeking pleasure; eager to enjoy, set on enjoying, oneself: C. 19–20. Cowper, *John Gilpin*, ca. 1782, 'Though on pleasure she was bent, she had a frugal mind'.

*on speaking terms; esp., **not to be . . .,** either 'not to know somebody well enough to do more than nod to him' or, generally, 'no longer to speak to him, because of a quarrel or a coldness': from ca. 1880.

*on tenterhooks, to be. To feel very impatient; to be in a state of painful suspense: mid C. 19–20. 'A young author, until his book is accepted, is on tenterhooks.' With nerves taut.

on the fence; esp., **to sit . . .,** to associate oneself with neither party or side: late C. 19–20; mostly political. One can then jump down into the safer field.

on the horns of a dilemma. Confronted with equally or almost equally awkward alternatives: late C. 19–20. From logic, where the phrase = 'refuted by a dilemma'.

on the knees (or **lap**) **of the gods.** Dependent on the dispensation of Providence; in the future: C. 19–20. The O.E.D. compares θεῶν ἐν γούνασι (on the knees of the gods).

*on the qui vive. Alert ; on the alert, the look-out; sharply watchful: C. 19–20. From *qui vive*, a sentry's cry of 'who goes there?' (*qui va là?*)

on the right side of the law; esp., **to keep . . .,** to abide by the laws: late C. 19–20. Connotation: from policy (and only just).

on the rocks (?). Destitute; penniless: colloquial: C. 20.

on the side of the angels, to be. To take the more spiritual view: from almost immediately after Disraeli's speech at the Oxford Diocesan Conference, 1864, 'The question is this: is man an ape or an angel? I, my lord, am on the side of the angels.' (Benham.)

on the spot. Present; there: late C. 19–20. 'It's the man on the spot who gets the job.' Lit., 'in the locality—at the very place' (of the context).

*on the spur of the moment. Impulsively; unthinkingly; in one's excitement or emotion: late C. 19–20. 'On the spur of the moment, he told a foolish lie.'

on the threshold of life, to be. At life's beginning: mid C. 19–20.—Cf. the common *threshold of manhood*, when a youth becomes a man.

on the tip of one's tongue. 'It was on the tip of my tongue, and yet I couldn't remember.'—'He had it on the tip of his tongue, as I could see.' Mid C. 19–20. (In C. 18: *at . . .*)

on the wrong tack, to be. To take a wrong line, to be on a wrong line, of action or conduct: C. 20. Nautical in origin.

on unimpeachable authority. From a sure source: C. 20. *On excellent authority* was, in C. 19, held to be adequate.

once and for all is a cliché-elaboration of *once for all*, 'finally; once and then it's done with': C. 20.

one and all. All, both collectively and individually: from ca. 1780. (The phrase has existed since early C. 16: see O.E.D.) —Cf. **all and sundry** and **each and every.**

'one crowded hour of glorious life (Is worth an age without a name)' is the second half of a quatrain, by Major Thomas Mordaunt, in *The Edinburgh Bee*, Oct. 12, 1791, and incorporated by Scott in verses appearing in *Old Mortality*, 1816: mid C. 19–20.

one flesh, to be. See **of one flesh.**

one foot in the grave; esp., **to have . . .,** to be old and feeble; sometimes applied to a young or middle-aged person suffering from cancer, phthisis, or other grave malady: occurring in 1632, it was not, I believe, a cliché before mid C. 19.

one in a thousand. An elect spirit, a very stout fellow: colloquial: C. 20.

one knows very well. A polite understatement of 'I am certain' or 'Absolutely everybody knows': late C. 19–20.

'one touch of nature makes the whole world kin.' Late C. 18–20. Shakespeare, *Troilus and Cressida*, III, iii. My brilliant friend Howard Phillips (killed in action, Sept. 1918) parodied it thus to me between two grim battles on the Somme (July–August, 1916):—'One touch of Nietzsche makes the whole world sin.'

onerous duties of public office, the. A political and journalistic perennial of C. 20.

*only too glad (or **happy** or **pleased**) **to** (do something), **to be.** This absurd C. 20 formula-cliché has been particularly rife since ca. 1925.—Cf. the next: in both, *only too* = 'extremely'.

only too well did he (or **she**) **know that . . .** He knew, with a connotation of fatefulness or compulsion: late C. 19–20.

open-mouthed surprise (?). 'He stood looking at it in (or, with) open-mouthed surprise.' Late C. 19–20.

open road, the. (The pleasures of walking along) country roads: late C. 19–20.—Cf. E. V. Lucas's delightful *The Open Road*, 1899: its popularity has done much to fix the phrase.

*open secret, an. A secret only in name: C. 19–20. Benham alludes to Carlo Gozzi's *Il Publico Secreto*, a play translated (1769) from Calderon's *El Secreto á Voces* (the noisy secret). *Secret de deux, secret de Dieu*, says a French proverb, to which, in 1927, I ventured to add: *mais secret de trois, secret de tout le monde*.

or one will know the reason why. 'I'll finish this book by the Greek Kalends, I suppose—or my publishers will know the reason why.' Late C. 19–20.

or words to that effect. Or words of that general significance: C. 20. 'He said she was a mercenary whore—or words to that effect.'

orb of day, the. The sun: C. 19–20; an obsolescent poetical and rhetorical cliché. Gray, 1757, 'Think'st thou yon sanguine cloud . . . has quench'd the Orb of Day?'

organ of the Press (or **press**), **an.** A newspaper: late C. 19–20. Here, *organ* = 'a means of communication'; *of the Press* is descriptive or classificatory.

other things being equal. See **ceteris paribus.**

'où sont les neiges d'antan?' 'Where are the snows of
yester year?', in the best-known rendering (D. G. Rossetti's)
of Villon's famous *Ballade Des Dames du temps jadis*: from
ca. 1880

'our rough island-story'; or, more fully, **'not once or
twice in our** rough island-story | The path of duty was the
way to glory', (Tennyson, *Ode on the Death of Wellington*,
1852): from ca. 1870.

'our withers are unwrung.' We are not moved to pity:
C. 19–20. Shakespeare, 'It touches us not: let the galled jade
wince, our withers are unwrung' (*Hamlet*, III, ii).

out and about. In the open air, and active; applied to a person
after illness or accident: colloquial: late C. 19–20. *Outside* and
about one's work or hobby.

out at elbows (?). To be ragged or obviously poor and in
poor condition: from ca. 1840. From a coat worn out at the
elbows.

*out-Herod Herod, to. To go to excess in evil or extravagance; 'to be more outrageous than the most outrageous':
mid C. 19–20. Shakespeare, 'It out-Herod's Herod. Pray you
avoid it' (*Hamlet*, III, ii). Herod in the Mystery Plays was
represented as a blustering tyrant. (O.E.D.)

out of one's depth. In an enterprise, a situation, a position,
a task, a circle, a conversation that is too difficult for one: mid
C. 19–20.

out of the blue. Unexpectedly; unlooked for: C. 20.—
Cf. **bolt from the blue.**

'out of the mouths of babes (often misquoted as **fools)
and sucklings'** (with a significant pause): C. 19–20. *Psalms*,
viii. 2; *Matthew*, xxi. 16, 'Out of the mouths of babes and
sucklings thou hast perfected praise': 'Ἐκ στόματος νηπίων καὶ

164

θηλαζόντων . . ., 'from mouth of infants [etymologically, non-speakers] and [those] sucking [at the breast]'.

*out of the wood (U.S.A.: **woods**), **(not) to be.** (Not) to be safe yet: mid C. 19–20. Mme D'Arblay, 1792, 'Mr Windham says we are not yet out of the wood, though we see the path through it' (O.E.D.).

outbreak of hostilities, the; esp., **on the . . .,** at the beginning of a war: late C. 19–20.

outstanding features; esp., **one of the . . .,** one of the prominent or conspicuous features: C. 20.

outstanding figure, an. A prominent or pre-eminent person: from ca. 1890.

*over and above. Over; in excess of, more than, besides: C. 18–20, though common as early as C. 16.

over and done with. Finished; passed; past: C. 20. 'Now that the war is over and done with, we may return to normality.'

over and over again. Many times; repeatedly: C. 19–20. Gillespie, 1637, 'Upon this string they harp over and over again' (O.E.D.).

over head and ears; esp., **over head and ears in love,** very much in love: late C. 18–20; recorded, as to the longer phrase, in 1690, as to the shorter in C. 16.

overcome by emotion. See **emotion . . .**

overwhelming force; esp., **in . . .** 'The enemy came in overwhelming force.' Mid C. 19–20.

overwhelming odds, against. Against circumstances far too difficult; esp., against an enemy or opponents numerically much superior: late C. 19–20.

own flesh and blood, to be (one's). To be one's children or parents; to be close relatives: see **flesh and blood.**

*own master, to be one's. To have the control of oneself, to the exclusion of the power of others: late C. 19–20. 'I am my own master' = 'I myself (and no other) am master of what I do'; there is no contrast with someone else's master. (O.E.D.)

own worst enemy, to be one's. To be more harmful to oneself than anyone else is: C. 20. Applied esp. to drunkards and the feckless.

P

pageant of history, the. History, regarded as a pageant; history in its decorative and illustrative aspect (cf. the idea behind Noel Coward's *Cavalcade*): late C. 19: mostly literary and educational. Augustine Birrell, in 'The Muse of History' (*Obiter Dicta*, 1884–7), declares that 'History is a pageant and not a philosophy'.

paid on the nail. See **pay on the nail.**

pains and penalties. Suffering and punishment: a legal phrase that has, in mid C. 19–20, become a cliché.—Cf. **trials and tribulations.**

pale(s) into insignificance. Become(s) insignificant, unimportant, in comparison with something else; late C. 19–20.

*palmy days, in one's (or **its**). In one's prosperous, in its flourishing, days: late C. 19–20.—Cf. Shakespeare's 'In the most high and palmy state of Rome' (*Hamlet*, I, i, 113).

palpable lie (occasionally **untruth**), **a.** An obvious or easily perceived lie: mid C. 19–20. One that can almost be felt (L., *palpare*, to touch softly).

Pandora's box. Some event, incident, action that releases ills or benefits (the latter disappearing)—generally the former:

C. 19–20 (though common in C. 17); obsolescent. From Classical mythology.

*par excellence. Pre-eminently; superior to (and to the exclusion of) all others of that name or kind: C. 19–20. 'Christians were once called Nazarenes; the Nazarene *par excellence* was Christ.' A French phrase (L., *per excellentiam*, 'by excellency') that gained much ground in England during the Restoration.

paramount importance. See **supreme importance.**

parlous state; esp., **in a . . .** (*As You Like It*, III, ii), 'in a dangerous condition', hence 'in a perilous situation': C. 19–20.

*part and parcel. 'An essential or integral portion; something essentially belonging to a larger whole' (O.E.D.): from ca. 1830; in C. 16–18, common in its legal sense. 'This being part and parcel of my subject' (1837).

parting of the ways, the; esp., **at the . . .** and **come to the . . .,** to reach a point (in one's life or in an enterprise) at which one is compelled—or at which it is advisable—to choose between two courses of action or behaviour: from ca. 1870. 'Who hath not . . . Stood doubtful at the Parting of the Ways' (J. R. Lowell, in a poem thus entitled, 1869). Lit., the point at which a road divides into two or more. (O.E.D.).

parting shot, a. An effective remark that one makes as one is departing: late C. 19–20. A folk-etymologizing of *Parthian shot*; Parthian horsemen used to 'discharge their missiles backwards while in real or pretended flight' (O.E.D.).

passing belief. Incredible: C. 19–20; obsolescent. *Passing = surpassing =* 'beyond the compass of'; a participle used as a preposition.

passing fair. Very or exceedingly beautiful: C. 19–20; obsolescent. *Passing = passingly =* 'surpassingly'; an adverb.

past and gone. 'Over and done with' (q.v.); past and out of mind: C. 19–20.—Cf. Shakespeare's 'My day's delight is past, my horse is gone' (*Venus and Adonis*, 380).

*patience of Job, the. Pre-eminent forbearance or long-suffering: C. 19–20. Fielding, 1749, 'You would provoke the patience of Job' (O.E.D.). The patriarch Job (who also typifies destitution: *as poor as Job*) bore his trials with exemplary patience. There is no such phrase in the Bible; the Book of Job does not contain the word *patience*.

pay (someone) **back**—or simply **to pay**—**in his own coin, to.** To treat him as he has treated oneself; to render tit for tat: mid C. 18–20. Lit., in the same currency or in coins of the same denomination.

pay on the nail, to. To pay immediately a sum is due or an invoice is received: C. 18–20, though common in C. 17. Origin obscure; perhaps from flipping a coin with (and from off) one's nail to a pot-boy.

*pay the piper (and call the tune), to. To pay the expenses (or the loss) incurred and—for the longer phrase—say what is to be done: mid C. 18–20. Lit., to pay the piper for his piping at a dance.

pay up and look pleasant, to. To pay cheerfully: C. 20. —Cf. **grin and bear it.**

peace be on his (or **her**) **ashes!; peace to his . . .!,** may he be at peace in his grave, for he deserves it!: mid C. 19–20. A commendation of merit.

peace in our time. Freedom from war during our lifetime: C. 20, but esp. since September, 1938.

peace that passeth all understanding, a (or **the**). A sense of peace and security: mid C. 19–20. An adaptation of 'The peace of God, which passeth all understanding' (*Philippians*, iv. 7): ἡ εἰρήνη τοῦ Θεοῦ, ἡ ὑπερέχουσα νοῦν, the undisturbedness [tranquillity] of [= given by] God, surpassing [being beyond] the reasoning faculty. A wit described the Munich agreement between Hitler and Chamberlain as 'the peace that passeth all understanding'.

peace with honour. Recorded as early as 1650, it was popularized—and virtually made a cliché—by Disraeli when, in 1878, he returned from the Congress of Berlin. (Benham).

pearls before swine. See **cast pearls** . . .

*peg to hang (something) **on, a.** An opportunity; a pretext or excuse; a theme: mid C. 19–20. 'War provides many pegs to hang articles on.'

Pelion on Ossa. See **pile** . . .

penny plain, twopence (or **tuppence**) **coloured.** Plain and unpretentious, adorned (or embellished) and vivid: from ca. 1890. In 1884, R. L. Stevenson entitled an essay *A Penny Plain and Twopence Coloured*. In reference to prints in black and white and in (those and) other colours.

perfidious Albion. Treacherous or deliberately faithless England: mid C. 19–20. A translation of *la perfide Albion*, which occurs in a poem published in 1821 though probably known a lustrum or even a decade earlier. Bossuet, ca. 1665, had spoken, in a sermon, of 'la perfide Angleterre'. (Benham.)

perform (or **do**) **yeoman service, to.** To do efficient, useful work, render good service: C. 19–20. Recorded for 1613; in 1602, Shakespeare has *yeoman's service*. 'Such as is rendered by a faithful servant of good standing' (O.E.D.).

persistent rumour, a; persistent rumours. A rumour or rumours that do not die down; constantly repeated rumours: late C. 19–20.

*persona grata. A person (or personage) acceptable to one or many: mid C. 19–20. 'Count X was *persona grata* at the Court.' From diplomatic phraseology. Lit., 'a person pleasing (to another)'.

personal affront. An affront or insult aimed at an individual: C. 20. 'Hitler regarded the boarding of the *Altmark* as a personal affront.'

personal attack. An attack, bodily or written (or spoken): late C. 19–20.—Cf. the preceding.

personal factor, the; personal factors. Human nature; the human element; human feelings, emotions, opinions: C. 20. 'Before Ruskin, the personal factor was ignored by economists.'

pet aversion, one's. See **bête noire.**

Phœnix-like (or **like the Phœnix**) **from the ashes, to rise.** To spring from the ruins or ashes of one's or its predecessor: used by Shakespeare in 1591, but not a cliché until ca. 1870. From that fabled bird the Phœnix, which, burnt, emerges from its ashes to cycles of renewed life.

pick and choose, to. To choose or select fastidiously (v. intransitive): recorded for 1665 (O.E.D.), but not a cliché until ca. 1720. A C. 18 variant was *pick and cull.*

pick of the bunch, the. The best of a group of persons, a set or batch of things: colloquial: C. 20. Rather commoner than *the best of the bunch* and the much older *the pick of the basket.*

pick up the threads, to. To resume a piece of work (e.g., a book) or an occupation after an appreciable or considerable absence: C. 20. 'After the war he will pick up the threads precisely as if there has been no interruption.' From picking up—resuming—a discourse or conversation.

picture of health, the (very). A very symbol or emblem of good health: from ca. 1880. *Punch*, 1871, 'He looks the picture of health' (O.E.D.).

pile Pelion on Ossa. To heap, excessively or outrageously, one thing upon another: late C. 18–20. Pelion, now Zagora, is a high Thessalian mountain that is the continuation of Ossa (now Kissovo). An allusion to Virgil's *ter sunt conati imponere Pelio Ossam* (Georgics, I, 281), 'thrice did they strive to set Pelion on Ossa'. Horace's variant is *Pelion imposuisse Olympo* (Odes, III, iv, 52).

*pillar of the church, a. A main or enthusiastic supporter of a particular church or (*Church*) of the Church in general: C. 19–20. There are anticipations in C. 14 (see O.E.D.) and in *Galatians*, ii. 9, 'James, Cephas [Simon], and John, who seemed to be pillars' or στύλοι; Gibbon speaks of 'the scourge of Arianism' as being also 'the pillar of the orthodox faith'.

pious fraud, a. 'A deception practised for the furtherance of what is considered a good object; esp. for the advancement of religion' (O.E.D.): mid C. 19–20. A translation of French *fraude pieuse*.

piping times of peace, the; esp., **in the . . .,** in peace-time, when people amuse themselves (with pastoral pipes instead of martial drums and fifes): late C. 18–20. An allusion to Shakespeare's 'in this weak piping time of peace' (*Richard III*, I, i, 24).

pity of it (!), the. A most regrettable, sad, shameful state of affairs!: late C. 19–20.

*place in the sun, a. 'Ma place au soleil' occurs in C. 17 (Pascal, *Pensées*), but the English phrase did not become a cliché until ca. 1880. A variant is Hitler's *Lebensraum*, 'living room', as though there were not plenty of space for him in that place to which he belongs. In 1926, Mr Anthony Eden published, in *Places in the Sun*, his thoughts on the subject in its political aspects.

*plague, to avoid like the; to shun as one would the plague. To avoid a person as though he had—a thing as if it were—the bubonic plague: late C. 19–20.

play fast and loose (with), to. To repudiate obligations that one acknowledges before and after; to be fickle, inconstant, unreliable (towards another person): common from mid C. 16; a cliché in C. 18–20.

play the devil with, to (colloquial). To make havoc with, to ruin, to cause much trouble to: C. 19–20. I.e., to act *diabolically*.

*play the game, to. To act honourably; to be 'a decent fellow': late C. 19–20. 'Men do not talk about their honour nowadays—they call it "playing the game"', *The Daily Chronicle*, May 2, 1904 (O.E.D.).

play the sedulous ape. See **sedulous ape.**

play to the gallery, to. To play a game, to talk, to demonstrate, so as to win applause (contrast **team spirit**): late C. 19–20.

play with edged tools, to. To play with danger—fool about with dangerous persons—employ dangerous means, which may injure him who uses them: late C. 18–20. Earlier, *edge-tools*, formerly knives or swords, now chisels, planes, axes, etc.

play with fire, to. To trifle with danger, 'esp. at the risk of moral disaster' (O.E.D.); esp. applied to men and women in their sentimental attachments: late C. 19–20. See, e.g., Kipling's 'His Wedded Wife' in *Plain Tales*, 1888.

plot thickens, the. The plot or action becomes more complex or intense: mid C. 19–20. Villiers, 1671, uses it literally of a dramatic plot.

plough the sands, to. To engage in fruitless labour; to make a useless or a foredoomed effort: C. 18–20; first in Greene, 1590 (O.E.D.). Benham gives it as *to plough the sands and sow the waves*; he does not mention that the original of the shorter phrase is the Latin proverbial saying, *arare litus*, which Ovid uses twice.

pluck out the heart of a (or **the**) **mystery, to.** To solve a mystery, detect a subtle crime: late C. 19–20.

plunge heavily, to. To gamble or speculate heavily: late C. 19–20.

plus ça change, plus ça reste [= remains] **la même chose.** Late C. 19–20. An adaptation of *plus . . ., plus c'est . . .*, 'the more it changes, the more it is the same thing', Alphonse Karr, in *Les Guêpes*, Jan. 1849. (Karr wrote a delightful book entitled *Voyage autour de mon jardin.*)

point-blank refusal, a. A very blunt or direct refusal: late C. 19–20.

police have the matter well in hand (and an arrest is expected at any moment), the. Journalistic: C. 20.

pomp and circumstance. Splendour of the whole and magnificence of the details: mid C. 19–20. The title of a celebrated musical composition. *Othello*, III, iii.

pomps and vanities. Worldly shows and personal vanity: from ca. 1830. In the Catechism (C. of E.), it is 'the pomps and vanity of this wicked world'.

pool our (or **your** or **their**) **resources, to.** To share, and utilize in common, the resources from all quarters; or even between two persons: C. 20. From *pool*, 'a combine'.

poor but honest (when used facetiously). Since ca. 1910. It partly owes its rise (to the rank of cliché) to a popular ballad.—Cf. Shakespeare's 'My friends were poor but honest' (*All's Well That Ends Well*, I, iii).

poor thing, but mine own,—('tis) a. A mid C. 19–20 misquotation-cliché from Shakespeare's 'An ill-favoured thing, sir, but mine own' (Touchstone concerning Audrey in *As You Like It*, v, iv.)

popular member(s) of the younger set. A C. 20 American journalistic counter.

possess one's soul in patience, to. To be patient: C. 19–20. A misapprehension of *Luke*, xxi. 19, 'In your patience possess ye your souls', i.e., win them, come into possession of them: ἐν τῇ ὑπομονῇ ὑμῶν κτήσεσθε τὰς ψυχὰς ὑμῶν, 'in your steadfast endurance, win your souls'.

possible sympathy, all or, loosely, **every.** 'He showed the widow all possible sympathy.' C. 20.

[**post haste** (adverb). With all possible speed; with the utmost expedition: C. 19–20. But if treated as one word, it is obviously not a cliché.]

postpone (often **put off**) **the evil hour, to.** To defer an unpleasant task or experience: late C. 19–20.

pound of flesh, one's; esp., **to ask** or **demand** or **exact** or **want . . .**, to ask, want, or exact one's dues (esp., in money): from ca. 1870. In allusion to Shakespeare's 'The pound of flesh which I demand of him . . . 'tis mine, and I will have it' (Shylock in *The Merchant of Venice*, IV, i, 99).

*pour oil on troubled waters, to. 'To appease strife or disturbance': mid C. 19–20. 'In allusion to the effect of oil upon the agitated surface of water' (O.E.D.).

power behind the throne, the. Applied to a person that, unobtrusively, sways the king or queen, as Rasputin did the last Czar: late C. 19–20.

*powers that be, the. Those in authority (in a specified matter): late C. 19–20. 'The powers that be are ordained of God' (*Romans*, xiii. 1).

praise to the skies, to. To praise very *highly*; to eulogize extravagantly: mid C. 19–20. (Earlier, *extol to the skies*.)

prancing steed(s). A poetical and rhetorical cliché of mid C. 18–20; now only jocular.

preconcerted arrangement, a. An arrangement made beforehand; esp., a carefully made one: late C. 19–20.

prepared to say (or **state**), **to be.** To state firmly; often little more than 'to state': public speakers': C. 20.—Cf. **venture** . . .

present (someone) **with a token of one's esteem, to.** To make somebody a presentation: late C. 19–20. This token (witness Sullivan) is as popular in the U.S.A. as in the British Empire.

*pretty kettle of fish, a (colloquial). A disagreeable state of things, a predicament, a muddle, 'a lovely mess': C. 19–20. Fielding, 1742.

prey on one's mind, to. To worry extremely, to influence deleteriously: from ca. 1880, though current eighty years earlier.

prick up one's ears, to. To become attentive (and then listen carefully): C. 19–20. From a horse on the alert.

pride of place. Ostentatious pride of position (or occasionally of rank): mid C. 19–20.—Cf. the Biblical *pride of life* (ἡ ἀλαζονεία τοῦ βίου: *superbia vitæ*).

*prime of life, the; esp., **in the** . . ., at the most vigorous period of life: mid C. 19–20. In C. 17, *the prime of age*.

primrose path (of dalliance), the. The longer phrase is a quotation from *Hamlet*, I, iii: C. 19–20; the shorter is a cliché of mid C. 19–20.

principalities and powers. Sovereigns and political officials or great men: C. 19–20. From *Titus*, iii. 1, 'Put them in mind to be subject to principalities and powers, to obey magistrates, to be ready to every good work': ἀρχαῖς καὶ ἐξουσίαις, 'to rulers and earthly powers'.

*pro bono publico. For the public good: C. 19–20: political and sociological. Much used by writers to the Press. Originally a legal phrase.

proclaim upon (or **from**) **the house-tops, to.** To make public proclamation or profession: mid C. 19–20. 'Proclaim upon the house-tops' is the R.V. reading of *Matthew*, x. 27.

progressive and enlightened policy, a. Late C. 19–20: political and journalistic.

prolonged absence; a p.a. An extended—hence simply a long—absence: C. 20.

prominent citizen, a; prominent citizens. Distinguished persons, regarded civically: from ca. 1890.

promise. See **full and hearty . . .**

'proper study of mankind is man, the.' Pope, *An Essay on Man*, Epistle II (1733): C. 19–20. A translation from the French of Pierre Charron († 1603). (Benham.)

prophet without honour (in his own country), a. A mid C. 19–20 cliché adapted from 'A prophet is not without honour, save in his own country, and in his own house' (*Matthew*, xiii. 57).

proud parents (generic or, with *the*, particular). Journalistic and domestic: late C. 19–20.

prunes and prism (incorrectly, **prisms**). Applied to a prim, affected manner of speaking: from ca. 1880; hence to superficial accomplishments: C. 20. Dickens, *Little Dorrit*, 1855–7, in Part II, ch. v.

psychological data. Facts requisite for psychological research or analysis: from ca. 1910: originally, academic; now also literary.

psychological moment. See **at the . . .**

public-school spirit, the. The spirit inculcated by public-school education and environment: from ca. 1916. Kipling, 1899 (O.E.D.).

*pukka sahib, the. A true gentleman (not merely a poor, benighted 'Nature's gentleman'): Regular Army's and ruling classes': from ca. 1910. Now often jocular or sarcastic, as in 'I found him quite a pleasant change after all the regimental hearties and terribly pukka little sahibs who seem to come here so much' (Hugh Clevely, *The Wrong Murderer*, ca. 1938).

pull one's weight, to. To do a fair share of the work; to merit one's salary or wages: from ca. 1918. Not to be a passenger: boating (or rowing) phraseology.

pull the chestnuts out of the fire, to. To do the illicit or dangerous work for someone else: late C. 19–20. Adumbrations in C. 17–18. From the fable of the monkey that used the cat's paw to pull chestnuts out of the fire.

pull the strings, to. To control affairs; to be the actual operator of what is ostentatiously or apparently done by another: from ca. 1880; originally and still mainly political. From puppetry. (O.E.D.)

pure and simple; purely and simply. Without addition, qualification, modification; mere and sheer: late C. 19–20. 'It's nonsense pure and simple.'

purple, in the; born in (or **to**) **the purple,** born in a Royal or noble (or, even, wealthy and distinguished) family; born to power: from ca. 1870.—Cf. *the purple*, 'imperial or Royal rank'.

pursuit of happiness, the. Active search for—a striving to attain—happiness: late C. 19–20.

push and go. Enterprising energy; vigorous perseverance: colloquial: C. 20. 'He has plenty of push and go.'

put a good face (up)on, to. 'To make (a matter) look well; to assume or maintain a bold bearing (with regard to)': from ca. 1880. (O.E.D.)

put a spoke in someone's wheel, to. To circumvent, thwart, or hinder him (or it): C. 17–18, but not a cliché before C. 19. 'Capitalists . . . were trying to put a spoke in the wheel of Socialism', *The Manchester Examiner*, 1885 (O.E.D.). *Spoke* = a bar.

*****put all one's eggs in one basket, to.** To risk all one's money (and property) in a single venture; to trust to one source or means: late C. 19–20.

put back the clock, to. To put back the hand of time: C. 20. 'There is no putting back the clock: life and events are inexorable.'

put down one's foot, to; generally **put one's foot down, to.** To take a firm stand with regard to another's or other people's behaviour, policy, actions: from ca. 1890.

put (a person) **in good heart, to** (?). To succeed in encouraging him or cheering him up: late C. 19–20.

put off. See **postpone** . . .

put on one's thinking (or **considering**) **cap, to.** To take time to consider a matter: C. 20.

put one's best foot forward, to. To do one's utmost to succeed: mid C. 19–20. Variants were current in late C. 16–18.

put (or **set**) **one's hand to the plough, to.** To undertake something difficult or long to do: C. 18–20. In C. 16–17, mainly in allusion to *Luke*, ix. 62, 'No man, having put his hand to the plough, and looking back, is fit for the kingdom of God': ἐπιβαλὼν τὴν χεῖρα αὐτοῦ ἐπ' ἄροτρον.—Cf. the next entry but one.

put one's pride in one's pocket, to. To suppress one's pride; to ignore an insult or a humiliation: from ca. 1890.

put (occasionally **set**) **one's shoulder to the wheel, to.** To go, set oneself, vigorously to work: mid C. 18–20. From assisting a wheeled vehicle to proceed.

put pen to paper, to. To begin to write (esp., a letter, an article): from ca. 1880; slightly obsolescent.

put the cart before the horse, to. See **cart** . . .

put through the mill, to. To compel a person to learn by experience: from ca. 1840. From grain that is milled.

put too fine a point on it, to. See **not to put** . . .

put words into the mouth of (or **into someone's mouth**), **to.** To tell or suggest to him what he is to say: C. 19–20.—Cf. 2 *Samuel*, xiv. 3, 'So Joab put the words in her mouth'.

Pyrrhic victory, a. A victory as disastrous to the victors as to the vanquished: late C. 19–20. King Pyrrhus, victorious at Asculum, 269 B.C., 'Another such victory and we are lost'; Herodotus records, as a proverbial saying, Καδμεία νίκη 'a Cadmæan victory'. (Benham.)

Q

Q.E.D. (in non-geometrical contexts). Lit., 'which had to be proved' (*quod erat demonstrandum*, in Euclidean geometry); freely, 'there's your problem solved!': C. 20.

'quality of mercy is not strained, the.' One must not be niggardly in clemency or kindliness: C. 19–20. Shakespeare, *The Merchant of Venice*, IV, i.

quarrel with one's bread and butter, to. To speak ill of one's livelihood: common from ca. 1730; in C. 19–20, a cliché.

queer fish, a (colloquial). A strange, odd, or mysterious fellow: C. 19–20.

queer the pitch, to (colloquial). To spoil things: late C. 19–20. From one cheapjack spoiling another's market; *pitch* is here a cheapjack's or costermonger's stand.

'quem deus vult perdere, prius dementat.' Whom the god wishes to destroy, he first makes mad: C. 19–20.

'quis custodiet ipsos custodes?' Who will watch over the wardens themselves? or who will supervise the super-visers?: mid C. 19–20. From Juvenal, *Satires*, VI, 347–8.

quite frankly I should (or **shouldn't**) . . . An introductory formula: late C. 19–20. Almost = 'you ought to . . .'

quite providential; esp., **it is** (or **was**) . . . It is very lucky; it's an extremely lucky chance: late C. 19–20.

*****quite the opposite** (incipient) and **quite the reverse** (fully qualified; incipiently **very much the reverse**). The opposite; the reverse: C. 20.

'quorum pars magna fui.' Lit., 'of which events I was an important part'; hence, 'in which events I was a principal participator': mid C. 19–20. Virgil, *Æneid*, II, 6. Neatly varied in the Preface to G. V. Carey's *Mind the Stop*, 1939.

'quoth the raven, ("Nevermore").' From Edgar Allan Poe's *The Raven*, 1845: a literary cliché since ca. 1880.

R

Rabelaisian humour. A mid C. 19–20 literary cliché, often used by book-reviewers who have not read their Rabelais. A coarse, extravagant humour and wit.

race is to the swift, the. An adaptation (mid C. 19–20) of 'The race is not to the swift, nor the battle to the strong' (*Ecclesiastes*, ix. 11).

*rack and ruin; esp., **to go to r. and r.,** (of a building, a farm, etc.) to fall into ruinous disrepair or neglect: late C. 18–20, though recorded so early as 1599 (O.E.D.). *Rack = wrack* or *wreck.*

rack one's brains (or **memory**), **to.** See **cudgel . . .**

radiantly happy. So happy that one's face glows; loosely, very happy: from ca. 1910. 'The bride was radiantly happy.'

rags and tatters, in. In tattered clothing: C. 19–20. From early C. 17.

*rain cats and dogs, to. 'It was raining cats and dogs, so I didn't go out.' Recorded for 1738 (O.E.D.); cliché in mid C. 19–20.

rain (or **heavy rain**) **interrupted the festivities.** American journalists': late C. 19–20. (Sullivan.)

rain or shine. Lit., whether it rains or shines, i.e., **no** matter what the weather: mid C. 19–20.—Fig., no matter what happens; in any case: C. 20. 'I'll be there, rain or shine.'

rake's progress, the. A rake's progressive—i.e., onward— course in dissipation (and evil); his downward path: mid C. 18–20. William Hogarth's famous series of oil-paintings so entitled (cf. his 'The Harlot's Progress') appeared ca. 1724.

rank and file, the. Ordinary people, without high rank or good position or wealth: from ca. 1880. E.g., the rank and file of a political party. From the military sense of the phrase: privates and corporals.

rank treason. Gross treason; utter treason: mid C. 18–20. Recorded for 1766 (O.E.D.). **Rank heresy** is (C. 18–20) on the border-line.

rap on the knuckles, a (figurative) (?). A reprimand: C. 20.

rapid stream of time, the (?). The swift passage of time: C. 20

rara avis and its translation, **a rare bird** ('You're a rare bird, these days'): respectively C. 18–20 (obsolescent) and C. 19–20. The original is Juvenal's *rara avis in terris, nigroque simillima cygno*, Satire VI, 165, ('a rare bird upon the earth, and exceedingly like a black swan', Benham).—Cf. *white blackbird*.

rash act, a. A hasty (and foolish) act; a reckless act: C. 19–20.

rattling good yarn, a. A most readable story, adventurous or packed with incident: from ca. 1870. Not disguised propaganda nor psychological study.

ravening wolves (?). Persons as greedy and cruel as wolves: C. 19–20. In allusion to *Matthew*, vii. 15, 'False prophets . . . inwardly . . . ravening wolves': λύκοι ἅρπαγες, 'greedy wolves'.

raze to the ground, to. To destroy (towns or buildings) completely: mid C. 19–20. Gibbon, 1781, 'The fortifications were razed to the ground' (O.E.D.).

read between the lines, to. To discern a hidden meaning in words or writings; to discover a meaning or purpose not explicit, not obvious: from ca. 1880.

'read, mark, learn, and inwardly digest.' Read carefully and, having learnt it, assimilate it: C. 19–20. *The Book of Common Prayer*, Collect for the 2nd Sunday in Advent.

read the riot act, to (?). To put (a person or persons) to order; to declare that a certain course of action or conduct must cease: from ca. 1925. The Riot Act was made law ca. 1720.

ready for the fray. See **eager for the fray**.

ready response, a. A prompt response: late C. 19: mostly journalistic. 'The appeal for funds met with a ready response.'

ready to drop in one's tracks. 'He was exhausted—ready to drop in his tracks.' Late C. 19–20. From hunted animals.

*really and truly. Very; indeed; certainly or positively; (*really and truly!*) yes, it's true!: colloquial: from ca. 1880. 'Really and truly, he was sorry for what he had done.'

receive every consideration, to. To be solicitously treated: C. 20.

record for all time, a. A lasting—a permanent—record: from ca. 1880.—Cf. Young's *Night Thoughts*, 'In records that defy the tooth of time'.

red-letter day, a. An important or memorable, fortunate or prosperous, or very happy day: C. 19–20. From the ecclesiastical sense (a saint's day).

*red rag to a bull, a. 'Communism to him was like a red rag to a bull': it infuriated him, as a red rag does a bull: late C. 19–20.

red ruin. Destruction by fire and massacre: from ca. 1870; slightly obsolescent. Tennyson, 'Guinevere' (420–21) in *Idylls of the King*, 'The children born of thee are sword and fire, | Red ruin, and the breaking up of laws'.

reduced to a skeleton. (Much) emaciated: C. 20.—Cf. that battered simile, *as thin as a rake*.

refined irony. Subtle and/or delicate irony: from ca. 1880.

regrettable affair (or **incident**), **a**; esp., **a most . . .,** an unfortunate incident: late C. 19–20.

reliable source, a; esp., **from . . .,** authoritative, dependable, accurate: C. 20. 'The information does not, I fear, come from a reliable source.'

reply in the affirmative (or **the negative**), **to; the answer is in . . .** To reply Yes (or No); the answer is Yes (or No): from ca. 1880. Before that, *answer* . . . was the usual form.

*representations are (or were) being made, or were made. A protest or expostulation is (or was) made (or being made); the case is being formally put: a diplomatic formula (late C. 17–mid 19) that is, in C. 20, a political and journalistic cliché.

resist to the death, to. To resist even unto death, death being no deterrent: C. 20.

resplendent uniform, a. A bright and splendid uniform: from ca. 1880; slightly obsolescent.

rest in peace, to. To rest quietly, undisturbed: jocular: late C. 19–20. From the *R.I.P.* (*requiescat in pace*, may he rest in peace!) of tombstones.

'rest is silence, (and) the.' Mid C. 19–20. Shakespeare, *Hamlet*, v, ii.

rest (up)on one's laurels, to. To be content with one's success; to be no longer actively ambitious: from ca. 1870. With reference to an athletic victor's prize-laurels.

resume one's customary avocations, to. To return to one's usual occupation or employment: from ca. 1880; slightly obsolescent.

retort courteous, the. A courteous retort or reply: C. 19–20. In allusion to *As You Like It*, v, iv, 'The retort courteous . . . the lie direct' (six types of retort).

return to one's vomit, to. To backslide into one's evil and disgusting ways; to relapse into sin: C. 18–20; now literary. 2 *Peter*, ii. 22, 'But it is happened unto them according to the true proverb, The dog is turned to his own vomit again; and the sow that was washed to her wallowing in the mire'.

return to the charge, to (figuratively). To try again, make another attempt; to reopen a subject, renew a complaint: late C. 19–20.

return to the fold, to. 'The sinner, repenting, returned to the fold.' Applied to a spiritual or intellectual estray: C. 19–20. Perhaps in allusion to *John*, x.

revenons à nos moutons! Let us return to our sheep, i.e., to the subject in hand: C. 19–20. (The facetious *let us return to our muttons* is itself almost a cliché of mid C. 19–20.) From the return-to-earth (and their duties) of amorous shepherds and shepherdesses in French pastoral poetry of C. 17–18.

*rich beyond the dreams of avarice. Immensely rich; a multi-millionaire; also, ecstatically happy [in context of felicity]: C. 19–20. Edward Moore, 'I am rich beyond the dreams of avarice' (*The Gamester*, produced in 1753: II, ii); Dr. Johnson, 1781, 'The potentiality of growing rich beyond the dreams of avarice'. (Benham.)

rich in . . . See **this world's goods.**

ride rough-shod over, to. To tyrannize over; to treat without consideration: mid C. 19–20. From horses with shoes that have projecting nail-heads. (O.E.D.)

rift within the lute, a. A hint of quarrels or trouble to come; a mark or sign of incompatibility: from ca. 1880. An adaptation of Tennyson's 'It is the little rift within the lute, | That by and by will . . . slowly silence all', 'Merlin and Vivien' (1869), lines 388–90, in *Idylls of the King*.

right and proper. Correct and seemly, in moral or behaviouristic context; often *very right and proper*: late C. 19–20.

right royal; esp., **to have a right royal time,** a splendid or thoroughly enjoyable time: colloquial: late C. 19–20

right side. See **on the right side.**

'rigour of the game, the.' Applied, since ca. 1830, to a game played fairly but in strict accordance with the rules. From Lamb's 'Mrs Battle's Opinions on Whist', in *Essays of Elia*, 1820–22. 'Next to her devotions', she 'loved a good game of whist'. Bridge-players will note that she *loved* the game.

ring down the curtain, to. To close the proceedings; to write *finis*: late C. 19–20. 'To direct (a theatre-curtain) to be . . . let *down* by making a bell ring' (O.E.D.).—Cf. **world's a stage.**

riotous living. Extravagant and dissolute, very gay living: C. 19–20. Recorded by the O.E.D. for 1389. Often **waste one's substance with riotous living,** as in *Luke*, xv. 13.

rise as one man, to. To stand up simultaneously, as if the crowd were one man: late C. 19–20.

rise Phœnix-like. See **Phœnix-like.**

rise with the lark, to. To rise with the sun; to rise early: C. 19–20. Lyly, 1580, 'Go to bed with the lamb, and rise with the lark' (O.E.D.).

risk life and limb, to. To risk death or the loss (or serious injury) of a limb: from ca. 1840 (*life and limb* current since C. 17).

road to perdition (or **ruin**), **the.** The path of folly and sin: mid C. 19–20; late C. 19–20. An English proverb runs, 'The road to ruin is in good repair; the travellers pay the expense of it'.

roar a welcome, to. 'The milling crowd roared a welcome to Roosevelt.' A C. 20 American cliché, esp. among journalists. (Sullivan.) And why, by the way, are there always '*milling* crowds' in the U.S.A. of C. 20?

*roast beef of old England, the. English roast beef; beef as an English national dish: C. 19–20. Fielding, in *The Roast Beef of Old England*, ca. 1740, cries, 'Oh! the roast beef of Old England! | And oh! the old English roast beef!' (Benham).

*rob Peter to pay Paul, to. To take from one person in order to pay another; to incur a debt in order to pay an earlier debt: from ca. 1400: a cliché in C. 18–20. Origin dubious.

rod in pickle, a; esp., **to have a . . .,** to intend to, be ready to, punish someone: late C. 18–20. From rods kept in lye, which preserves their chastising virtue.

*Roland for an Oliver, a. A fair exchange; an equal reciprocation; 'as good as one gets'; tit for tat: late C. 18–20. Two celebrated knights (*primi inter pares*) in *La Chanson de Roland* and other medieval romances.

rolling wave, the. The sea; the ocean. 'Life on the rolling wave.' Mid C. 19–20; obsolescent.

Roman virtue. Stern Roman courage and fortitude (*virtus Romana*): literary: C. 19–20; obsolescent.

root and branch (adverb), thoroughly, utterly; esp., **destroy** something **root and branch,** to destroy it utterly, with the connotation of not only destroying the thing itself but also of preventing or counteracting its evil effects: the shorter, late C. 17–20; the longer, mid C. 19–20. In allusion to *Malachi*, iv. 1.

*root of all evil, the. Money: mid C. 19–20. Based on a misapprehension of 1 *Timothy*, vi. 10, 'The love of money is the root of all evil', where the stress is on *love*.

root of the matter, the. The quintessence or the most important part or aspect: mid C. 19–20. Originally in allusion to *Job*, xix. 28, 'Seeing the root of the matter is found in me'.

'rooted in dishonour'; or in full, **'his honour rooted in dishonour stood'** (And faith unfaithful kept him falsely true): from ca. 1880. Tennyson, 'Lancelot and Elaine' (*vv.* 871–2), published in 1869 in *Idylls of the King.*

*rose between two thorns, a. A proverbial saying, but so hackneyed in C. 19–20 as to be a cliché during that period.

'roses and raptures (of vice), the.' From ca. 1870.—See **lilies and languors.**

rotten to the core. Utterly corrupt, morally, politically, socially, or personally: C. 19–20. 'He is rotten at the core, and his soul is dishonest', 1718 (O.E.D.). From rotten fruit.

rough and ready. (Of things) only just good enough: mid C. 19–20.—(Of way, manner, method, etc.) effective though unskilful or inelegant: from ca. 1870.

rough and tumble, a (?). A scuffle; a disorderly set-to: from ca. 1890.

*rough diamond, a. An uncouth person (usually, male) with much ability and/or **a heart of gold**: from ca. 1890. Cf. Dryden's famous description of polished Chaucer as 'a rough diamond'!

rough idea, a. 'He asked me to give him a rough idea of what I wanted.' Here, *rough* = 'approximate', 'fairly accurate (though not detailed)', 'adequate—not final'. Late C. 19–20.

round dozen, a. A full dozen; neither more nor less than a dozen, an exact dozen: C. 18–20; recorded for ca. 1572 (O.E.D.).—Cf. **in round numbers.**

round oath, a. A downright oath; an oath not toned down; a hearty oath: from ca. 1840. Dickens, 1843, 'To swear a few round oaths' (O.E.D.).

rousing cheers. Loud, hearty, stirring cheers: C. 20.

royal road to success, the. The highway—the *best* road (hence, way)—to success; the *smooth*, hence easy, way or method: late C. 19–20.

rub (a person) **the wrong way, to.** To irritate, annoy, or offend him: from the 1880's. From rubbing a cat's hair the wrong way.

*ruin stared him in the face (actual cliché); **he was faced with ruin** (potential). His ruin was obvious to him, and imminent: respectively from ca. 1820 and from ca. 1890.

rule the roost, to (?). To be, rather ostentatiously, obviously, or arrogantly, the dominant person, the person in effective charge: colloquial: C. 20. From the farmyard.

ruling precedent, a. A precedent that constitutes a rule; a precedent that determines a rule; an important and accepted precedent: late C. 19–20.

rumour hath it (that . . .). It is rumoured that . . .: late C. 19–20; slightly obsolescent.

run amuck, to (figurative). To act with extreme folly or recklessness; to act wildly, very extravagantly: from ca. 1880. From Malay *amoq*, 'indiscriminately murderous'.

run one's head against a stone wall, to. To ignore facts, essay the obviously impossible, oppose fate or predominant circumstance: C. 20.

run to earth, to. To catch or find (something) after a long search: from ca. 1880. From chasing a fox to its earth.

run to seed, to. To become slack physically or mentally; to deteriorate or degenerate: late C. 19–20. From farming or gardening.

*run with the hare and hunt with the hounds, to. To associate oneself with both parties to a war, a quarrel or a contract: a proverbial saying (C. 15 onwards), which in late C. 19–20 is fairly to be classified as a cliché.

runs in the blood, (generally) **it.** It is hereditary in the family or, less often, characteristic of the nation specified: mid C. 18–20. 'Cruelty runs in the Tartar blood.'

rus in urbe. Country in town; a rural effect within a city; a garden suburb: mid C. 18–20. Martial, *Epigrams*, XII, lvii, 12: but no longer apprehended as a quotation—except by Classical scholars.

Russian Bear, the. Russia or the Soviet; the Russian nation personified: journalistic: late C. 19–20. The Russian bear is one of the three or four chief kinds of bear.

S

sackcloth and ashes; esp., **in sackcloth and ashes,** abjectly penitent or, now only occasionally, grief-stricken: late C. 18–20. Biblically, clothes of sackcloth and ashes sprinkled on the head conventionally and ritualistically betokened penitence or lamentation: as, e.g., in *Matthew*, xi. 21, 'They would have repented long ago in sackcloth and ashes': πάλαι ἂν ἐν σάκκῳ καὶ σποδῷ μετενόησαν 'they would long ago have changed the inner man—the soul—in sacking and ashes'.

sacred edifice, a or **the.** A (or the) church: C. 19–20. John Gloag crystallizes its 'clichéness' in his distinguished novel, *Sacred Edifice*, 1937.

*'sadder and a wiser man, a.' Mid C. 19–20. Coleridge, *The Rime of the Ancient Mariner*, 1797, Part 7.

sadly at fault, to be (esp., **to have been**), much at fault; very much in the wrong: late C. 19–20.

sæva indignatio. A severe and fierce indignation, befitting a satirist: literary: C. 19–20. Often applied to Juvenal and Dryden.

*safe and sound. Safe: from ca. 1870. Properly, safe and uninjured.

[**safety first.** In the corner formed where three provinces meet: those of official formulas, catch-phrases, and clichés. It is rapidly becoming predominantly the third.]

sail near the wind, to. To keep only just inside the law; to be almost **beyond the pale**; to do shady things that aren't illegal: from ca. 1880. Nautical.

sail the seven seas, to. See **seven seas**.

sailor's yarn, a. An improbable or exaggerated story: late C. 19–20.—Cf. the almost obsolete *a traveller's tale*.

salad days; esp., in one's. In one's youth; inexperienced and very, very *green*: 1606, Shakespeare, *Antony and Cleopatra*, 'My salad days, | When I was green in judgement'; but it did not become a cliché until ca. 1840 or 1850.

*salt of the earth, the. Mid C. 19–20. 'In recent trivial use', says the O.E.D. in 1914, 'the powerful, the aristocratic, the wealthy'; but, from 1920 at latest, the prevailing sense, surely, has been that of 'the staunch and true, the essentially good, generous, humane and kindly'. In *Matthew*, v. 12–13, Christ, addressing those persecuted and/or reviled because of their loyalty to His cause, says, 'Rejoice, and be exceeding glad: for great is your reward in heaven . . . Ye are the salt of the earth': ὑμεῖς ἐστε τὸ ἅλας τῆς γῆς: that which gives life its savour and preserves civilization.

sanctity of the home, the. The inviolability of the home ('an Englishman's home is his castle'): C. 20. D. C. Murray, 1888, 'We have grown quite accustomed nowadays to the invasion of what used to be called the sanctity of private life' (O.E.D.).

sanctum sanctorum. A person's study or 'den', where he is—or should be—free from intrusion: from ca. 1880: journalistic. Lit., holy of holies.

[**sans cérémonie** (without ceremoniousness or ceremony)
and **sans gêne** (free-and-easy; casual): not quite clichés. But
guard against them!]

saunter to and fro, to. To stroll about carelessly or idly:
mid C. 19–20.

save (another's, or one's own) **good name, to.** To preserve one's or another's honour or credit: mid C. 19–20.

saving for a rainy day. Putting money by against old age,
illness, unemployment, crisis: mid C. 19–20. An old proverb
runs, *keep some till more come*.

saving grace, a or **one's.** A redeeming quality or feature:
late C. 19–20. From the theological grace that delivers a
person from sin and/or hell-fire.

*say 'boh!' to a goose, not to. 'That quiet fellow wouldn't
say "Boh" to a goose,' is too timid to open his mouth. A
proverbial saying (recorded, in Apperson, for 1588): from
ca. 1880, a cliché.

say nay, to; esp., **there is no one to say** or **who dares to
say** (e.g., him) **nay,** to deny, withstand, forbid or prohibit
(him): from ca. 1870.

say the least. See **to say the least . . .**

scales of Justice, the. Justice with its scales that weigh the
good and the ill; Justice: C. 19–20.

scantily attired (or **clad**). Wearing few clothes (and those,
rather less than opaque): mid C. 19–20; late C. 19–20.
Dickens, 1840, has the former.

Scarlet Woman, the. The Church of Rome: pejorative-
religious (*odium theologicum* . . .), much commoner among
Nonconformists than among Church of Englanders: from
ca. 1870 (Southey, 1816). Of *Scarlet Lady, Whore, Woman,*
only the third has survived; cf. Joseph Hocking's anti-

Roman novel, *The Scarlet Woman*, 1899, and his return-to-the-charge, *The Woman of Babylon*, 1906. See *Revelation*, xvii. 1 ('the great whore'), 4 ('the woman . . . arrayed in purple and scarlet colour'), 5 ('Babylon the Great, the Mother of Harlots').

scathing sarcasm; scathingly sarcastic. Withering, or sharp and damaging, sarcasm; cuttingly or searingly sarcastic: late C. 19–20.

scotch—not kill—a snake, to. To render only temporarily harmless something that is, or is regarded as, dangerous: C. 19–20. From Theobald's proposed emendation, 'We have scotch'd the snake, not kill'd it': *Macbeth*, III, ii, 13.

scrap of paper, a; esp., **a mere scrap . . .** A political pact: from mid August 1914. Used by von Bethmann-Hollweg, the German Chancellor: noted by Sir Edward Goschen, to whom it was said, in his ambassadorial despatch, Aug. 4, 1914, from Berlin.

screw one's courage to the sticking-point, to (obsolescent); **to screw up one's courage.** To intensify one's courage to achieve a particular purpose: C. 19–20; late C. 19–20. The longer phrase is a misquotation (and adaptation) of Shakespeare's 'Screw your courage to the sticking place, | And we'll not fail' (*Macbeth*, I, vii, 60–1).

sculptured. See **living rock**.

*Scylla and Charybdis; e.g., **between S. and C.** 'Used allusively . . . of the danger of running into one evil or peril in seeking to avoid its opposite' (O.E.D.): late C. 17–20. Charybdis, dangerous Sicilian whirlpool, stands over against Scylla, Italian rock. *Incidis in Scyllam cupiens vitare Charybdim* (Walter de Lille, *Alexandreis*, Bk V, 301: Benham).

sea-change, a; esp., **to suffer a sea-change.** To be almost miraculously and certainly much changed for the

better: mid C. 19–20. 'Full fathom five thy father lies. . . .
Nothing of him that doth fade | But doth suffer a sea change |
into something rich and strange' (Shakespeare, *The Tempest*,
I, ii).

seamy side of life, the. The worst—the most degraded—
side or aspect of life: from ca. 1870 (Carlyle, 1865). In
allusion to *Othello*, IV, ii, 146–8. From the under sides of
garments.

seasonable weather. Weather suitable to the time of year
(and often to nothing else); such weather as you would
expect: from C. 15, but not, I believe, a cliché before C. 19.
To tell a man shivering with cold and a fever that 'it's nice
seasonable weather' is an incitement to murder: such crass
remarks should be made an indictable offence.

second to none. Inferior to none: adumbrated by Chaucer,
used by Shakespeare (*A Comedy of Errors*, v, i, 7–8), cliché'd
since ca. 1860.

sedulous ape; esp., **to play the sedulous ape.** To
imitate closely: late C. 19–20. Stevenson, ca. 1880, 'I have
played the sedulous ape to Hazlitt, to Lamb, to . . .'

see eye to eye; esp., **not to see eye to eye (with** a
person), to differ in opinion, not to think alike: from ca. 1870.
A misapprehension of *Isaiah*, lii. 8, 'Thy watchmen . . .
together will they sing: for they shall see eye to eye [*oculo ad
oculum videbunt*, Vulgate], when the Lord shall bring again
Zion'.

*see how (or **which way**) **the cat jumps, to.** To see—
to ascertain—which way things will go: from ca. 1830. Scott,
Journal, Oct. 7, 1826 (Apperson).

see how the land lies, to; to spy out the land (figurative). To make preliminary investigations for a project; to
discover what a place is like: mid C. 19–20. The latter from
Numbers, xiii. 16.

see it through, to (colloquial). To go through with it to the end; to finish or complete something: late C. 19–20.

see no further than one's nose, to. To be mentally and/or morally (very) short-sighted; to have no vision: mid C. 19–20.

see red, to. To become extremely angry; to lose one's self-control, so angry has one become: from ca. 1915. *Red*, the colour of blood, fire, violence.

see the finger of God in (something), **to.** To see the working or interposition of God in an accident, a piece of good fortune, etc.: C. 18–20. 'The finger of God is used to mean his power, his working. Pharaoh's magicians discovered the finger of God in the miracles which Moses wrought (*Exodus*, viii. 19). This legislator gave the law written with the finger of God to the Hebrews, *Exodus*, xxxi. 18' (Irwin's recension of *Cruden's Concordance*); cf. *Luke*, xi. 20.

*see the wood for the trees, not to be able to. To be unable, because of the multitude of details, to obtain a general or comprehensive view: from C. 16; in C. 20, if not in C. 19–20, a cliché.

see which way the cat jumps, to. See **see how the cat . . .**

see with half an eye, to (?). To see effortlessly or at a glance: implied in 1579, but a cliché only in C. 19–20. (O.E.D.)

see with one's own eyes, to. To see; to see for oneself: late C. 18–20. Current since ca. 1700.

seek one's virtuous couch, to. To go to bed alone; occ., with one's wife (cf. the cynical French saying, *faute de mieux, on couche avec sa femme*): jocular: from ca. 1880.

seething masses of humanity. Agitated multitudes; vast crowds; vast populations: C. 20.

select few, the. Connoisseurs; experts; the very discerning: late C. 19–20.

*sell like hot cakes, to. To be sold very quickly: U.S.A., late C. 19–20; British Empire, C. 20.

sell one's soul, to. To sacrifice one's conscience for money, rank, fame: late C. 19–20. From *to sell one's soul to the Devil*.

sell the pass, to. To give valuable information to the enemy; to betray one's cause or country: mid C. 19–20; obsolescent. Originally an Irishism, with the connotation of giving information to the authorities.

send about ... See **business.**

*send to Coventry, to; esp., **to be sent to Coventry,** to be cold-shouldered by one's fellows: dating from the Civil War (English), when it was equivalent to *to Stellenbosch*, it became a cliché in C. 18 (see my annotated edition of Grose's *Vulgar Tongue*).

separate. See **grain.**

sere and yellow leaf, the. Old age; **in the ...,** old and withered (person): mid C. 19–20. A misquotation of 'My way of life | Is fall'n into the sear [or sere], the yellow leaf', *Macbeth*, v, iii, 25–6.

sermons in stones. C. 19–20. No longer apprehended as a quotation from Shakespeare, 'Finds tongues in trees, books in the running brooks, | Sermons in stones, and good in everything' (*As You Like It*, II, i).

serve (or **wait on**) **hand and foot, to.** To wait upon, attend to, assiduously: mid C. 19–20; late C. 19–20.

serve one's turn, to. To answer one's purpose (adequately, with a connotation of slight imperfection): mid C. 18–20. Current since ca. 1530.

set by the ears, to. To cause (persons) to quarrel or to be friends no longer; late C. 18–20. From causing dogs to fight.

set one's face against, to. To be determinedly hostile towards; to take up such an attitude towards: 1611, *Leviticus*, xx. 3, 'I will set my face against that man'; cliché in C. 19–20.

set one's hand to the plough. See **put . . .**

set one's heart on, to. To long, to determine, to have or achieve (a thing, an aim or ambition): recorded for C. 14; cliché in C. 18–20. 'He set his heart on a knighthood.'

set one's house in order, to. To put one's affairs in good order; to arrange one's affairs so that they are no longer in confusion or danger: late C. 19–20.

set one's teeth, to (?). To become grimly determined, to oppose foes, overcome opposition, face danger: 1672, Dryden (O.E.D.); cliché in C. 19–20.

set (a person's) **teeth on edge, to.** To cause one an unpleasant feeling (of repulsion or, generally, distaste); to make an unpleasant impression on a person: C. 18–20. Cf. Shakespeare, 1 *Henry IV*, III, i, 133–4 ('mincing poetry'); and *Jeremiah*, xxxi. 29 and *Ezekiel*, xviii. 2.

*set the Thames on fire, to. 'To make a brilliant reputation' (O.E.D.): generally in the negative: mid C. 19–20. In German it is the Spree.

set to with a will, to; to work with a will. To eat or engage in some work vigorously and willingly: late C. 19–20.

seven-leagued boots. Allusively applied to great speed or enormous size: from ca. 1820. From the fairy tale of Hop o' my Thumb. French *bottes de sept lieues*. (O.E.D.)

seven seas, the; esp., **to sail the seven seas,** to sail all over the world: from ca. 1890. Kipling's *The Seven Seas* appeared in 1896. The seven seas are the Arctic and Antarctic, the North and South Atlantic, the North and South Pacific, the Indian Oceans.

seventh heaven of delight, (in) the. (In) a state of ecstasy, keen delight or happiness: mid C. 19–20. From the later-Jewish and, derivatively, the Moslem highest heaven or *seventh heaven* (or *heaven of heavens*), the abode of Jahveh, or Allah, and the most exalted angels (O.E.D.).

shadow and the dust, the. This C. 19–20 literary cliché, now obsolescent, is a translation of the Latin *pulvis et umbra* (*sumus*: Horace, *Odes*, IV, vii, 16).

shadow of death, the. See **valley of the shadow . . .**

shadow of one's (former) self, to be but the. To have become feeble and/or emaciated; to have lost one's intellectual vigour and distinction, or one's position or fame (cf. the near-cliché, *the shadow of a name*, from Latin *nominis umbra*): mid C. 19–20.

shake in one's shoes, to. To tremble with fear (or extreme nervousness): from ca. 1860.

*shake (off) the dust from (originally **of**) **one's feet, to.** To depart from an uncongenial place, with a connotation of finality and determination: late C. 18–20. Originally in allusion to *Matthew*, x. 14 (cf. *Mark*, vi. 11 and *Luke*, ix. 5), Jesus to the twelve disciples, 'And whosoever shall not receive you, nor hear your words, when ye depart out of that house or city, shake off the dust of your feet': ἐκτινάξατε τὸν κονιορτὸν τῶν ποδῶν ὑμῶν: *excutite pulverem de pedibus vestris* (which has determined the modern form of the phrase).

shaken to its (or their) foundations. Tottering: mid C. 19–20.

shape of things to come, the; also **things to come.** The foreshadowed form of future events; the future: as a cliché, since ca. 1935. H. G. Wells's *The Shape of Things to Come* appeared in 1933; the film-story, *Things to Come*, in 1935. With the shorter, cf. Shakespeare's 'giant mass of things to come' (*Troilus and Cressida*, I, iii, 345–6); with the longer, the prophetic scenes in *Macbeth*.

shape or form; esp., in any . . . ('He cannot eat crustaceans in any shape or form.') The longer phrase = 'of any kind; in any manner; at all': late C. 19–20. The doubling of the sense arises from the Biblical use of *shape* for the more usual *form* (L. *forma*, Gr. μοϱφή): see O.E.D.

share and share alike, to. To share equally: late C. 19–20. Macaulay, 1841, 'In Kent the sons share and share alike' (O.E.D.).

shattering effect, a; with (a) shattering effect, destructively; stupefyingly or astoundingly effective or effectual: C. 20.

*she is (or was) no chicken; esp., she's . . . She is no longer young: C. 19–20. Swift, 1720, 'Your hints that Stella is no chicken' (O.E.D.).

shed light. See light on . . .

sheer physical exhaustion; sheer physical inability. Utter exhaustion; powerlessness, excessive weakness: respectively late C. 19–20 and from ca. 1915.

shining armour. Resplendent armour: C. 19–20. Bellenden, 1533, 'vi knichtis in schynyng armoure' (O.E.D.).

ship of state, the; often, to steer . . ., to guide the State, to control it: late C. 19–20. The shorter phrase occurs in the 1675 translation of Macchiavelli's *The Prince*.

*ships that pass in the night. Persons that meet and pass on, never (or unlikely) to meet again: from ca. 1880. Longfellow, *Tales of a Wayside Inn*, 1863, Part III, 'Theologian's Second Tale', Canto iv. (Benham.)

shipshape and Bristol fashion. Seamanlike; orderly, trim, tidy: mid C. 19–20; slightly obsolescent.

shoot one's bolt, to; esp., to have shot . . ., to have done all that one is able to do; to be intellectually or creatively exhausted: mid C. 19–20. From the proverb, *a fool's bolt is soon shot*.

short and sweet. Brief but pleasant (or lively): late C. 19–20. A proverbial saying, which dates from C. 16; but it has become a cliché (e.g., in Hugh de Sélincourt's *The Saturday Match*, 1937, of a very short, spirited innings). *Short and sweet like a donkey's gallop* is a Lancashire proverbial elaboration.

*short life and a merry one, a. A brief but joyous (or adventurous) life: mid C. 19–20.

shoulder the burden, to. To take up the figurative burden, to undertake and/or discharge a duty, a task, a debt: late C. 19–20.

show a bold front, to. To appear undismayed or un-afraid: mid C. 19–20.

show a clean pair of heels, to. To flee (and escape): from C. 16, but a cliché only in C. 19–20.

show one's hand, to. See **lay one's cards on the table.**

show one's teeth, to (figurative). To show malice or hos-tility; to behave threateningly: mid C. 19–20. From dogs about to bite.

show the cloven hoof, to. See **cloven hoof.**

*show the white feather, to. To show signs of cowardice: from ca. 1830. 'A white feather in a game-bird's tail is a mark of inferior breeding' (O.E.D.).

shreds and patches, rags and/or scraps of cloth; but a cliché only in *a thing of shreds and patches*, a poor creature (in motley): from ca. 1830. Originally in allusion to Shake-speare's 'A king of shreds and patches' (*Hamlet*, III, iv, 102).

shuffle off this mortal coil, to. To die: mid C. 19–20. In allusion to Shakespeare's 'When we have shuffled off this mortal coil' (*Hamlet*, III, i, 67).

shun ... See **plague.**

'si jeunesse savait, si vieillesse pouvait.' If youth but knew; if old age but could (i.e., had the physical power): mid C. 19–20. This French epigram, No. CXCI in *Les Prémices*, 1594, by Henri Estienne, has been parodied as 'If youth could only forget and if old age could only remember' (Rupert Penny: not verbatim).

'sic transit gloria mundi'. So well known, in C. 19–20, is this Latin quotation from the Service of the Pope's Enthronement (cf. Thomas à Kempis's *o quam cito transit gloria mundi*, 'Oh how quickly passes away the glory of the world', Benham), that a detective-story writer adapted it for the title of one of his novels: *Sic Transit Gloria* (name of the murdered girl).

sick at heart. Deeply sorrowful or regretful; longingly desirous: mid C. 19–20.

Sick Man of Europe, the. Turkey. This political and journalistic cliché is obsolescent: Kemal Ataturk changed all that. It was coined in a conversation between the Czar Nicholas I and Sir G. Seymour on Feb. 21, 1853; the phrase caught on almost immediately. (O.E.D.)

sickening thud, a; esp., **with a . . .** 'He fell with a sickening thud.' From ca. 1910.

sight for sore eyes, a (colloquial). A scene, a person, that it is a pleasure to see: late C. 19–20. 'Easy to look at.'

signed, sealed, and delivered. Completed in a thoroughly satisfactory manner; ratified: as applied to legal deeds, it is a legal formula; used in non-legal contexts, it is a C. 20 cliché.

*silence reigns (or **reigned**) **supreme.** There is, or was, utter silence: late C. 19–20.—Cf. Edward Lear's 'When awful darkness and silence reign' (ca. 1870) and Reginald Heber's 'Majestic silence' (ca. 1820).

silver lining, a. With reference to the proverb, 'Every cloud has a silver lining', it = the happier or more fortunate side or aspect of a misfortune, a grief: from ca. 1870.

silver sea, the. The sea, lustrous-white, like silver: late C. 19–20. As a cliché (merely 'the sea'), the phrase is trivial, but originally it was used in allusion to Shakespeare's England, 'set in the silver sea'.

'simple, my dear Watson!'; often shortened to **my dear Watson!** That's easy!; nothing difficult in that!: from ca. 1905. From Conan Doyle's Sherlock Holmes stories (1892–1905). Originally and correctly: *Elementary* . . .

simple truth, the. The truth, unadorned: from ca. 1860. 'The simple truth is that he was bored.'

simply and solely. Simply; solely; in brief: late C. 19–20. 'What has been done is simply and solely to adjust our domestic legislation to the pressing requirements of a particular occasion' (*The Daily Telegraph*, February 15, 1940, in leader on English enlistment for Finland).

sin against the light, to. To sin against the Holy Ghost—against one's conscience and higher nature: mid C. 19–20. Often applied to one who is a traitor to the things of the spirit.

sine qua non, a or **the.** An indispensable condition or thing: C. 19–20. Literally, 'without which [thing], nothing'.

*sinews of war, the. Money: dating from ca. 1550, the phrase has been a cliché since ca. 1750. From Cicero's *nervi belli pecunia* (money: the sinews of war). (O.E.D.)

single blessedness. The unmarried state: from ca. 1830. In Shakespeare (*A Midsummer Night's Dream*, I, i, 78–80), the phrase = 'divine blessing accorded to a life of celibacy' (O.E.D.); in C. 20, it is jocular.

single iota. See **not one iota.**

sink or swim, to. 'It was a case of sink or swim', failure or success: common already by 1538 (O.E.D.); cliché in C. 18–20.—'We are determined to do it, sink or swim', i.e. without regard to the circumstances, or despite probable failure: C. 19–20.

*sit on the fence, to. To be an indifferentist, esp. politically: from ca. 1870. By an American university wit, a *mugwump* has been defined as 'a man who sits on the fence, with his mug on one side and his wump on the other'.

'sitting at the receipt of custom'; to sit . . . Sitting at the cash-desk: from ca. 1860. The quoted phrase occurs in *Matthew*, ix. 9, '[Jesus] saw a man, named Matthew, sitting at the receipt of custom' (εἶδεν ἄνθρωπον καθήμενον ἐπὶ τὸ τελώνιον)—*Mark*, ii. 14—*Luke*, v. 27: where *receipt of custom* = 'an office for the receipt of taxes'. (See my *A New Testament Word-Book* at *receipt*.)

six of one and half a dozen of the other; esp., **it is** (or **was**) **. . .,** there is little (or no) difference; there is no real choice: from ca. 1870.

skate on thin ice, to. To act in dangerous and/or delicate and difficult circumstances: from ca. 1860. Emerson, 'In skating over thin ice our safety is in our speed'.

skeleton at the feast, the (?). A reminder (or a source) of gloom or sadness in the midst of enjoyment: C. 20. The alternative *banquet* is now rare.

skeleton in the cupboard, a. Such a source of shame to a family (or a person) as is unknown outside the family: from ca. 1860.

skin and bones; esp., **to be all** (or **nothing but**) **skin and bones.** To be extremely lean or emaciated: mid C. 18–20.

*sleep the sleep of the just, to. To sleep soundly: C. 19–20. Racine, 'Elle s'endormit du sommeil des justes'. (Benham.)

'slings and arrows of outrageous fortune, the.' C. 19–20. In Shakespeare's famous 'To be or not to be' speech (*Hamlet*, III, i, 50).

slipshod reasoning. Careless argument(s); superficial or unthought-out argument: late C. 19–20.

Slough of Despond, the. A phrase, formed on 'The name of the slough was Despond' (*Pilgrim's Progress*, 1678: Part I); it = a state of despondency: C. 19–20.

slow but sure; slowly but surely. Steadily; ploddingly trustworthy: a proverbial saying (more often in form, *slow and sure*), but in mid C. 19–20 a cliché.

slow to anger. Not easily angered; equable: C. 19–20; since ca. 1880, mainly literary. Biblical: *Nehemiah*, ix. 17, 'A God . . . slow to anger' (Vulgate, *Deus longanimis*).

smack of the soil, to. To be suggestive or reminiscent of the land, country life, farming: from ca. 1870.

smack one's lips, to. Employed literally, it is not a cliché (how otherwise say it?—so briefly?—so well?); but allusively, of keen relish (cf. **lick one's chops**) and delighted anticipation of things other than food and drink, it is, in late C. 19–20, a cliché.

*smell a rat, to. To suspect that something is wrong or that there is danger: current since mid C. 16: a cliché in mid C. 18–20.—Cf. *Hamlet*, III, iv, 'How now! a rat? Dead, for a ducat, dead!': Hamlet, stabbing Polonius, lurking like a rat in the arras.

smell of the lamp, to. This slightly obsolescent literary (esp., literary critics') cliché arose, as a cliché, ca. 1750; recorded as early as 1579; meaning, 'to show signs of being worked at by lamp-light'—laboured and artificial. (O.E.D.)

smell to heaven, to. 'Bribery and corruption smelt to heaven in Urbitavia.' From ca. 1870. *Hamlet*, 'Oh, my offence is rank, it smells to heaven' (III, iii, 36). Here *smell* is intransitive, and it = 'to stink metaphorically'.

smiling hypocrite, a. A blandly hypocritical person: mid C. 19–20.—Cf. **pious fraud.**

smite (a person, one's enemies) **hip and thigh, to.** To attack unsparingly or very vigorously, to defeat by vigorous means (esp., overwhelming blows), to rout utterly: mid C. 19–20; since ca. 1910, only literary. *Judges*, xv. 8, 'He'—Samson—'smote them hip and thigh with great slaughter': Vulgate, *Percussitque eos ingenti plaga.*

smoke the pipe of peace, to. To renew a friendship, after a period of enmity, over a glass of beer: mid C. 19–20. From the calumet or peace-pipe of the Red Indians.

snake in the grass, a. A suspicious or dangerous person; a spy; a traitor, a treacherous deceiver: common since early C. 17, but a cliché not before C. 19. (Virgil, *Eclogues*, III, 93, 'Latet anguis in herba'.)

snapper-up of unconsidered trifles, a. One who gleans what others omit—or scorn—to gather: C. 19–20. Shakespeare, *The Winter's Tale*, IV, ii.

snatch a hasty meal, to. To make a hurried meal; to eat hurriedly, bolt a meal: C. 20.

sneaking doubt, a. An undeclared but firmly held doubt: late C. 19–20. The once very common *a sneaking kindness* (feeling of kindness; sympathy) is now hardly common enough to qualify; but *to have a sneaking sympathy for* (someone) must, in late C. 19–20, be almost—if not quite—a cliché.

snow blankets (or **blanketed**) **the city** (or **country**). This is an American journalists' cliché of C. 20.

so far as in one lies. See **all that . . .**

so (or **as**) **far as that goes** . . . is an introductory formula that limits the applicability (and validity) of the preceding statement: C. 19–20.

so far—so good! 'Used to express satisfaction with matters up to a certain point': from ca. 1840.

'so shines a good deed in a naughty world.' C. 19–20. Shakespeare introduces the line thus, 'How far that little candle throws his beams!' (*The Merchant of Venice*, v, i, 90). Here, *naughty* = 'wicked'.

. . . **so to say** (or **speak**). As it were; one might so put it: mid C. 19–20; slightly obsolescent.

social amenities. Social advantages; service, shops, entertainments such as one would expect in a civilized city: from ca. 1920.

social whirl, the. The social round; Society's supposedly gay life: late C. 19–20.

Society butterfly, a; Society butterflies, (young, youngish, or at least not aged) women moving in Society and enjoying themselves in a frivolous manner; generally with the implication of a deficiency of brains: from ca. 1880.

soft impeachment, the; esp., **to admit**—or **to deny**— **the** . . . , to admit or deny an accusation (of a not very serious fault): mid C. 19–20. The original is 'I own the soft impeachment', Mrs Malaprop *loquitur*, in Sheridan's *The Rivals*, 1777, Act v, sc. iii.

soft place in one's heart, a; esp., **to have** . . . **for** (some one), to be very kindly disposed towards someone: late C. 19–20.

solvitur ambulando is a Latin proverbial saying, which = 'The matter—the difficulty—is settled or solved by walking': C. 19–20.

something in the wind; esp., **there's . . .,** there is something afoot; something important or significant is happening —or about to happen: C. 19–20. Current since ca. 1530 (O.E.D.).

something must be done (about it). We (or I or you) must act: late C. 19–20.

*****son of the soil, a;** esp., **a horny-handed son . . .,** a hard-working farmer or farm-labourer: from ca. 1890. One who both spiritually and physically *glebæ ascriptus* (as Roman law has it).

sooner or later (?). At some time or other in the future (something is certain to happen): late C. 18–20.

sop to Cerberus, a; to give a sop to Cerberus, to pacify, appease, buy off with a promise, a present, a bribe: mid C. 18–20. Cerberus was the watch-dog that guarded the entrance to hell: a sop stopped, momentarily, his three mouths (*Æneid,* VI, 417).

sore trial, a. A continual vexation: late C. 19–20.

sorry jest, a. An inferior, a pointless joke: from ca. 1820; obsolescent, except as a literary cliché.

sort of day that makes one glad to be alive, the. C. 20.

sotto voce, adj. and adv. In an undertone, in a subdued voice: mid C. 19–20. (Italian; lit., 'under voice'.)

soul of honour, the. Strictly honourable: C. 19–20. Goldsmith, 1766, 'My brother indeed was the soul of honour' (O.E.D.). The very personification of honour.

'sound and fury, (signifying nothing).' Much furious talk, of no importance and little or no meaning: C. 19–20. 'It is a tale | Told by an idiot, full of sound and fury, | Signifying nothing' (*Macbeth,* v, v, 26–28).

*sound in wind and limb. Healthy and unmaimed; healthy: C. 19–20. (Massinger, 1636: O.E.D.)

sound policy (generic); **a sound policy** (particular). A good policy; a policy free from wrong principle and logical fallacy: from ca. 1880.

'sounding brass.' Noise without (much) sense; a braggart; one who speaks much but performs little: C. 19–20. In allusion to 'Though I speak with the tongues of men and of angels, and [= but] have not charity, I am become as sounding brass, or a tinkling cymbal' (1 *Corinthians*, xiii. 1): γέγονα χαλκὸς ἠχῶν ἢ κύμβαλον ἀλαλάζον, 'I have become resounding bronze or a clanging cymbal'.

*sour grapes. Short for *the grapes are sour*, which is a semi-proverb based on Æsop's fable, 'The Fox and the Grapes': C. 19–20. Applied to a person heard to disparage that which he would—it is suspected—gladly possess.

sovereign remedy, a. Lit., an efficacious remedy; fig., a means, method, process, act that is very effectual: C. 18–20. 'Work is a sovereign remedy against discontent.'

*sow one's wild oats, to. To be dissipated (and wild) when one is young and to reform afterwards: C. 18–20. (Current since ca. 1570.) 'In reference to the folly and mischief of sowing wild oats instead of good grain' (O.E.D.).

sow the wind and reap the whirlwind, to. To cause or begin strife and/or trouble and receive 'more than one bargained for' (q.v.): C. 19–20. *Hosea*, viii. 7, 'For they have sown the wind, and they shall reap the whirlwind': Vulgate, *Quia ventum seminabunt, et turbinem metent* ('Ils sèment le vent, et ils récolteront la tempête', Verdunoy).

spacious times of good Queen Bess (or **of Queen Elizabeth**), **(in) the.** An adaptation (in late C. 19–20, a cliché) of Tennyson's 'The spacious times of great Elizabeth' (*A Dream of Fair Women*, st. 2).

spare no pains, to. To labour most carefully (to do something): mid C. 19–20. 'No pains have been spared ... to make it superior to any other work of the kind', Sir Gurney Benham, Preface to the latest edition of *Benham's Book of Quotations*, to which I, like so many others, am much (and gratefully) indebted.

speak by the book, to. To speak formally, authoritatively or accurately (as if reading from a book): implied in C. 16 (cf. Shakespeare's 'kiss by the book'); in C. 19–20, a cliché.

speak the King's English, to. See **King's English, the.**

speaks volumes for, it (or **this** or **that**). It is extremely significant or expressive; it is figuratively eloquent: mid C. 19–20.

spectators line the streets (in U.S.A.: **curbs**), generally preceded by **many thousand** or **thousands of**: late C. 19–20. (Sullivan.)

*speed the parting guest, to. To hasten him on his way; properly, to wish him God-speed: C. 19–20. Pope, *The Odyssey*, 1725–26, Bk XV, 83–84, 'True friendship's laws are by this rule express'd, | Welcome the coming, speed the parting guest'.

spend money like water, to. To spend money recklessly and/or very freely: late C. 19–20.

spent rocket, a. A brilliant person that has 'shot his bolt' and is now intellectually unproductive: from ca. 1880; slightly obsolescent.

spick and span (colloquial). Very neat or trim, esp. if new or almost new: from ca. 1870.

spicy breezes. Sweet-scented breezes: mid C. 19–20. Pope, 1713, has 'spicy gales' (O.E.D.).

spike someone's guns, to. To circumvent him or, figuratively, block his way; to render a plan impossible, a project unfeasible, an act ineffectual: from ca. 1820.

spirit is willing, but the flesh is weak,—the. An adaptation (in late C. 19–20, a cliché) of *Matthew*, xxvi. 41, 'Watch and pray, that ye enter not into temptation: the spirit indeed is willing, but the flesh is weak': τὸ μὲν πνεῦμα πρόθυμον, ἡ δὲ σὰρξ ἀσθενής, 'man's higher nature is zealous (or eager), but the flesh weak': *Spiritus quidem promptus est, caro autem infirma* (Vulgate).

*spirit of the troops (less often: **men**) **is excellent, the.** The Army is cheerful and full of courage: from late 1914: official and journalistic.

spiritual home, one's. The country to which one is most akin and towards which one feels the profoundest sympathy, esp. if it is not one's own country: ca. 1910, Viscount Haldane of Cloan (1856–1928) said that Germany was his 'spiritual home': owing to the stir made by this statement, the phrase became very widely known and it has, since ca. 1920, been a cliché. In his *An Autobiography*, 1929, he says (p. 285), 'I had gone to Germany too often, and had read her literature too much, not to give ground to narrow-minded people to say that Germany was my "spiritual home".'

splendid isolation. Britain's political isolation, hence any other country's: from 1896, when Sir Wm. Laurier and Viscount Goschen popularized it. The technical name is *isolationism*.

spoil the Egyptians, to. To despoil, to plunder one's enemies: C. 19–20. *Exodus*, iii. 22, 'Ye shall spoil the Egyptians' (Vulgate, *spoliabitis Ægyptum*).

springtime of life, (in) the. (In one's) youth: from ca. 1860.

square deal, a; a straight deal. An equitable arrangement: C. 20. 'What he desires is a square deal, what he needs is a square meal.'

square meal, a. A substantial meal, a full meal: from ca. 1880.—Cf. the preceding entry.

*square peg in a round hole, a. A man (usually, an able man) in a position unsuited to his abilities and/or knowledge and training: from ca. 1870.—Cf. John Masefield's novel, *The Square Peg*; Sydney Smith, *Sketches of Moral Philosophy*, 1804–6, in Lecture IX, 'We shall generally find that . . . a square person has squeezed himself into the round hole'.

stab in the back, a; to stab . . . A treacherous disservice; to render one to (a person): C. 20.

stab to the heart, to. To wound exceedingly, to pain extremely: C. 20.

*staff of life, the. Bread: mid C. 19–20. (Penkethman, 1638, 'Bread is worth all, being the staff of life': O.E.D.)

stage whisper, a. A whisper that carries distinctly: late C. 19–20. From the theatrical use of the phrase.

stagger humanity, to. To bewilder mankind, to astound and horrify the world: from ca. 1910.

stamped on every link. Indubitably or indubitable: mid C. 19–20. From official hall-marks, etc.

stand in awe of, to. To be respectfully and admiringly afraid of or daunted by: mid C. 18–20, though recorded in early C. 14.

stand not upon the order of one's going, to. To depart, careless of ceremony in general and precedence in particular: from ca. 1820. From Lady Macbeth's 'Stand not upon the order of your going, but go at once' (at the end of the banquet at which Macbeth sees the murdered Banquo's ghost).

stand on one's own legs (or **feet**), **to.** To be independent: from C. 16; cliché only in C. 19–20.

stand or fall (**by** something—rule, principle, or esp. an uncertain event), **to.** Applied to a person (less often a thing) dependent on fate, event, rule, principle: mid C. 18–20.

stand (or **stay**) **the pace, to.** To be able to resist, actually to resist, hard work, hard living, fast running: late C. 19–20. From horse-racing.

stand with ... See **back to the wall.**

*__star has set, one's.__ One's fortune and fame are diminishing: from ca. 1880.

star of the first magnitude, a. See **of the first magnitude.**

starry heavens, the. The star-filled and star-lit sky: from ca. 1870. Originally, *the starry heaven* (in the singular) meant, 'the "sphere" of the fixed stars' (O.E.D.).

stars in their courses, the. Destiny (regarded as under the control of the stars): C. 19–20. In allusion to *Judges*, v. 20, 'The stars in their courses fought against Sisera': Vulgate, *Stellæ, manentes in ordine et cursu suo, adversus Sisaram pugnaverunt.*—Cf. **not in our stars.**

stately homes of (old) England, the. From ca. 1870. The shorter phrase occurs in Felicia Hemans's *The Homes of England* (ca. 1830), thus:—'The stately homes of England! | How beautiful they stand, | Amid their tall ancestral trees, | O'er all the pleasant land!'

stay one's hand, to. To cease from work or from attacking an enemy: C. 19–20 (in late C. 19–20, mostly literary).—Cf. Shakespeare, 1 *Henry VI*, at I, ii, 104.

stay the course, to (?). To endure; to pursue a task, a course of conduct, to the appointed end: colloquial: C. 20. From horse-racing.—For **stay the pace,** see **stand the pace.**

steady improvement, a. An unfaltering, regular, equable or evenly maintained improvement: late C. 19–20.

***steal a march (on), to.** To obtain, secretly, an advantage over an opponent, a rival: mid C. 19–20. From the original (the military) sense, 'to move troops without the enemy's knowledge'.

steal someone's thunder, to. To use his methods or system, so as to destroy (or damagingly lessen) the effect of his actions, writings, words: since ca. 1925. Owing to literary historians' revival of the words of John Dennis († 1733): see Benham or the O.E.D.

steer clear of, to. To avoid completely or entirely: from ca. 1840. From the lit., nautical sense (Defoe, 1723; fig. used as early as 1789: O.E.D.).

stem the tide, to. To check or stop the course (of, e.g., public opinion); loosely, to make headway: late C. 19–20.

step by step. With gradual regularity; with a regular but slow, gradual progress; by successive degrees: mid C. 19–20.

step in the right direction, a. An act, a decision, that will assist one to achieve an aim: from ca. 1880.

step into someone's shoes, to. To take someone's place (in a business, in employment): from ca. 1860.

'stepping-stones of their dead selves.' One's past, regarded as being or having been made to serve, to benefit, one's future: from ca. 1870. Tennyson, *In Memoriam*, 1850, 'Men may rise on stepping-stones | Of their dead selves to higher things'.

sterling worth. Excellent character; qualities, principles, habits, abilities, well tested and thoroughly dependable: mid C. 19–20. Washington Irving, 1832, 'A young man of sterling worth' (O.E.D.).

stern reality (?). Hard or inexorable facts: from ca. 1915. **Stern necessity** (from ca. 1860) is indubitably a cliché.—Cf. **hard facts.**

stew in one's own juice, to; esp., **to leave** (or **let**) **someone stew in his own juice,** to leave him to do what he can for himself: from ca. 1880. Earlier *stew in one's own grease* (Benham).

stick in one's gizzard, to. Applied to something that one cannot stomach (figuratively) or remains offensive or disagreeable to one: C. 19–20. Current since ca. 1660.

stick to one's guns, to. To refuse to abandon one's point, aim, ambition: from ca. 1870. Not to abandon one's battery though under heavy fire.

still, small voice,—a or **the.** Conscience: late C. 19–20. Sir Richard Burton, *The Kasidah of Haji Abu*, 'El-Yadzi', ix, 19, 'Enough to thee the small still voice aye thundering in thine inner ear'. Ultimately from 1 *Kings*, xix. 12, 'And after the earthquake a fire; but the Lord was not in the fire: and after the fire a still small voice' (Vulgate, *sibilus auræ tenuis*: 'le murmure d'une brise légère', Verdunoy).

stink in the nostrils of, to. To be extremely offensive—to be abhorrent—to (a person): mid C. 19–20; since ca. 1910, only literary.

stir up strife, to (?). To provoke a quarrel; to cause trouble: from ca. 1840.

*stolen fruit (figurative). Anything stolen; esp., illicit love: C. 19–20. In allusion to the apple 'stolen' by Eve.

stone dead and **stone deaf** are clichés (C. 19–20), according to some. They represent 'utterly dead' or, rather, 'dead and cold', and 'completely deaf'. I think that whereas the former is, the latter is not a cliché.

*storm brewing, a (lit. or fig.); esp., **there's a storm brewing,** a war, a fight, a riot—strife, trouble—anger, resentment—is working up, 'coming to the boil': from ca. 1870. Josiah G. Holland, 1860, 'A storm was brewing in the domestic sky' (O.E.D.).

*storm in a tea-cup, a. 'Much ado about nothing'; a great fuss about a trifle (or in a very small community): from ca. 1880.—Cf. the Duke of Ormond's 'a storm in a cream-bowl' (1678) and Lord Thurlow's 'A storm in a wash-hand basin' (1830). 'Probably after Latin *fluctus excitare in simpulo* (Cicero)': O.E.D. The exact reference is *De Legibus*, III, xvi, 36, and the phrase may be rendered, 'To stir up waves in a ladle': Benham.

straight and narrow path, the. Virtuousness, virtue: mid C. 19–20. Also **the strait and narrow path,** probably in allusion to *Matthew*, vii. 14, 'Strait is the gate, and narrow is the way, which leadeth unto life'—i.e., to eternal life; to salvation.

straight deal. See **square deal.**

straight from the horse's mouth (colloquial), adjective and adverb. On very good authority: from ca. 1910.—Cf. *a straight tip.*

straight from the shoulder (adverb). Bluntly; in a direct, outspoken manner: C. 20. 'I let him have it straight from the shoulder.' Pugilistic.

straight off the reel. Uninterruptedly; without stopping: from ca. 1870. 'To look through three photograph albums straight off the reel is too much of a good thing.'

strain at a gnat, to. To make a difficulty of accepting (some point, theory, etc.), esp. after accepting readily a much greater difficulty: C. 19–20. From a misunderstanding of *Matthew*, xxiii. 24, 'Ye blind guides, which strain at a gnat' (i.e. strain the liquor if they find a gnat in it), 'and swallow a camel': see esp. the O.E.D., at *strain*, v^1, 21.

strain every nerve, to. To exert oneself (physically) to the utmost: from ca. 1830. (Milton, 1671, 'Straining all his nerves': O.E.D.) Here, *nerve* = 'sinew'. Hence, figuratively, to do one's utmost (late C. 19–20).

strait and narrow path, the. See **straight and . . .**

strange but true. Late C.19–20.—Cf. **stranger than fiction.**

stranger in a strange land, a. A foreigner in a country unfamiliar to him: C. 19–20. *Exodus*, ii. 22, 'I have been a stranger in a strange land': Vulgate, *Advena fui in terra aliena.* Cf. **stranger within . . .**

stranger than fiction. A late C. 19–20 cliché from 'Truth is stranger than fiction'.

stranger within their gates, the. A stranger or a foreigner in a community, a household, that receives (and shelters) him: C. 19–20. *Exodus*, xx. 10, 'Thy stranger that is within thy gates' (2nd Commandment): Vulgate, *advena qui est intra portas tuas.*

strapping wench, a. See **great strapping . . .**

stress and strain; esp., **in times of stress and strain,** in times of strained effort and tension, hence loosely of distress and nervous strain: from ca. 1915. It has almost superseded *storm and stress.*

stretch one's legs, to (?). To go for a walk (properly, in order to relieve stiffness or for exercise): C. 19–20.

strictly accurate. Accurate in every detail; *to be strictly accurate* (introductory formula), to be precise: late C. 19–20.

*strike while the iron is hot, to. To act at the propitious moment, when action will have the most effect: a proverbial saying (from C. 14); in C. 19–20, a cliché.

striking example, a. An impressive, remarkable, or (extremely) apposite example: C. 20.

*strong silent man, a. Beloved of women novelists (Maud Diver, Elizabeth Page, Eleanor M. Hull *et hoc genus omne* [q.v.]): from ca. 1905.

strong support (figurative). Support from an influential quarter; keen and sustained assistance: late C. 19–20.

struck all of a heap (colloquial); **struck dumb with surprise; stunned with surprise.** 'Flabbergasted'; astounded: late C. 19–20.

stuff and nonsense; it's all . . . !, it's all nonsense (or rubbish)!: mid C. 19–20; Fielding used it in 1749 (O.E.D.). An elaboration of the obsolescent *stuff*, 'nonsense'.

stung to the quick. Very much annoyed, offended, or (in one's feelings) hurt: C. 19–20. (Fairly common in C. 18.) Earlier, *touched* or *galled to the quick*. Here, *the quick* is the sensitive flesh in any part of the body, esp. that under the nails. (O.E.D.)

stunned with surprise. See **struck . . .**

stupendous success, a. An astounding success; an amazingly great success: from ca. 1910.

sturdy independence. Robust and/or uncompromising independence (in thought and act): from ca. 1870. Charles Kingsley, 1866, 'They were distinguished . . . for sturdy independence and for what generally accompanies it—sturdy common sense' (O.E.D.).

Sturm und Drang. Storm and stress: literary: mid. C. 19–20. Chiefly in reference to a German literary movement of C 18, from a play of that title (1776).

*sub rosa. Secretly; clandestinely; 'on the quiet': C. 19–20. Lit., under the rose. Harpocrates, god of silence, was bribed with a rose by Cupid not to divulge the amours of Venus. A rose hanging over the table indicated that words spoken at table were to remain secret. *Est rosa flos Veneris,* 'the rose is the flower of Venus'. (Benham.)

submerged tenth, the. 'That part of the population which is permanently in poverty and misery (contrasted with [*the*] *upper ten*)', O.E.D.: from the 1890's: sociological and journalistic. Apparently used first in Booth's *In Darkest England*, 1890.

substantial agreement; esp., **to be in . . .,** agreeing as to the most important aspects or parts; agreeing in the main: C. 20. 'Conservatives, Liberals, and Labour men are in substantial agreement in respect of the British war-policy.'

subterranean manœuvres. Machinations existing, and operating, secretly: from ca. 1930; mostly journalistic.

'such men are dangerous.' See **'lean and hungry look'.**

'such stuff as dreams are made on' (often misquoted **of**). C. 19–20. 'We are such stuff | As dreams are made on, and our little life | Is rounded with a sleep' (Shakespeare, *The Tempest*, IV, i).

suck (someone's) **brains, to.** To draw out and use for oneself the results of another's intelligence: late C. 19–20.

suffer. See **fate worse than death** and **sea-change.**

suffer fools gladly, (not) to. (Not) to be patient with the stupid and the foolish: C. 19–20. 2 *Corinthians*, xi. 19, 'For ye suffer fools gladly, seeing ye yourselves are wise': ἡδέως γὰρ ἀνέχεσθε τῶν ἀφρόνων φρόνιμοι ὄντες : *libenter enim suffertis insipientes, cum sitis ipsi sapientes.*

suffer in silence, to. To suffer or endure without complaint; in grievous circumstances to wait patiently: mid C. 19–20.

suffer the tortures of the damned, to. To suffer such torture or anguish as is inflicted on the souls in hell: C. 19–20. 'The payne . . . that dampned [i.e. damned] have in hell' (O.E.D.).—Cf. *torment* in *Revelation*, xiv. 11.

sui generis. Of its own particular sort; peculiar; in a class by himself or itself: from ca. 1830. Lit., of its own kind or sort.

suit all tastes, (not) to. 'There was something to suit all tastes.'—'Such a book will not suit all tastes.' Late C. 19–20.

suit one's book, to. To be convenient or agreeable to one; to answer his requirements or accord with his plans: late C. 19–20. Originally, a bookmaker's *book*.

suitably inscribed. Appropriately inscribed: C. 20. 'He sent her a book suitably inscribed.'

sum and substance, the. The gist (of a matter); the essential part (of something): current since late C. 16; a cliché in C. 19–20. Robertson, 1852, 'The Sermon on the Mount contains the sum and substance of Christianity' (O.E.D.).

sumptuous repast, a. A costly meal magnificently set forth; hence, loosely, any excellent meal: from ca. 1880.—Cf. Milton's 'Their sumptuous gluttonies, and gorgeous feasts'.

sunnier climes. Countries where the sun is more constant, more kindly: late C. 19–20; mostly journalistic. E.g., California as compared with New York; Egypt as compared with England.

sunny South, the. The South coast of England: an *English* cliché, which has been a cliché only since ca. 1920.

superhuman effort, a; esp., **to make a . . .,** to make a tremendous effort or an effort much beyond one's normal powers: late C. 19–20. *Superhuman energy* is a candidate.

supply and demand. In *the law(s) of supply and demand*, the phrase is not a cliché; but in the loose usage of C. 20, it is a cliché. From Political Economy.

supreme (or **paramount**) **importance, of.** Of the utmost importance; most important of all: from ca. 1870. J. D. Chambers, 1877, 'Matters of paramount importance' (O.E.D.).

supreme moment, the. Not 'the moment of death' (the original sense: French *le moment suprême*), but the moment of greatest happiness, the acme of triumph: C. 20.

supreme sacrifice. See **make the . . .**

sure and certain hope, the; esp., **in the . . .,** an adaptation of 'Earth to earth, . . . dust to dust; in sure and certain hope of the Resurrection to eternal life' (Burial of the Dead, *The Book of Common Prayer*): mid C. 19–20. In the steadfast hope of something that is certain to happen.

*survival of the fittest; or **the survival . . .,** when used without direct or apposite reference to the theory of natural selection; for instance, when used of non-living things: C. 20. 'He [an old bull, monarch of the herd] had to fight again, in obedience to that law which respected only the survival of the fittest' (Zane Grey, *The Thundering Herd* (English edition), 1926).

sustain cuts, contusions, and abrasions, to. An American journalistic cliché, dating from ca. 1910; esp. in reference to an automobile accident.

*Swan of Avon, the. Shakespeare: mid C. 18–20. 'Sweet Swan of Avon!' occurs in Ben Jonson's verses prefacing the First Folio of Shakespeare, 1623.

*swan-song, a or **one's.** One's final, one's last, poem (hence, speech, etc.): C. 19–20.—Cf. Shakespeare's 'He makes a swan-like end, | Fading in music', swans being fabled to 'sing' just before they die.

swear by all the gods, to. To swear by all the divinities one knows of; to swear or assert solemnly: mid C. 19–20.

*swear that black is white, to. To swear, or declare, against the clear evidence; to be a shameless perjurer; to be flagrantly contradictious: C. 19–20.

sweat of one's brow, the; esp., **by the . . .,** by hard manual labour: C. 19–20. Adapted from 'In the sweat of thy face shalt thou eat bread', God to Adam on banishing him from Eden.

sweep the board, to. To carry off all the prizes, gain all the distinctions: from ca. 1830. From a card-player's winning all the stakes.

sweeping statement, a. An indiscriminately all-inclusive statement; hence, a rashly comprehensive statement: late C. 19–20.

'sweetness and light.' Dean Swift in *The Battle of the Books*, 1604, but popularized by Matthew Arnold in *Literature and Dogma*, 1873—'Culture is the passion for sweetness and light, and . . . the passion for making them prevail' (Benham).

swim into one's ken, to. To come to one's knowledge, to be discovered by a person: mid C. 19–20. Keats, 'Then felt I like some watcher of the skies | When a new planet swims into his ken' (*On First Looking into Chapman's Homer*).

*swing of the pendulum, the. A natural oscillation between opposite opinions: mid C. 19–20.

sword of Damocles, the. An impending or imminent danger: mid C. 18–20. Over the head of flatterer Damocles, Dionysius Tyrant of Syracuse hung a sword suspended by a hair, to impress him with the tenuous and perilous nature of happiness.

T

tablets of memory, the. The memory as a book wherein events and incidents are recorded: late C. 19–20; obsolescent. Novelettish, as in 'indelibly impressed upon the tablets of her memory'.

Tadpoles and Tapers; properly, **Tadpole and Taper;** a frequent misquotation, **Tapers and Tadpoles.** Professional politicians that are the hacks of a party: from ca. 1890. From Disraeli's *Coningsby*, 1844: see, e.g., II, ii, and esp. I, i, 'Tadpole and Taper were great friends. Neither of them ever despaired of the Commonwealth' (Benham).

take a hand in the game, to. To participate, unexpectedly or graspingly: C. 20. From card-playing.

*take a leaf out of someone's book, to. To imitate; follow the example of: from ca. 1870.

take a (or the) long view, to. To look far ahead; to have —and show—vision: C. 20. Esp. among politicians.

take (a person) as one finds (that person), **to.** Mid C. 19–20. 'But still, now you are here, you must just take us as you find us, as the saying is' (Charles Rushton, *Murder in Bavaria*, 1937).

take away one's breath, to (?). To astound; to nonplus: mid C. 19–20.

take by storm, to. To make very rapidly a deep impression on, to win rapidly the affections of, to convince rapidly and vigorously: late C. 19–20. From warfare.

*take French leave, to. To do something, esp. to go away, without notice or permission: from ca. 1780. From a usage of French society.

take heart of grace, to, is probably an elaboration of—for it is exactly synonymous with—*take heart*, 'to pluck up courage': recorded in 1530; in C. 18–20, a cliché.

take immediate steps, to (?). To set about attaining—to take immediate action to attain—an end: late C. 19–20.

take into (due) account, to. To take proper or sufficient notice of: late C. 19–20. Here, *account* = 'estimation' or 'consideration'.

*take it as read, to. To take it for granted, presume and assume it done: C. 20. From parliamentary or legal procedure.

take it or leave it, to; esp., **take it or leave it!,** either take it or leave it, but make up your mind: from ca. 1920.

take one's Bible oath, to. To swear solemnly, to give one's solemn word of honour: colloquial and non-aristocratic, non-cultured: from ca. 1880.

take one's courage in both hands, to. To summon one's courage and take the risk: late C. 19–20.

take one's life in one's hands, to. To embark on a hazardous enterprise: mid C. 19–20.

take one's name in vain, to. To mention a person's name lightly, casually, disrespectfully: jocular: from ca. 1880. From the Biblical phrase for 'to utter blasphemy'.

take one's pleasures sadly, to. Not to be whole-hearted in one's pleasures, not to be joyous: late C. 19–20. From 'The English take their pleasures sadly'. Generally (but on what evidence?) attributed to the Duc de Sully, ca. 1630, 'Les Anglais s'amusent tristement, selon l'usage de leur pays' (Benham).

take pot-luck, to. (Of a guest) to accept an invitation to a meal not specially prepared: from ca. 1770. I.e., what happens to be in the pot.

take the bit in one's teeth, to. To become unmanageable, to spurn restraint: mid C. 19–20. From horse-lore.

take the bread out of a person's mouth, to. To take away (or to lessen considerably) a person's livelihood: mid C. 19–20.

*take the bull by the horns, to. To meet a danger, risk, difficulty with courage: from ca. 1880. From the farmyard.

*take the gilt off the gingerbread, to. To lessen the value or attractiveness of something: from ca. 1880. Culinary.

take the rough with the smooth, to. To accept hardship and disappointment as calmly or cheerfully as one accepts comfort and good fortune: C. 20.

take the wind out of a person's sails, to. To nonplus or perplex; to abash: late C. 19–20. Nautical.

take the word(s) out of a person's mouth, to. 'Why! you took the very word out of my mouth.' To anticipate what he is on the point of saying: C. 19–20, though used by Shakespeare—and before.

take the wrong turning, to. To en.bark on an evil (less often, a foolish or mistaken) course: late C. 19–20.

take things as one finds them, to. To accept life as it comes; to be tolerant: C. 19–20.

take time by the forelock, to. To act promptly; to seize one's opportunity: from ca. 1770. Phædrus, 'Calvus, comosa fronte, nudo occipitio, ... Occasionem rerum significat brevem' (O.E.D.).

take (a woman) **to one's bosom, to.** To marry her: from ca. 1880. *The wife of one's bosom*, 'one's wife', is so archaic that it can no longer be classified as a cliché.

take to one's heels, to. To flee; to run away: mid C. 19–20.

take up the cudgels, to. To engage vigorously in a contest, quarrel, debate: common in latter half of C. 17; a cliché by 1800 at latest. From cudgel play.

take with a grain of salt, to. See **cum grano salis.**

taken aback. Unpleasantly astonished, visibly perturbed: from ca. 1880. *Set back* in confidence, repelled, discomfited.

taken in the toils. See **in the toils.**

talk double Dutch, to. To talk in a manner unintelligible to the listener: late C. 19–20.

*talk of the Devil! A mid C. 19–20 cliché; applied to the appearing of one who is being or has just been talked about. It is a shortening of the proverb, *talk of the Devil and he'll appear*.

talk through one's hat, to (colloquial). To talk nonsense; to talk ignorantly: late C. 19–20.

Tapers and Tadpoles. See Tadpoles and Tapers.

*tarred with the same brush. Having the same faults or objectionable habits or qualities: mid C. 19–20. Rather colloquial.

task confronts (or confronted) one, a; esp., a difficult task . . ., there is hard or difficult work that must be done: C. 20.

tastefully arranged (esp. of flowers or a table). Arranged with good taste: late C. 19–20.

taxed to its utmost capacity. A C. 20 American cliché ('guyed' by Sullivan), comparable with the English *filled to capacity*, itself a virtual cliché, and *to play to capacity*.

teach one's grandmother, to. This mid C. 19–20 cliché is allusive—a shortening of the ancient proverbial saying, 'to teach one's grandmother to suck eggs'.

'teach the young idea how to shoot, to.' To instruct and form the young: C. 19–20. 'Delightful task! to rear the tender thought, | To teach the young idea how to shoot; | To pour the fresh instruction o'er the mind!' (James Thomson, *The Seasons*, 'Spring' (1728), vv. 1149–51).

team spirit, the. The spirit that moves one to play, to do things, for one's side, one's school, one's company, one's country, not in self-display: from ca. 1920. Mostly Public Schools' and ruling classes'.

tear one's hair, to. To give way to extravagant grief or rage: C. 19–20.

teeming earth, the (certainly); **teeming millions** (probably). The abundantly productive earth; swarming millions: late C. 19–20.

tell (someone) **a few home-truths, to.** To make pointed or searching or effectively personal remarks or statements or reproofs to: from ca. 1880.—Cf. the archaic *home-thrust*: in both expressions, *home* was originally adverbial, 'going home to one' (slang 'where one lives').

'tell it not in Gath!'; often misquoted as **whisper . . .** Do not make it public!: C. 19–20. 'How are the mighty fallen! Tell it not in Gath, publish it not in the streets of Askelon' (2 *Samuel*, i. 19–20).

*tell tales out of school, to. To give damaging information, to betray damaging secrets: C. 18–20. In fairly common use, both literal and figurative, in C. 17–18; the literal sense has long been obsolete.

telling effect; esp., **with . . .,** effectively, forcibly, strikingly: late C. 19–20.

temper the wind to the shorn lamb, to. To make things tolerable—less harsh, less difficult—to the inexperienced or the helpless: late C. 18–20. Sterne, 1768, 'God tempers the wind, said Maria, to the shorn lamb'. (Most people think it to be of Biblical origin; the first record of the idea is in Henri Estienne's *Les Prémices*, 1594, 'Dieu mesure le froid à la brebis tondue'.)

[**tempus fugit**, 'time flies', is too proverbial to be strictly a cliché.]

tender a testimonial dinner, to. An American, mainly journalistic, cliché of late C. 19–20. (Sullivan.)

tender one's thanks (to a person), **to.** To thank him; to give thanks: public speakers' and journalists': late C. 19–20.

tender susceptibilities. Feelings very easily hurt; touchiness and/or tender-heartedness: late C. 19–20; obsolescent.

terminated fatally, it (or **the affair** or **incident**). It ended with—resulted in—a death, or disastrously: journalistic: C. 20.

terminated the proceedings. 'A vote of thanks terminated the proceedings.' C. 20.

terminological inexactitude, a. Winston Churchill, in a speech, on Feb. 22, 1906, 'Some risk of t.e.' (Benham).

***terra firma.** Firm land, dry land as opposed to the sea: mid C. 19–20. A Latinism now despised as an outmoded elegancy. (Cf. Ger. *Festland*.)

terrible (or **unspeakable**) **Turk, the.** Mid C. 19–20 clichés, both obsolescent. A famous Turkish wrestler of the early C. 19 (*tempore* Gough and Hackenschmidt) was nicknamed 'The Terrible Turk'.

thank from the bottom of one's heart. See **from the bottom . . .**

thank God . . . See **on bended knee.**

***thankful for small mercies.** Grateful for little things, modest sums, trifling kindnesses: late C. 19–20.

thanking you in anticipation. Thanking you beforehand or expectantly: commercial: C. 20.

that being the case (?). That being so: an introductory formula: late C. 19–20.—Cf. **this is not the case.**

'that way madness lies.' If I (or you or he . . .) persist in *that*, I shall become mad: C. 19–20. Shakespeare, 'O, that way madness lies; let me shun that!' (*Lear*, III, iv).

that will be all for the present. That will do: late C. 19–20.

that's flat! Often **and that's flat!**, q.v.

then and there (?). As 'at that precise time and in that particular place; immediately and on the spot', it is brief, unimprovable, and certainly not a cliché; but loosely as 'immediately', it is extremely common and a virtual cliché.

their name is Legion (or **legion**). See **name is . . .**

there are more things in heaven and earth, Horatio, than are dreamt of in your philosophy.' C. 19–20; from *Hamlet*, I, 5. ('The original reading is "our philosophy" ', Benham.) The universe is a mystery.

'there, but for the grace of God, goes' (the speaker)—or **. . . go I.** C. 19–20: based on a remark, ca. 1550, by John Bradford (burnt at the stake in 1555) 'on seeing some criminals going to execution' (Benham).

'there is a tide . . .' See **turn of the tide.**

there is (or **was**) **more in it than meets** (or **met**) **the eye.** See **more in it . . .**

there is (or **was**) **not a breath of air.** See **not a breath . . .**

*thereby hangs a tale and its original **'and thereby . . .'** (several times in Shakespeare): C. 19–20.

'there's a divinity that shapes our ends, rough-hew them how we will.' C. 19–20. *Hamlet*, v, ii.

*there's something 'rotten in the state of Denmark'. The correct form is 'Something is rotten in the state of Denmark' (*ibid.*, I, iv): C. 19–20.

*'there's the rub' or **'ay, there's the rub',** C. 19–20. 'To sleep! perchance to dream;—ay, there's the rub', in reference to death: *ibid.*, III, i.

these little things are sent to try us. We must bear patiently with (these) annoyances and (not necessarily little) misfortunes: said in humorous resignation and fortitude: C. 20.

---

*thin end of the wedge, the. The beginning of an influence; the creation of a (dangerous) precedent: C. 19–20. From the proverb, *the thin end of the wedge is to be feared.* From wood-splitting.

thin on top. See **little thin** . . .

'thing of beauty is a joy for ever, a.' Mid C. 19–20. Keats, *Endymion*, 1818, Book I, 1; the passage continues, 'Its loveliness increases'. Parodied by literary flappers as 'A thing of beauty is a boy for ever'.

thing of shreds and patches, a. See **shreds** . . .

thing of the past, to be (or **become**) **a.** To have become, or to become, out of date or forgotten: late C. 19–20. 'Tyranny is not a thing of the past.'

things to come; esp., **the shape of things to come.** See **shape of** . . .

think no small beer of oneself, to. To think well of oneself: colloquial: late C. 19–20. *Small beer* is weak beer.

thirst for someone's blood, to. To desire eagerly to strike, reprimand, vituperate, or reproach someone: mid C. 19–20.

this is a bloody business. A jocularity of late C. 19–20. Adapted from Shakespeare's 'It is the bloody business which informs thus to mine eyes' (*Macbeth*, II, i, 48).

this (or **that**) **is not the case;** esp., **but this is** . . . or **this, however, is** . . ., it is not so; it is untrue or incorrect: mid C. 19–20. From the law-courts.

this is the happiest moment of my life. See **happiest moment** . . .

this vale of tears. The world: late C. 18–20; recorded in 1554 (O.E.D.). Sir David Lindsay († ca. 1557) spoke of 'this vaill of miserie and wa' (woe).

this world's goods, rich in or **well endowed with.** See **endowed** . . .

*thorn in one's flesh, a. A mid C. 19–20 adaptation of '[They] shall be pricks in your eyes, and thorns in your sides' (*Numbers*, xxxiii. 55) and 'They shall be as thorns in your sides' (*Judges*, ii. 3); but see also 2 *Corinthians*, xii. 7.

'though I says it as shouldn't.' A late C. 19–20 modification of *though I say it myself*, a cliché of C. 19–20, anticipated in Langland, *Piers Plowman*, VIII, 192 (Benham).

thousand ills that flesh is heir to, the. A misquotation-cliché (late C. 19–20) of 'the thousand natural shocks . . .' (*Hamlet*, III, i).

thousands flock to beaches to seek relief (from a heat wave): American journalists': from ca. 1912. Chiefly as a head-line.

threadbare excuse, a. A hackneyed excuse; an excuse made too often by a specific person: late C. 19–20.

threescore and ten (years). The natural or average life of man; 'the allotted span': C. 19–20. From its frequency in the Bible: cf. 'The days of our years are threescore years and ten' (*Psalms*, xc. 10).

through and through (adverb). Thoroughly, entirely; in all respects: late C. 19–20. 'We were wet, through and through'; 'He's a good fellow, through and through'. Originally of penetration.

through (or **throughout**) **the ages.** From the beginning (and/or during the entire course) of recorded time: mid C. 19–20.—Cf. **time out of mind.**

*through thick and thin. Despite difficulties, hardships, or dangers, disgrace or persecution; esp., *to stick to a person through thick and thin*: C. 19–20. Originally in reference to *thicket* and *thin* wood (O.E.D.).

throw a veil over, to. To hide or conceal; to say nothing more about (a sexual incident or process): mid C. 19–20.

throw down the glove, to. To issue a challenge: mid C. 19–20; slightly obsolescent.—Cf. **trail one's cloak.**

throw dust in a person's eyes, to. To deceive or delude him: mid C. 19–20.

throw off the scent, to. To divert the attentions or suspicions of: C. 19–20. From hunting.

throw oneself on another's generosity, to. To commit oneself, or to trust, utterly to another's generosity or forgiveness: C. 20.

thrust and parry. Stroke and counterstroke, applied esp. to debate and witty conversation: late C. 19–20. 'He much enjoys the cut and thrust of riposte and repartee.' From fencing.

thrust down someone's throat, to (?). To force (e.g., an opinion) upon him: mid C. 19–20.

thus far—and no farther. To this point, extent, degree, but no further: C. 20.—Cf. 'Hitherto [= to this point] shalt thou come, but no further' (*Job*, xxxviii. 11).

tied. See **apron-strings** and **hand and foot.**

tighten one's belt, to (?). To brace oneself against hunger or penury: C. 20. To tighten one's belt is supposed to reduce the pangs of hunger.

tilt at windmills, to. To attack imaginary foes or abuses: mid C. 19–20. With reference to *acometer molinos de viento*, 'to attack w.' (Cervantes, *Don Quixote*, I, 8).

time and time again. Very often; repetitiously: late C. 19–20. An elaboration of *time and again* (a C. 19 variant of **again and again**).

time immemorial. See **from time immemorial.**

time is not far distant when . . ., the. Soon: public speakers': late C. 19–20. An oratorical rotundity.

time is (or **was**) **ripe, the.** It is, or was, a very suitable occasion or period (for something to happen or be done); time is sufficiently advanced: late C. 19–20. Ripe-fruit opportunity.

time marches on. See **march of time.**

time out of mind. 'From a time or during a period beyond human memory' (O.E.D.): mid C. 18–20. Synonymous with the obsolete *time out of memory*.

time (or **Time**) **stood still.** 'There seemed to be no such thing as time', is applied to moments or periods of ecstasy or profound absorption: late C. 19–20.

time (or **the time**) **was when** (one did or was able or accustomed to do something). There was a time when: mid C. 19–20; rather literary. 'Time was when we had a national style', Micklethwaite, 1870 (O.E.D.).

time (or **Time**) **with his sickle** (less often: **hour-glass**). Time personified: mid C. 19–20. In the conventional representation, Time has an hour-glass in one hand, a sickle in the other.

'timeo Danaos et dona ferentes.' I fear the Greeks even when they bring gifts; *their* (or *his* or . . .) friendliness is suspect: C. 19–20. Virgil, *Æneid*, II, 49.

times are out of joint, the. The age is restless, disturbed, 'quite unsatisfactory, don't you know!': late C. 19–20. Based on 'The time is out of joint' (*Hamlet*, I, v).

tinkling cymbal, a; tinkling cymbals. A chattering, brainless person: C. 19–20. And see **sounding brass.**

tip from the stable, a (colloquial). Confidential information: late C. 19–20. From horse-racing.

'tis a mad world, my masters. Gentlemen, it is a mad world we live in: C. 19–20. Originally, it was probably a quotation; John Taylor, 'the Water Poet', gave it in this form ca. 1620 (Benham).

tit for tat (?). A fair (or a natural) return or reciprocation; a retaliation: C. 19–20; originally of one blow for another. Cf. the proverb *tit for tat is fair play*.

to a fault. See **generous** . . .

to all intents and purposes. Virtually: mid C. 19–20.

'to be, or not to be; that is the question.' C. 19–20. *Hamlet*, III, i. Often parodied.

*to say the least of it. To put it mildly or temperately: mid C. 19–20.

*to tell the truth, . . . ; truth to tell (an elegant variation). A (generally, introductory) formula of mid C. 19–20; the latter is obsolescent.

to that effect. See **or words** . . .

to the bitter end. To direst extremity; to death itself: from ca. 1870.—Cf. the title of John Brophy's fine war-novel, *The Bitter End*, 1928.

to the end of the chapter. To the end; until death; always: late C. 19–20.—Cf. Thackeray's 'Yet a few chapters more, and then the last: after which, behold Finis itself comes to an end, and the Infinite begun' (*Roundabout Papers*, 1860–62), cited by Benham.

to the finger-tips, 'entirely' (late C. 19–20), is a border-line case; ***have at one's finger-tips,** 'to know thoroughly and have at ready command; to be readily familiar with', is a fully qualified cliché, dating from ca. 1880.

to the manner born; esp., **as to the . . .,** with natural ease, as though one were born with the knowledge of what to do or how to do it: mid C. 19–20. From *Hamlet*, I, iv.

to the tune of. To the extent, amount, sum of: mid C. 18–20. Generally in reference to money, as in 'fined to the tune of £20'. Developed from the earlier sense, 'according to, in accordance with'. (See O.E.D. at *tune*, n., 6.)

toe the mark, to. To conform wholly and immediately to a rule, a principle, a policy: mid C. 19–20. Synonymously *toe the line*, which is rather less common—not a cliché.

toiling millions (or **multitudes**), **the** . . . Those who work hard for little money: late C. 19–20.—Cf. 'Too long, that some may rest, | Tired millions toil unblest', Sir William Watson.

token of one's esteem, a. See **present with** . . .

*Tom, Dick, and Harry, every; any T., D., or H. Everyone—anyone—of no matter what social grade or degree of ability: C. 19–20, though recorded, in other forms, centuries earlier. ' "We can't have every Tom, Dick and Harry throwing the damned thing in our teeth" ' (F. W. Crofts, *Fatal Venture*, 1939). From the commonness of these pet-forms of *Thomas, Richard, Henry.*

*tongue in one's cheek; esp., **to have one's** . . . and **speak with one's** . . ., to speak insincerely: from ca. 1870. I.e., with unexpressed reservations.

tongues of rumour, the (?). The voice of rumour; active rumour; rumours: mid C. 19–20; obsolescent.

too (e.g., **thrilling**) **for words.** Very thrilling, etc.: colloquial: late C. 19–20.

too much . . . See **have too much** . . .

too numerous to mention. Too numerous to particularize: late C. 19–20.

tooth and nail. See **fight tooth and nail.**

top of one's bent, the. See **fool** . . .

torn asunder. Painfully divided between desire and duty, between integrity and worldly interest, or between two loyalties: late C. 19–20. Lit., torn apart, torn in two.

tortures of the damned, the. See **suffer the . . .**

touch and go. A very narrow escape; a delicate, ticklish, precarious state of things: mid C. 19–20. 'It was touch and go whether reinforcements would arrive in time.' A mere touch would cause disaster (O.E.D.).

touch with a pair of tongs, not to; . . . with a barge-pole. 'I would not touch it with a pair of tongs!'—'with a barge-pole!': colloquial: from ca. 1810, 1880.

touched on the raw; touched to the quick. Annoyed (the former only); painfully or exquisitely or poignantly affected: respectively, colloquial, C. 20, and Standard English, mid C. 19–20. For the semantics, cf. **wring one's withers.**

touched to finger issues is an adaptation of Shakespeare's 'Spirits are not finely touched but to fine issues' (*Measure for Measure*, 1, i); in C. 20, a cliché, literary rather than general.

toujours la politesse! Always politeness; always polite: from ca. 1880. Often in reference to Frenchmen.

*tower of strength, a. A powerful or a most reliable, resourceful person: mid C. 19–20. Tennyson, *Ode on the Death of the Duke of Wellington*, 1852, 'O fall'n at length that tower of strength'. God is, in the Bible, often alluded to as a tower, 'a strong tower'—a source of protection.

towering passion, a; esp., **to be in a . . .** A *mounting* passion; great and increasing anger: C. 19–20. Shakespeare and Scott have *in(to) a towering passion.*

town mouse. See **country mouse.**

traffic is (or was) at a virtual standstill. An American newspaper reporters' cliché, dating from ca. 1905.

235

trail one's cloak, to. To be provocative; to give offence deliberately: from ca. 1920. A medieval provocation to a duel.

'trailing clouds of glory.' In reference to human beings, who are endowed with glory at birth: mid C. 19–20. 'Not in utter nakedness, | But trailing clouds of glory do we come' (Wordsworth, *Intimations of Immortality*, 1803).

trashy fiction (?). Sensational and/or worthless novels and stories: from ca. 1880.

*treat (someone or something) **with the contempt** (he or it) **deserves, to,** is exceedingly common in C. 20.

trials and tribulations. Trouble and hardship; troubles: late C. 19–20. From the frequency of *trial(s)* and *tribulation(s)* in the Bible.

tried and found wanting is a mid C. 19–20 adaptation of 'weighed in the balances and found wanting' (*Daniel*, v. 27).

trifles light as air. Airy trifles; baseless suspicions: C. 19–20. Shakespeare, 'Trifles, light as air, | Are to the jealous confirmations strong' (*Othello*, III, iii).

Triton among minnows, a. A person far pre-eminent above his fellows: late C. 19–20; earlier, *among the* . . .; originally *of the* . . ., Shakespeare, 'This Triton of the minnows' (*Coriolanus*, III, i). (A sea-god among the fish.)

trouble brewing; esp., there is . . ., trouble is coming, is being prepared: mid C. 19–20. Richardson, 1741, 'There is mischief brewing' (O.E.D.). Perhaps from the brewing of beer.

true blue. Staunch; unwavering in one's faith or principles: mid C. 18–20. *True blue will never stain*, a proverb recorded in 1672. In late C. 19–20 politics, it = 'staunchly Tory' (Conservative): the predominant C. 20 sense. (Benham; O.E.D.)

true inwardness. The inner merit; the quintessence: literary: late C. 19–20; obsolescent.

true to one's colours. Loyal to a cause, an ambition, an aim: late C. 19–20. *Colours* = flag.

truly representative. Genuinely representative; admirably illustrative: C. 20. 'He is truly representative of his age.'

trusty sword, one's. One's trustworthy sword: late C. 19–20; in C. 20, jocular. Spenser, 1596, 'His trusty sword, the servant of his might' (O.E.D.).

truth is beauty, beauty truth is a misquotation (late C. 19–20) of ' "Beauty is truth, truth beauty ",—that is all | Ye know on earth, and all ye need to know' (Keats, *Ode on a Grecian Urn*).

truth to tell. See **to tell the truth.**

tug at one's heart-strings, to. To be poignantly appealing to: late C. 19–20. 'The child, happily playing in the grimy street, tugged at his heart-strings.'

tug of war, the. See **when Greek . . .**

turn a blind eye to, to; to turn a deaf ear (to), to. To pretend to be blind or deaf, so as to enable something illicit or 'unconstitutional' to be done: C. 19–20. The former was probably popularized by Nelson's masterly blindness at the battle of Copenhagen, 1801.

turn a hair, not to; without turning a hair. See **hair.**

turn an honest penny, to. See **honest penny.**

turn in one's grave, to. See **enough . . .**

*turn of the tide, a or **the.** A or the change in fortune: C. 19–20. From the literal sense.—Cf. Shakespeare's 'There is a tide in the affairs of man, | Which taken at the flood, leads on to fortune' (*Julius Cæsar*, IV, iii, 218–19), itself a cliché of C. 19–20.

237

turn out en masse, to. An American (witness Sullivan) and English cliché of late C. 19–20.

*turn over a new leaf, to. To adopt a better course of conduct: C. 19–20. Recorded for 1597 (O.E.D.). From turning the pages of a book.

turn tail, to. To flee; to retreat: mid C. 19–20. Originally a phrase in falconry.

*turn the other cheek, to. To be meek under insult, provocation, punishment, oppression: C. 19–20. With reminiscence of 'Unto him that smiteth thee on the one cheek offer also the other' (*Luke*, vi. 29).

turn the tables on, to. To obtain advantages, or the upper hand, of one who held the upper hand; to reverse the relative position or condition: C. 18–20. From players that reverse the position of the board in order to reverse their relative positions (O.E.D.).

turn up like a bad penny, to. To arrive, to arrive continually, as a bad (counterfeit or defaced) penny seems to do; applied to ne'er-do-wells and scamps: mid C. 19–20.

turn up one's nose at, to. To scorn; to despise: mid C. 19–20. This action (often accompanied with a sniff) indicates contempt.

turn up trumps, to. Applied to something that turns out favourably: C. 19–20; originally colloquial. From games of cards.

twelve. See **good men and true**.

Twelve Tribes, the. A jocular, not unkindly, reference to Jews: late C. 19–20.

*twist round one's little finger, to. A cliché variant of *twist round one's finger* (late C. 18–20; obsolescent): late C. 19–20. To have completely in one's control or under one's influence.

two of a kind (or a trade). Two persons of the same trade (or profession) or of the same sort of character—or lack of it. Mid C. 19–20.

two strings to one bow. See **have two . . .**

U

ugly duckling, an or **one's.** The plainest or stupidest child in a family, but turning out to be the handsomest or cleverest of all: 1869, Dickens. From Hans Andersen's tale of the cygnet hatched with a brood of ducklings and at first despised for its ugliness. (O.E.D.)

unalloyed pleasure. Pleasure unmixed with pain, discomfort, or doubt: from ca. 1880. From unalloyed (unmixed) metal.

unavoidable delay, an; unavoidable delays. From ca. 1890.

Uncle Sam. See **Brother Jonathan.**

unconfirmed rumour (or report), an. Uncorroborated rumour or report: C. 20; originally journalistic.

unconsidered trifle(s). See **snapper-up.**

uncrowned king of (some country), the. A person that, by virtue of his power, is the virtual ruler (of a country, a district, a commercial activity): from ca. 1910.

und so weiter. And so forth: from ca. 1875. (German phrase.)

***under a cloud, to be.** In (temporary) disgrace: mid C. 18–20; recorded as early as ca. 1500 (O.E.D.).

under a rough exterior. Applied to a person that, in appearance rough, has **a heart of gold**: late C. 19–20. 'Under his rough exterior, he possessed many admirable qualities.'

under one's breath (?). In a faint whisper or a very low voice: mid C. 19-20. 'He swore under his breath.'

under the aegis of. Under the powerful protection of; protected by: literary: mid C. 19-20. From the αἰγίς or shield of Jupiter and/or Minerva.

under the Southern Cross. In the Southern Hemisphere: an Australian cliché, dating from ca. 1880.

under the sun. 'It was, they thought, the richest country under the sun', in the world; anywhere on earth: 1382, Wyclif; a cliché in C. 17-20.

under the thumb of, to be . . . To be utterly and easily controlled by (another person); subservient to him: C. 19-20.

undetermined origin. 'The fire was of undetermined origin.' American: C. 20. (Sullivan.)

'uneasy lies the head that wears a crown.' C. 19-20. Shakespeare, *King Henry IV*, Part 2, Act III, sc. i.

unfathomable designs; an unfathomable secret (?). Designs—a secret—that cannot be discovered, discerned, guessed: C. 20.

unfortunate pedestrian(s). Luckless walker(s) across city streets or along arterial roads: from ca. 1925. 'There are only two kinds of pedestrians—the quick and the dead' (Vernon Rendall, ca. 1930).

unfortunate women. Prostitutes: from ca. 1820. (Hence Hood's 'One more Unfortunate . . . Gone to her Death', *The Bridge of Sighs*, 1844.) Originally a London Society expression (Grose, 1796).

unkindest cut of all, the; 'the most unkindest cut of all'. The former is an incipient cliché (late C. 19-20; by misquotation), the latter (C. 19-20) a fully qualified one, from Shakespeare, *Julius Cæsar*, III, ii, 187.

unleash the dogs of war. See **let loose . . .**

unmistakable symptom, an. A sure sign of disease, malady, love, etc.: C. 20. Medical at first.

unprecedented situation, an. A situation without precedent, generally with a pejorative connotation: from ca. 1890.

unsavoury reputation, an. A bad and/or unpleasant reputation: C. 20. 'The sort of people with the reputation that we journalists describe as unsavoury' (Somerset Maugham, *Christmas Holiday*, 1939).

unshakeable alibi, an. A crime reporters' and detective-story writers' cliché: from ca. 1925.—Cf. the next.

unsolved mystery, an. From ca. 1880, but esp. since ca. 1920.

unspeakable Turk, the. See **terrible Turk.**

unsubstantiated report, an (?). An uncorroborated report: C. 20. In C. 19, *unsubstantiated rumour* was almost a cliché.

until death do us (or them) part. *Us* is the original form; from *The Book of Common Prayer*; from ca. 1870. The latter dates, as a cliché, from ca. 1890: see the Introduction, para. 2.

untimely end, an; esp., **come to . . .** To die prematurely: mid C. 19–20. Addison, 1709, 'Souls of infants . . . snatched away by untimely ends'; Prescott, 1847, 'An untimely and miserable end' (O.E.D.).

untold advantages (perhaps); **untold riches** (certainly). Very numerous advantages; vast wealth; late C. 19–20; mid C. 19–20 (in C. 17–18, *untold gold*). And *untold wealth* (late C. 19–20) is gaining ground.

'unwept, unhonoured, and unsung.' Of a dead person: mid C. 19–20. From Scott, *The Lay of the Last Minstrel*, 1805. Anticipated by Euripides (*Antigone*) and Pope (*Odyssey*).

unwritten law, the. The 'rules' of decency and, as Hobbes put it (ca. 1670), 'right reason': mid C. 19–20. From *unwritten law* (Common Law).

up and doing, to be. To be actively busy, esp. after an illness or a rest: colloquial: late C. 19–20.

up in arms (figuratively used). Actively ready to take offence—and action: C. 19–20; perhaps longer, for cf. Swift, 1704, 'All the men of wit . . . were immediately up in arms' (O.E.D.).

up like a rocket and down like a stick. Applied to a person that 'fizzles out', starts well and ends as a failure: from ca. 1880; obsolescent.

up to one's eyes in work (colloquial). Extremely busy: late C. 19–20.

up to scratch (or **the scratch**), **to come.** To do one's duty, or what is expected of one: mid C. 19–20. From the line drawn on the ground or floor to divide a boxing-ring.

*up to the hilt. Completely, entirely, to the furthest degree possible: mid C. 19–20 (in C. 17, '. . . hilts'). From a dagger inthrust right to the hilt. Often used absurdly.

ups and downs. Vicissitudes: mid C. 19–20. From irregularities on the surface of ground.

*upset the apple-cart, to. To upset a plan or intention: mid C. 19–20. Originally *the apple-cart* signified 'the human body'.

use and wont. Habit and custom; accustomed practice and custom: C. 19–20; obsolescent. Recorded by the O.E.D. as early as 1609.

utter darkness, in. In complete darkness: mid C. 19–20.

V

væ victis! Woe to the conquered!: C. 18-20. Livy, V, xlviii, 9, ascribes to Brennus the exclamation: *væ victis! intoleranda Romanis vox*. It corresponds to the Greek *οὐαί* and the English *woe!*

vagaries of the English climate, the. The seemingly unaccountable and rapid changes in English weather: C. 20.— Cf. the once very common phrase, *the vagaries of fashion*.

valley of the shadow (of death), the (or with capitals). An almost fatal illness; experience thereof. First in Coverdale, 1535, but thoroughly popularized by Bunyan in *Pilgrim's Progress*, 1678. See *Psalms*, xxiii. 4. Hence, the shadow of death, in the same sense, is also a cliché: C. 19-20.

valued guest of honour, a. An Americanism: late C. 19-20. (Sullivan.)

*vanish into thin air. To vanish; to depart and be seen no more: mid C. 19-20. Originally of ghosts.

vast difference, a (?). A very great difference: C. 20. 'A rise of a pound a week will make a vast difference to him.'

venerable pile, a or **the.** An ancient (and impressive) edifice: mid C. 19-20.

'veni, vidi, vici.' I came, I saw, I conquered: C. 18-20. Julius Cæsar's famous statement.

venture a guess (or **an opinion**), **to; *I venture to say.** To hazard a guess or an opinion; I dare say: late C. 19-20.

'verray parfit, gentil knyght,—a.' Literally 'a truly perfect, noble knight', it is often used of a very courteous, knightly gentleman: mid C. 19-20. Chaucer, *Canterbury Tales*, Prologue, 72.

very much the reverse. See **quite the opposite.**

***very present help in (time of) trouble, a.** 'A cliché, like a lie, is a very present help in trouble' (H. A. Vachell). Mid C. 19–20. Here, *present* = 'practical', and the short, the correct form comes from *The Book of Common Prayer*.

very right and proper. Correct and fitting: late C. 19–20. ' "He married her, you know."—"Very right and proper, I'm sure." ' Mostly lower middle-class.

vested interests (?). Established or definitely assigned shares or privileges: from ca. 1840. (Cf. *a vested legal right*.)

vexed question, a. A translation of Latin *quæstio vexata* (or *vexata quæstio*): mid C. 19–20. I.e., a difficult question, and often posed.

via dolorosa. Latin for 'dolorous way or road', it is a mid C. 19–20 literary cliché when used figuratively. (*Dolorosus* is late Latin; the Classical L. would probably have been *via tristis*.)

vicious circle, a. Applied esp. to an argument that comes full circle: mid C. 19–20. Carlyle, 1843.

'vicisti, Galilæe!' Thou hast conquered, O Galilean: C. 19–20. Julian the Apostate, apostrophizing Christ.

view the prospect with complacency, to. To regard a probability (or an outlook) without fear, uneasiness, or doubt: late C. 19–20.

violation of sacred principles, a. An American political cliché of C. 20. (Stuart Chase, *The Tyranny of Words*, 1938.)

virgin page, a. A page unwritten on: mid C. 19–20. In 1785, Crabbe spoke of 'the virgin copies' of books and newspapers: unbought, unread.

visible to the naked eye. Visible without microscope: late C. 19–20.

vital spark, the. That which distinguishes the living person from the corpse; the principle or essence of the physical human being: C. 19–20. F. Reynolds, 1826, 'For some moments it was supposed that the vital spark was extinct' (O.E.D.).

voice an opinion, to. To utter an opinion, esp. in public: from ca. 1890. Originally and still mostly journalistic.

voice (crying) in the wilderness, a. A C. 19–20 adaptation of St. John's 'I am the voice of one crying in the wilderness' (i, 23); esp. of precursive messages or warnings.

'vox et præterea nihil.' A sound (or voice or word) and nothing else: C. 19–20. Often jocular or sarcastic.

vox populi, vox Dei. The voice (i.e., expressed opinion) of the people is the voice of God: C. 17–20. 'Frequently cited or alluded to in English works from C. 15 onwards' (O.E.D.). A Roman maxim.

vulnerable spot, esp., the. The vulnerable point or place: C. 20; but chiefly since September 1938. From the military *vulnerable part* or *point*, much used during the Napoleonic Wars.

W

wages of sin, the; 'the wages of sin is death'. The payment—wages paid—for sin is death; sin results in death: C. 19–20. *Romans*, vi. 23 (τὰ γὰρ ὀψώνια τῆς ἁμαρτίας θάνατος).

waifs and strays (figuratively). Oddments; things not classified elsewhere, things unclassifiable: C. 20. Prob. from the Waifs and Strays Society—for children homeless or lost.

wait on hand and foot, to. See **serve hand and foot.**

*walk on (or **upon**) **air, to;** esp., **to feel as if** (or **though**) **one were walking on air.** To feel 'on top of the world', to be exultant: late C. 19–20.

walking encyclopædia, a. A polymath; a person with a great fund of information at command: mid C. 19–20. (A *walking library*, 1691: O.E.D.)

wallow in the mire, to. To give oneself whole-heartedly and without restraint to sensual enjoyment: late C. 19–20. The phrase occurs in its literal sense in 1577 (O.E.D.).

war impends. War is obviously near; war threatens to come shortly: from ca. 1910; mostly journalistic.—Cf. Cicero's 'Belli magni timor impendet' (the fear of a big war hangs over us).

war-path. See **go on the war-path.**

war to end war, a. Since late 1914. 'This war, like the next war, is a war to end war', anonymous (cited by Benham).

war to the knife; esp., **it is** (or **was**) **war . . .** Relentless and/or fierce war; war to the death: not a cliché in its literal sense (Spanish *guerra al cuchillo*: the origin of the English phrase, O.E.D.), but in its figurative: mid C. 19–20.

'wars and rumours of wars'; often adapted to **war and rumours of war.** Actual warfare and hints, talk, reports of war(s): respectively mid C. 19–20 and C. 20. The quotation is from *Matthew*, xxiv. 6 (πολέμους καὶ ἀκοὰς πολέμων).

*warm the cockles of one's heart, to. Applied to something that causes one to rejoice or feel very happy: mid C. 19–20. (Scott, 1821; earlier as *rejoice, please, delight*: O.E.D.) A cockle is zoologically *Cardium*, from Greek καρδία, 'heart'.

warm to one's work, to. To become animated in, or eager about, one's work: from ca. 1880. *Warm to one's subject* (mid C. 19–20) is almost a cliché.

was not to be, (but) it or **that.** Fate ordained otherwise: sentimentalists': late C. 19–20, though common throughout the Victorian era.

---

*wash one's dirty linen in public, to. To make public one's disgrace or scandalousness; to discuss in public what should be talked about only at home: from ca. 1860.

wash one's hands of, to. To disown; to refuse to have anything more to do with: mid C. 18–20. Originally (C. 16) in allusion to Pilate's washing his hands (*Matthew*, xxvii. 24).

waste one's breath, to. To speak to no purpose: C. 19–20. (Dryden, 1667; *waste words*, C. 15–20. O.E.D.)

watch and ward. See **keep** . . .

*'water, water everywhere, and not a drop to drink.' A misquotation of 'water, water everywhere, nor any drop to drink' (Coleridge, *The Ancient Mariner*): mid C. 19–20.

wave of optimism, a (?). A not easily resisted optimistic mood or movement sweeping over a country: C. 20.

way of all flesh, the; to go the way . . ., to die, or rather, to decline, die, and be buried: C. 20. This is a misquotation of 'This day I am going the way of all the earth' (dying), *Joshua*, xxiii. 14; cf. 1 *Kings*, ii. 2. Erewhon Butler's novel, *The Way of All Flesh*, appeared posthumously in 1903.

'way of transgressors is hard, the'; often misquoted as **the way of the transgressor is hard.** C. 19–20: both forms are border-line cases. *Proverbs*, xiii. 15.

ways and means. See **discuss ways and means.**

we all come to it sometime (or **sooner or later**). In reference, esp. the former, to death or, esp. the latter, to love: mid C. 19–20.

'we are none of us infallible, not even the youngest.' From ca. 1880. W. H. Thompson (1810–86), Master of Trinity, Cambridge.

'we are not amused.' Queen Victoria's icy remark (ca. 1880): late C. 19–20.

'we are such stuff . . .' See 'such stuff . . .'

we shall not look upon his like again is an adaptation (a C. 19–20 cliché) of Shakespeare's 'He was a man, take him for all in all, | I shall not look upon his like again' (*Hamlet*, I, ii).

weaker vessel, the. A wife; a man's female partner: C. 19–20. 'Likewise, ye husbands, dwell with them . . ., giving honour unto the wife, as unto the weaker vessel' (I *Peter*, iii. 7): ἀσθενεστέρῳ σκεύει (utensil).

weal or woe; esp., **for weal or woe,** for (or in) prosperity and hardship, happiness and grief: C. 19–20, although *weal and woe* occurs so early as ca. 1000. (The earliest sense of *weal* is 'wealth'.)

wealth of meaning, a; esp., **with a . . .,** richly significant (or significant), often with a sense of innuendo: late C. 19–20. *Wealth* here = 'abundance'.

*****wear one's heart on one's sleeve, to.** To show one's feelings, esp. one's affections, for all the world to see: C. 19–20. Originally in reference to Shakespeare's 'I will wear my heart upon my sleeve | For daws to peck at' (*Othello*, I, i).

wear the trousers, to (colloquial). Of a woman ('the grey mare is the better horse') that dominates her husband: C. 18–20. Adumbrated in C. 15: see Apperson.

weariness of the flesh, a. Applied to something that wearies: mid C. 19–20. *Ecclesiastes*, xii. 12, 'Much study is a weariness of the flesh'.

(good, bad, etc.) weather (has) occurred over widespread areas. American journalistic of C. 20. (Sullivan.)

weather the storm, to. To sustain crisis, adversity, danger, without disaster: mid C. 19–20. Macaulay, 1849, 'Who weathered the fiercest storms of faction' (O.E.D.). From a ship's withstanding a storm.

wedded bliss. Happiness in marriage: late C. 19–20. Contrast **single blessedness.**

weighed in the balance and found wanting. A reminiscence and adaptation (and a C. 19–20 cliché) of 'Thou art weighed in the balances, and art found wanting' (*Daniel*, v. 27).

weighty reasons. Forcible or potent reasons: late C. 19–20. (Cf. *weighty arguments*.)

*welcome with open arms, to. To welcome warmly or eagerly; to receive affectionately or eagerly: late C. 18–20. 'The envoy was received with open arms.'

well and good. (It is) all right, permissible, understandable: C. 19–20. 'If you like to write such trash, well and good; after all, it's your concern.' (Cf. French *à la bonne heure*.)

*well and truly. Thoroughly; properly or fittingly; duly: late C. 19–20. 'I declare this [foundation] stone to be well and truly laid' (a formula). An elaboration of *truly*, 'accurately, rightly'.

well-earned rest. Deserved repose or relaxation or holiday: from ca. 1880. 'The statesman is now enjoying a well-earned rest.'

well he (or **she** or **they** or . . .) **know(s)—or knew—it.** 'He knows (or knew) it', in intensive form: late C. 19–20.

well-known resident, a. American, slightly more than English: mid C. 19–20. (Sullivan.)

well nigh. Almost (wholly); very nearly: C. 19–20. 'He was well nigh dead, exhausted, killed.' If regarded as one word, it is then a vogue-word.

Welsh Wizard, the. The Rt. Hon. David Lloyd George (b., Jan. 17, 1863), M.P. for Caernarvon in 1890–1931; Chancellor of the Exchequer in 1908–15, Prime Minister in

1916–22: from ca. 1910; obsolescent. With reference to his eloquence and his financial magic.—Cf. **Wizard of the North.**

*wend one's way, to. To go: from ca. 1830. Current in C. 14–16, it was revived (esp. by Scott) early in C. 19. Literally, to turn one's way: cf. *turn one's steps* (in a specified direction).

wet to the skin. Drenched; thoroughly wet: recorded for 1526, but not a cliché until mid C. 19.

what a wonderful place the world would be if (or **if only**), e.g., kindness or even good sense prevailed: C. 20.

what with one thing and another. Mid C. 19–20. 'What . . ., he doesn't know what to do.'

'what's Hecuba to him, or he to Hecuba?' C. 19–20. From Shakespeare, *Hamlet*, II, ii (completed by 'that he should weep for her').

*wheels within wheels. A semi-proverbial saying: C. 19–20. Probably from *Ezekiel*, x. 10, 'As if a wheel had been within a wheel', Revised Version. (Benham.)

when all is said and done. From ca. 1870. 'When . . ., it is not his fault but yours.'

*'when Greek meets Greek (then comes the tug-of-war).' A late C. 18–20 cliché that is a misquotation of Nathaniel Lee's 'When Greeks joined Greeks' (i.e., engaged in battle) 'then was the tug-of-war' (*The Rival Queens* (IV, ii), a poetic tragedy, 1677).

when one's ship comes home. When one succeeds; when one's projects bear fruit: mid C. 19–20. Perhaps with a reminiscence of *The Merchant of Venice*.

where 'every prospect pleases, and only man is vile.' As a quotation-cliché, it has been common throughout C. 19–20; in mid C. 19–20, it is often incorporated into the text, thus, 'It was like being in a little universe of her own where every prospect pleased—and only man was vile' (George Goodchild, *Yellowstones*, 1938). The quotation is from Reginald Heber's († 1826) *Hymns*, where it is *though*, not *where*.

whip-hand. See **have the whip-hand.**

whirligig of time, the. Time in its whirling course: C. 19–20. (Shakespeare, *Twelfth Night*, v, i, 385.)

whisper it not in Gath. See **tell it not . . .**

white blackbird, a. Applied to rarity: C. 19–20; obsolescent. An adaptation of Juvenal's *corvo quoque rarior albo*, 'rarer even than a white raven' (*Satires*, vii, 202): *rarissima avis*, in short.

white cliffs of Dover, the (figuratively for 'England on one's departure or arrival'): mid C. 19–20. With reference to the chalk.

*white elephant, a. A burdensomely costly and exasperatingly useless possession: late C. 19–20. The kings of Siam formerly—so the story goes—presented a white elephant to obnoxious courtiers, likely to be ruined by the expense of maintenance.

white feather. See **show the . . .**

'white flower of a blameless life, the' or **'wearing the . . .'** A mark, sign, indication of purity and integrity: from ca. 1870. Tennyson, 'Dedication' (1861) of *Idylls of The King*.

white man, to be a (colloquial). To be honourable: American (late C. 19–20), then (from ca. 1910) English. Originally in contradistinction to a negro.

*white man's burden, the. The white races' responsibility for the coloured races—or, at least, for the uncivilized coloured races: C. 20. From a famous poem addressed, Feb. 4, 1899, by Kipling to the U.S.A.

whited sepulchres. A lovely mockery; a beautiful (or agreeable) exterior with a foul interior: mid C. 19–20. *Matthew*, xxiii. 27, 'Ye are like unto whited sepulchres, . . . beautiful outward, but . . . within full . . . of all uncleanness'.

. . . who shall be nameless. Somebody, whose name we shall not mention: late C. 19–20.

'who shall minister to a mind diseased?' is a C. 19–20 misquotation of the passage cited at **minister . . .**

wholesome respect. See **to have a . . .**

whom the gods love die young. The usual form (C. 19–20) of 'He whom the gods love dies young' (Menander and Plautus).

*****why and (the) wherefore, the.** The immediate and the ultimate reasons: from ca. 1830. Often, it merely = 'the reason'.

wide open spaces, the. See **great open spaces.**

widow's mite, the (or **a**). A small contribution in money, the most one can afford: C. 19–20. From *Mark*, xii. 42, 'A certain poor widow . . . threw in two mites, which make a farthing', her action being praised by Christ in the next verse.

wild horses would not drag (originally: **draw**) **it from me.** Nothing could make me divulge it: mid C. 19–20. From a medieval form of torture.

will come into her (or **his** or **its** or **. . .**) **own, she** (or **. . .**). Will receive merited praise, reward, position: late C. 19–20. *Come into* = 'come into possession of'.

willingly let die, not to. See **world will not . . .**

win golden opinions, to. (E.g., of a book) to be very well received: late C. 19–20. Originally, with a reminiscence of 'I have bought | Golden opinions from all sorts of people' (*Macbeth*, I, vii).

win hands down, to (colloquial). To win easily: late C. 19–20. From a jockey's relaxing his hold on the reins and dropping his hands when victory is certain.

win (someone's) **heart, to.** To obtain, esp. by merit, someone's love: mid C. 19–20; slightly obsolescent (merit being out of fashion).

win (one's) **spurs, to.** To achieve one's first success: mid C. 19–20. From a squire's winning the spurs of knighthood by performing a gallant deed in battle.

wings of the wind; esp., **on the wings . . .,** swiftly: C. 19–20. A reminiscence of *Psalms*, xviii. 10, 'He [God] did fly upon the wings of the wind': Vulgate, 'Volavit super pennas ventorum'.

winter holds (e.g., the entire Eastern seaboard) **in its icy grip.** An American journalistic cliché of late C. 19–20. (Sullivan.)

wise after the event. A proverbial saying that, in C. 19–20, is a cliché. Anticipated in Homer, *Iliad*, XVII, 32; in Tacitus; in Livy: see Apperson.

*wise saws and modern instances. Shrewd sayings with up-to-date examples: C. 19–20. Originally in allusion to 'the justice [of the peace], . . . full of wise saws . . .' (*As You Like It*, II, vii).

wishful thinking. A cliché (from ca. 1930) among Freudians; cf. the proverb, 'the wish is father to the thought'.

witching hour of midnight, the. Midnight (to a romantic mind): mid C. 19–20. Probably with an allusion to Shakespeare's 'the very witching time of night, when graveyards yawn' (*Hamlet*, III, ii, 406–7).

*with a vengeance. Severely; to an extreme degree or unusual extent: mid C. 17–20. 'And then it rained with a vengeance.' Originally, 'with a curse'.

with all one's heart (and soul). See **heart and soul.**

with an eye to the main chance. See **eye to . . .**

with bated breath. With one's breathing restrained: late C. 19–20. 'He listened with bated breath to these stories of adventure.'

with flying colours; often **to come off with . . .,** to emerge with brilliant success from a struggle or an ordeal: C. 19–20. (Locke, 1692, as here.) Originally of a man-of-war.

with his blushing honours. See **blushing honours.**

with might and main. See **might and main.**

with one's tail . . . See **go off . . .**

with telling effect. See **telling effect.**

within limits (?). Within reasonable limits: late C. 19–20. 'He was to be given a free hand, within limits', i.e. a reasonably free hand.

without counting the cost. Recklessly; scorning, or forgetting, to foresee the expense or the grievous result: C.19–20. —Cf. the Scottish proverb, 'He that counts all costs will never put plough in the earth'.

*without let or hindrance. Without hindrance, unhampered; free or freely; mid C. 19–20. *Let* = 'hindrance'; earlier, *without let or stay* (C. 17–18).

without more ado. Without fuss or ceremony: mid C. 19–20.—Loosely: promptly; very soon: C. 20.

without rhyme or reason. See **neither rhyme . . .**

without turning a hair. See **turn a hair.**

Wizard of the North, the. Sir Walter Scott: literary: from ca. 1818: obsolescent. From his tantalizing anonymity (post-1918 journalism would speak of 'the Mystery Man of Scotland') and the fame of his novels.

woe betide (you, if you do something). You will get into (serious) trouble if . . .: from ca. 1830; slightly obsolescent.

*wolf in sheep's clothing, a. A dangerous or greedy person with a mild exterior: mid C. 18–20. As a proverbial saying, in various forms, it goes back to C. 15.

*woman of a certain age, a. A middle-aged woman: C. 19–20. 'She was not old, nor young, nor at the years | Which certain people call a "*certain age*", | Which yet the most uncertain age appears', Byron, *Beppo* (published in 1818), stanza 22.

woman's glory, a. Her long hair: mid C. 19–20; obsolescent (*où sont les cheveux d'antan?*) 'If a woman have long hair, it is a glory [δόξα, a divine glory] to her' (1 *Corinthians*, xi. 15).

woman's intuition. Her faculty (often abused and inaccurate) of guessing correctly: late C. 19–20.

won in a canter (colloquial). Won easily: sporting (originally, turf): from ca. 1870.

word has been received that . . . A message has been received, that . . .: late C. 19–20.

word in season, a. A late C. 19–20 cliché-adaptation (perhaps based on the Revised Version reading) of 'A word spoken in due season, how good is it!' (*Proverbs*, xv. 23).

word in your ear!, a. I want a few words with you: late C. 19–20.

word is as good as one's bond, one's. Mid C. 19–20. '[He] had been brought up in the old-fashioned belief that one's word should be as good as one's bond' (C. Rushton, *Murder in Bavaria*, 1937). *Bond* = written agreement or pledge.

words cannot describe; words fail me. I am at a loss to describe or account for this event or thing: mid C. 19–20.

*words of wisdom. Wise words; shrewd advice: mid C. 19–20.—Cf. 'the words of truth and soberness', *Acts*, xxvi. 25: ἀληθείας καὶ σωφροσύνης ῥήματα ('utterances of truth and sound sense').

work of national importance; esp., **engaged in . . .,** helping to win the war: from mid September 1939. A catholic phrase that cloaks many a cynical, many a shameful wangle.

work one's fingers to the bone, to. To work exceedingly hard: mid C. 19–20. Originally of sempstresses.

work with . . . See **set to.**

worked to death (figurative). Hackneyed; too common: late C. 19–20. 'The secret door is worked to death in fiction.'

world has ever seen, the (or, in full, **that—which— whom the world . . .**). The most outstanding or remarkable or . . . or . . .: C. 18–20.

'world must be made safe for democracy, the.' Woodrow Wilson, to Congress, on April 2, 1917.

world of good, the; esp., **something does** (or **did** or **will do) somebody the . . .** 'That medicine did the poor old man the world of good.' Late C. 19–20.—Cf. the next.

world of truth, a; esp., **there's a world of truth in it,** there is much truth in it, or much more than you would suppose: mid C. 19–20.

world of waters, the (?). The oceans of the world: C. 19–20; obsolescent. Perhaps in allusion to the Noachian Flood.

*world, the flesh, and the Devil,—the. The world, human frailty, and the Devil that tempts us always: C. 19–20. From 'the deceits of the world, the flesh, and the devil', *The Book of Common Prayer*, the Litany.

world well lost for love, the; esp., **to believe** (or **think**) **the world . . .,** to set love above one's worldly interests: late C. 19–20.

world-wide conflagration, a. A great war, such as that of 1914–18 and that of 1939–?: C. 20; at first, journalistic (as, in the main, it is still).

world will not willingly let die, such as (or **that**) **the.** Some person, institution, cause, ideal that mankind values very highly: mid C. 19–20. An adaptation of 'By intent and labour . . . I might perhaps leave something so written to after times as they should not willingly let it die' (Milton, Introduction to Book II of his *Church Government*, 1641). (With thanks to Professor A. W. Stewart.)

worldly wisdom. Knowledge, esp. extensive knowledge, of the ways of mankind: mid C. 19–20.

*'**world's a stage (and all the men and women merely players), the** (properly, **all the**). C. 19–20; from Shakespeare's *As You Like It*, II, vii; cf. 'The world . . . a stage, where every man must play his part', *The Merchant of Venice*, I, i.

'**world's mine oyster, the**', often with the continuation '**which I with sword will open**'. C. 19–20. Shakespeare, *The Merry Wives of Windsor*, II, ii.

worn threadbare (or **to a shred**). Worn-out (clothes, ideas, expressions): late C. 19–20.

worn to a shadow (?). (Of a person) thin from hard work, anxiety, grief: C. 20.

'**worth makes a man, the want of it the fellow.**' C. 19–20. Pope, *Essay on Man*, 1734.

***worth one's weight in gold.** Extremely valuable (or useful): mid C. 19–20; but in use since late C. 16.

worthy of a better cause; esp., **with a courage** (or **an ability**) **worthy** . . . Applied to a misplaced virtue: C. 20.

would give the world to . . ., **I** or **you** or **he.** (Not *I should.*) I should very much like to . . .: late C. 19–20.

would not do (something) **for anything in the world, I** (etc.). I certainly should not do it; it would pain me extremely to do it: colloquial: late C. 19–20.

*****wring one's withers, to.** To harrow a person's feelings; prevail upon him by appealing to his compassion: mid C. 19–20. With an allusion to 'Let the galled jade wince, our withers are unwrung' (*Hamlet*, III, ii). See also **our withers.**

*****writing on the wall, the.** An event or incident that clearly shows impending misfortune: C. 19–20. See *Daniel*, v: Belshazzar's feast, troubled by *mene, mene, tekel, upharsin.*

wry jest (?). An ill-natured, or a bitter, jest: late C. 19–20.

Y

year in (and) year out. Year after year; unceasingly for many years: mid C. 19–20. 'There she sleeps, year in and year out, while the people of Newport die off, one after another' (Bruce Graeme, *Racing Yacht Mystery*, 1939).

yeoman service. See **perform** . . .

yield to no man in one's admiration of, to. To admire (somebody or something) at least as much as anyone else does: from ca. 1870.

yielding inch by inch. Surrendering, giving way, only an inch at a time: late C. 19–20.

*****you could have knocked me down with a feather.** I felt extremely surprised or taken aback: late C. 19–20.

you know what I mean. You understand (? or !): late C. 19–20.

you know what I think? An introductory time-gainer; a formula serving to modify the egoism of one's ensuing statement: late C. 19–20.

(you) mark my words! Pay attention to what I say! You'll see I'm right: mid C. 19–20. (Either before or after a statement.)

you may (or **might** or **will** or **would**) **not believe it, but** (e.g. **it's true**). See **believe it or not.**

young in heart, the. Those who are spiritually and emotionally youthful: from ca. 1925. In 1939 there was a cinematographic film so entitled.—Cf. **young no matter . . .**

young man's fancy, a; and its original, **'in the spring a young man's fancy lightly turns to thoughts of love'.** A young man's mood, imagination and/or affections: C. 19–20.

young no matter what their age, the; the young of all ages. The morally, sentimentally, emotionally youthful: from ca. 1910.

your earliest convenience, at. As soon as you can, please: late C. 19–20. Originally and still mainly commercial.

your guess is as good as mine. After all, we're both of us guessing: American: late C. 19–20.

ADDITIONS[1]

(all) arrangements were in train: C.20.
aristocracy of the mind, the: since ca. 1950.
*****at this point in time:** see **in this day and age** below.
battle was in full swing, the: late C. 19–20.
blind with rage: C. 19–20.
by and large: late C. 19–20.
*****chapter and verse:** esp., **give . . .:** C. 19–20.

[1]Approximate periods during which the phrases have been clichés.

energy of despair, the: C. 20.
fact not widely recognized, a: C. 20.
***facts of life, the:** since ca. 1910.
follow to the ends of the earth: mid C. 19–20.
***food for thought:** late C. 19–20.
forty winks: late C. 19–20.
golden opportunity: mid C. 19–20.
greatest mistake of (one's) **life, make the:** C. 20.
hold the fort: late C. 19–20.
if you ask me, . . .: C. 20.
in point of fact: mid C. 19–20.
in the long run: late C. 19–20.
***in this day and age:** since ca. 1960. The most abhorrent of all post WW2 clichés.
***join the happy throng:** late C. 19–20.
live and learn: mid C. 19–20.
mend one's ways: C. 19–20.
moment of truth, the. A translation of the Spanish *el momento de la verdad*, applied to the moment at which the matador is about to kill the bull, or be himself killed; notably first Englished by Ernest Hemingway in *Death in the Afternoon*, 1932; heard occasionally ever since ca. 1940, but not become a cliché until 1962, especially in its application to the imminence of death—to a shattering revelation or confrontation —to a final attainment of complete truth or honesty or purpose.
mystery surrounds . . .: C. 20.
not to be sneezed at: late C. 19–20.
one fine day: late C. 19–20.
point of no return, the: since ca. 1955.
***Public Enemy No. 1:** since ca. 1924. Originally, American.
resume, or **take up, the threads of one's old life:** late C. 19–20.
rock bottom: esp., **down to . . .:** C. 20.
sad awakening: since ca. 1870.
signal victory, a: mid. C. 19–20.
snare and a delusion, a: late C. 19–20.

stony silence; esp., **maintain** or **preserve a . . .:** since ca. 1880.

stricken in years: mid. C. 19–20.

*tangled skein, a: late C. 19–20.

tender mercies (ironic): C. 20.

throw modesty to the winds: late C. 19–20.

tissue of lies: late C. 19–20.

toll of the road, the: since ca. 1930. Mostly journalistic.

turn the corner (metaphorical): C. 20.

wild and woolly: late C. 19–20. Originally, American and Australian.

wind of change, the: since 1945.

without a stain on one's character: mid C. 19–20.